D1555444

Who's Who in Sherlock Holmes

OREGON

JAN 12 1981

STATE LIBRARY

Who's Who in Sherlock Holmes

by

Scott R. Bullard

and

Michael Leo Collins

TAPLINGER PUBLISHING COMPANY

NEW YORK

WITHDRAWN

From EOU Library

La Grande, OR 97850

First edition
Published by
TAPLINGER PUBLISHING CO., INC.
New York, New York

Copyright © 1980 by Scott R. Bullard and Michael Leo Collins
All rights reserved
Printed in the United States of America

Library of Congress Cataloging in Publication Data

Bullard, Scott R.
  Who's who in Sherlock Holmes.

   1. Doyle, Arthur Conan, Sir, 1859–1930 — Dictionaries,
indexes, etc. I. Collins, Michael, joint author.
II. Title.
PR4623.B84   823'.8   79-66638
ISBN 0-8008-8281-4
ISBN 0-8008-8282-2 pbk.

The Annotated Sherlock Holmes by William S. Baring-Gould
quoted in this book is published in the United States by
Clarkson N. Potter

Acknowledgments

We wish to acknowledge the enormous debt of gratitude
we owe to Kathy Bullard and Kay Funk, Charles T. and
Wilma Adams, James D. and Yvonne Collins; Bobs Pinkerton and Sharon Webber; William S. Baring-Gould, Sir
Arthur Conan Doyle, and, of course, Sherlock Holmes
and Dr. Watson. Each of these persons, in his or her own
special way, served as an inspiration during the writing of
this book.

S.R.B.
M.L.C.

Preface

THE INITIAL INSPIRATION for *Who's Who in Sherlock Holmes* arose from the problems we encountered in our own Sherlockian pursuits. We might have recalled, for instance, that Sherlock Holmes had a hated rival on the Surrey shore named Barker, but where in the sixty Sherlock Holmes tales did he appear, and in what context? Thus the idea arose for an index of the proper names that appear in the tales, with reference to the stories in which they appear. From this simple goal, we quickly found that not only characters, but also places and objects were of significance to the student of the Holmesian epic.

Each entry is followed by the title, volume, and the page number(s) where it appears in Baring-Gould's two-volume *The Annotated Sherlock Holmes*. Everyone interested in the Great Detective is indebted to the late William S. Baring-Gould for the work and scholarship that went into producing that authoritative set.

If we have found more than one entry under the same heading, we have attempted to choose the most complete reference and annotate the others. However, occasionally we felt it best to include more than one reference per heading.

In undertaking as large a task as this, we are well aware of the possibility of omissions and errors, and we welcome any corrections.

Finally, we hope that this volume will bring the reader, for the first or fiftieth time, to the thrilling tales and adventures of "the best and wisest man" he or she will ever know, Sherlock Holmes.

A

ABBAS PARVA: A small village in Berkshire, it was the site of the murder of the famous showman, Ronder. *The Adventure of the Veiled Lodger*, II, 455.

ABBEY GRANGE: The residence of Sir Eustace and Lady Mary Brackenstall in Marsham, Kent. "The avenue ran through a noble park, between lines of ancient elms, and ended in a low, widespread house, pillared in front after the fashion of Palladio." *The Adventure of the Abbey Grange*, II, 492.

ABBEY SCHOOL: Holmes was clearing up the case of the Abbey School at the time James Dodd asked him to journey to Tuxbury Old Park. *The Adventure of the Blanched Soldier*, II, 715.

ABERDEEN: Holmes noted that there was a case parallel to *The Adventure of the Noble Bachelor* in Aberdeen, "some years back." *The Adventure of the Noble Bachelor*, I, 291.

ABERDEEN SHIPPING COMPANY: Mrs. Neville St. Clair had received a telegram "to the effect that a small parcel of considerable value which she had been expecting was waiting for her at the offices of the Aberdeen Shipping Company," which lay in Fresno Street, just off Upper Swandam Lane. *The Man with the Twisted Lip*, I, 374.

ABERGAVENNY MURDER: Holmes initially felt that he and Watson were too busy, having been retained in the case of the Ferrers Documents, and with the Abergavenny murder coming up for trial, to investigate the problem that Dr. Thorneycroft Huxtable brought to them. *The Adventure of the Priory School*, II, 608.

ABERNETTY FAMILY: "The affair seems absurdly trifling, and yet I dare call nothing trivial when I reflect that some of my most classic cases have had the least promising commencement. You will remember, Watson, how the dreadful business of the Abernetty family was first brought to my notice by the depth which the parsley had sunk into the butter upon a hot day." *The Adventure of the Six Napoleons*, II, 574.

ABRAHAMS: Holmes felt that he could not leave London while "old Abrahams is in such mortal terror of his life." So, he sent Watson to

Lausanne to try to find the whereabouts of the vanished Lady Frances Carfax. *The Disappearance of Lady Frances Carfax*, II, 658.

ACHMET: A merchant, he was "a little, fat, round fellow, with a great yellow turban, and a bundle in his hand, done up in a shawl." He was murdered for the great Agra treasure by the men bound by the sign of the four. *The Sign of the Four*, I, 679.

ACTING: Watson commented upon Holmes's expert use of disguise in his battle of wits with Irene Adler, "It was not merely that Holmes changed his costume. His expression, his manner, his very soul seemed to vary with every fresh part that he assumed. The stage lost a fine actor, even as science lost an acute reasoner, when he became a specialist in crime." *A Scandal in Bohemia*, I, 362; see also *The Sign of the Four*, I, 661.

ACTON: "A little, elderly gentleman," he was mentioned by Colonel Hayter: "Yes, we've had a scare in this part lately. Old Acton, who is one of our county magnates, had his house broken into last Monday. No great damage was done, but the fellows are still at large." *The Reigate Squires*, I, 332, 340.

ADAIR, HILDA: Daughter of the Earl of Maynooth and Lady Maynooth, she and her brother, Ronald, had accompanied their mother from Australia to England in 1894. Then, one night in the spring of that year, Hilda and her mother, after spending the evening with a relation, returned to their lodgings to find Ronald dead. *The Adventure of the Empty House*, II, 330.

ADAIR, THE HONOURABLE RONALD: "All London was interested, and the fashionable world dismayed, by the murder of the Honourable Ronald Adair, under the most unusual and inexplicable circumstances." Son of the Earl of Maynooth, "this easygoing young aristocrat ... moved in the best society, had, so far as was known, no enemies and no particular vices." He had been engaged once, but the engagement had been broken off by mutual consent. Also, he "was fond of cards, playing continually, but never for such stakes as would hurt him." Thus, there seemed to be no motive why, in the spring of 1894, he should have been killed, "his head ... horribly mutilated by an expanded revolver bullet." *The Adventure of the Empty House*, II, 330.

ADAMS: The criminal in the Manor House case. Sherlock Holmes solved the crime. His brother, Mycroft, had suspected Adams from the start. *The Greek Interpreter*, I, 594.

ADDLETON TRAGEDY: One of the many cases Sherlock Holmes handled in 1894 dealt with "the Addleton tragedy and the singular contents of the ancient British barrow." *The Adventure of the Golden Pince-Nez*, II, 350.

ADELAIDE: Mary Fraser was brought up in the free atmosphere of Adelaide, in South Australia. *The Adventure of the Abbey Grange*, II, 495; see also *The Disappearance of Lady Frances Carfax*, II, 662.

ADELAIDE-SOUTHAMPTON LINE: The larger of the two lines of steamers connecting South Australia with England, it maintained a shipping office at the end of Pall Mall. Two of the line's ships were *The Rock of Gibraltar* — "their largest and best boat" — and *The Bass Rock* — "their new ship." *The Adventure of the Abbey Grange*, II, 502.

ADLER, IRENE: She had become romantically involved with the King of Bohemia in Warsaw. They grew apart, but prior to his marriage to the second daughter of the King of Scandinavia, Adler refused to give up a compromising photograph of them both. She endured burglary and assault at the hands of the King's agents, but yielded up nothing. Eventually, the King sought Holmes's aid in recovering the picture. Adler was able to best Holmes in a battle of wits, thus winning his everlasting esteem. She married Mr. Godfrey Norton. Holmes had the following information concerning her in his massive index: "Born in New Jersey in the year 1858. Contralto — hum! La Scala, hum! Prima donna Imperial Opera of Warsaw — Yes! Retired from operatic stage — ha! Living in London — quite so!" Still, of all the accolades she ever received, it must be thought that one in particular held special significance: "To Sherlock Holmes she is always *the* woman. I have seldom heard him mention her under any other name. In his eyes she eclipses and predominates the whole of her sex." At the time of *A Scandal in Bohemia*, her address in London was Briony Lodge, Serpentine Avenue, St. John's Wood. *A Scandal in Bohemia*, I, 346, 354; see also *A Case of Identity*, I, 405; *His Last Bow*, II, 802.

AFGHAN CAMPAIGN: Watson: "I had remained indoors all day, for the weather had taken a sudden turn to rain, with high autumnal winds, and the jezail bullet which I had brought back in one of my limbs as a relic of my Afghan campaign, throbbed with dull persistency." *The Adventure of the Noble Bachelor*, I, 281; see also *The Sign of the Four*, I, 610.

Colonel Sebastian Moran, First Bengalore Pioneers, whom Holmes finally bagged through Oscar Meunier's waxen image, served in the Afghan Campaign. *The Adventure of the Empty House*, II, 346.

AFGHAN WAR, SECOND: The young Dr. Watson (University of London, 1878) was attached to the Fifth Northumberland Fusiliers as Assistant Surgeon when they were stationed in India, and participated in the second Afghan War. Watson was wounded in battle, contracted enteric fever, and eventually was sent home. *A Study in Scarlet*, I, 143.

AFGHANISTAN: Holmes's first words to Dr. Watson were, "How are you? You have been in Afghanistan, I perceive." *A Study in Scarlet*, I, 150.

Watson had only half an hour in which to join Holmes at Paddington to accompany him in the investigation of the murder of Charles McCarthy. "My experience of camp life in Afghanistan had at least had the effect of making me a prompt and ready traveller. My wants were few and simple, so that in less than the time stated I was in a cab with my valise, rattling away to Paddington Station." *The Boscombe Valley Mystery*, II, 134; see also *The Musgrave Ritual*, I, 123; *The Reigate Squires*, I, 331.

While they waited at Baker Street for Holmes's return and the results of his investigation of the disappearance of the stolen naval treaty, Watson tried to interest his old school friend, Percy Phelps, in a discussion of Afghanistan, India, and social questions. *The Naval Treaty*, II, 187.

AGAR, DR. MOORE: A Harley Street physician "whose dramatic introduction to Holmes" Watson hoped one day to recount. In March of 1897, after seeing that "Holmes' iron constitution showed some symptoms of giving way in the face of constant hard work of a most exacting kind, aggravated, perhaps, by occasional indiscretions of his own," Dr. Moore Agar "gave positive injunctions that the famous private agent would lay aside all cases and surrender himself to complete rest if he wished to avert an absolute breakdown." *The Adventure of the Devil's Foot*, II, 508.

AGATHA: Charles Augustus Milverton's housemaid, to whom Sherlock Holmes — in the guise of Escott, the swaggering plumber — had become engaged in order to obtain information from her about her master. She had enabled Escott to meet her at Milverton's estate, Appledore Towers, by locking up the large dog which usually roamed the garden. *The Adventure of Charles Augustus Milverton*, II, 564.

AGONY COLUMNS: Sherlock Holmes kept a "great book in which day by day, he filed the agony columns of the various London journals." He had mixed feelings about those columns, however, and he evidenced as much by saying, "What a chorus of groans, cries, and bleatings! What a rag-bag of singular happenings! But surely the most valuable hunting-ground that ever was given to a student of the unusual." *The Adventure of the Red Circle*, II, 694.

AGRA: A city in India where Jonathan Small sought refuge during the Indian Mutiny. *The Sign of the Four*, I, 675.

ACRA TREASURE: It was described by Jonathan Small as "a collection of gems such as I have read of and thought about when I was a little lad at Pershore." *The Sign of the Four*, I, 680.

AINSTREE, DR.: "The greatest living authority upon tropical disease," he was residing in London at the time when Watson proposed to consult with him for Holmes in *The Adventure of the Dying Detective*. *The Adventure of the Dying Detective*, I, 441.

AIR-GUNS: "You are afraid of something?" Watson asked.
"Well, I am," replied Holmes.
"Of what?"
"Of air-guns."
Holmes feared that the agents of Professor Moriarty would kill him with air-guns before he could secure the evil genius's arrest. *The Final Problem*, II, 302; see also *The Adventure of the Mazarin Stone*, II, 738.

ALDERSHOT: The First Battalion of the Royal Mallows regiment was stationed at Aldershot. It was here that Colonel James Barclay was found dead in a locked room with his wife, who had fainted. Holmes undertook the investigation of the singular affair. *The Crooked Man*, II, 226–27; see also *The Adventure of the Copper Beeches*, II, 121.

ALDGATE STATION: A station on the Underground system in London.

It was just outside Aldgate Station that the dead body of Arthur Cadogan West was found. *The Adventure of the Bruce-Partington Plans*, II, 434.

ALDRIDGE: Jim Browner, "a big, powerful chap, clean-shaven, and very swarthy," was something like Aldridge, who helped Holmes and Lestrade in the bogus laundry affair. *The Cardboard Box*, II, 204.

ALEXIS: He had been a member of the Russian Nihilist group known both as The Brotherhood and as The Order. A married woman, Anna, considered Alexis "the friend of [her] heart" and said that "he was noble, unselfish, loving—all that [her] husband was not." She also said that Alexis "hated violence" and that, because of his nonviolent nature, he had not—like most of his comrades—been implicated in the killing of a police officer, a crime for which "all [of the Brotherhood had been] arrested upon [her husband's] confession." Alexis had written letters to Anna which "would have saved him," but, as her husband had hidden the letters out of spite for Alexis's alienation of Anna's affections, the innocent man had been sentenced to work in a Siberian salt mine. *The Adventure of the Golden Pince-Nez*, II, *passim*.

ALGAR: Holmes's friend on the Liverpool force who did some investigation for him in the circumstances surrounding *The Cardboard Box*. *The Cardboard Box*, II, 203.

ALICE: Maid and confidante of Miss Hatty Doran, who had come from California and married Lord St. Simon. *The Adventure of the Noble Bachelor*, I, 289.

ALICIA: One of Holmes's unfinished tales, mentioned by Watson, involved "the cutter *Alicia*, which sailed one spring morning into a small patch of mist from where she never emerged, nor was anything further ever heard of herself and her crew." *The Problem of Thor Bridge*, II, 588.

ALISON'S ROOMS: Holmes fought three rounds with McMurdo there on the night of the latter's benefit. *The Sign of the Four*, I, 632.

ALLAHABAD, INDIA: "Young Edmunds, of the Berkshire Constabulary" was sent to Allahabad sometime after he had concluded his investigation of the Abbas Parva tragedy. *The Adventure of the Veiled Lodger*, II, 456.

ALLAN BROTHERS: Chief land agents in the village of Esher, Surrey.

It was from them that Aloysius Garcia rented Wisteria Lodge. *The Adventure of Wisteria Lodge*, II, 242.

ALLARDYCE'S: The butcher shop where Holmes spent a good part of one morning trying to transfix a dead pig hung by the rafter with a single blow of a harpoon. *The Adventure of Black Peter*, II, 399.

ALLEN, MRS.: "A buxom and cheerful person," she relieved Mrs. Jack Douglas, of Birlstone Manor, in Sussex, of some of her household chores. *The Valley of Fear*, I, 485.

ALPHA INN: A small public house in Bloomsbury at the corner of one of those streets which run down into Holborn, it was frequented by Mr. Henry Baker, who obtained his Christmas goose there from a goose club. *The Adventure of the Blue Carbuncle*, I, 459.

ALTAMONT: The great German spy, Von Bork, said of Altamont, "He is a wonderful worker. If I pay him well, at least he delivers the goods, to use his own phrase. Besides he is not a traitor. I assure you that our most pan-Germanic Junker is a sucking dove in his feelings towards England as compared with a real bitter Irish-American." Von Bork also noted that "Altamont has a nice taste in wines, and he took a fancy to my Tokay. He is a touchy fellow, and needs humouring in small things." Altamont was "a tall, gaunt man of sixty, with clear-cut features and a small goatee beard which gave him a general resemblance to the caricatures of Uncle Sam." *His Last Bow*, II, 795, 795–96, 797, 801.

ALUMINUM CRUTCH: One of Holmes's untold tales was the singular affair of the aluminum crutch. *The Musgrave Ritual*, I, 124.

AMATEUR MENDICANT SOCIETY: "The year '87 furnished us with a long series of cases of greater or less interest, of which I retain the records." Among the headings in Watson's list of cases during this twelvemonth period was the adventure of the Amateur Mendicant Society, which "held a luxurious club in the lower vault of a furniture warehouse." *The Five Orange Pips*, I, 389.

AMATI: As Holmes and Watson journeyed to NO. 3 Lauriston Gardens to investigate the mysterious death of Enoch J. Drebber in an empty house, the Great Detective "was in the best of spirits, and prattled away about Cremona fiddles, and the difference between a Stradivarius and an Amati." *A Study in Scarlet*, I, 166.

AMBERLEY, JOSIAH: "He was junior partner of Brickfall & Amberley, who are manufacturers of artistic materials.... He made his little pile, retired from business at the age of sixty-one, bought a house at Lewisham, and settled down to rest after a life of ceaseless grind.... Early in 1897 he married a woman twenty years younger than himself—a good-looking woman, too, if the photograph does not flatter. A competence, a wife, leisure—it seemed a straight road which lay before him. And yet within two years he is, as you have seen, as broken and miserable a creature as crawls beneath the sun." Watson agreed that Amberley was indeed pathetic, futile, and broken. Amberley had gone to Holmes with the sad tale of his wife's disappearance with their young neighbor and Amberley's fortune, but the truth turned out to be far more sinister! *The Adventure of the Retired Colourman*, II, 546, 548

AMERICA: "It is always a joy to me to meet an American, Mr. Moulton, for I am one of those who believe that the folly of a monarch and the blundering of a Minister in fargone years will not prevent our children from being some day citizens of the same world-wide country under a flag which shall be a quartering of the Union Jack with the Stars and Stripes," said Sherlock Holmes. *The Adventure of the Noble Bachelor*, I, 298.

AMES: The butler at Birlstone Manor, in Sussex. Watson viewed him as a "prim... quaint, gnarled, dried-up person." *The Valley of Fear*, I, 485, 492.

ANCIENT BRITISH BARROW: One of the many cases Sherlock Holmes handled in 1894 dealt with "the Addleton tragedy and the singular contents of the ancient British barrow." *The Adventure of the Golden Pince-Nez*, II, 350.

ANDAMAN ISLANDER: Watson believed that he would always associate "the dreary marshes of the Thames and the long, sullen reaches of the river" with his and Holmes's "pursuit of the Andaman Islander," Tonga, in *The Sign of the Four*. *The Adventure of the Golden Pince-Nez*, II, 357.

ANDAMAN ISLANDS: Situated 340 miles to the north of Sumatra, in the Bay of Bengal. The men who were bound by the sign of the four had all been incarcerated there. *The Sign of the Four*, I, 654–55.

ANDERSON: In the Boer War, Anderson was in the same squadron as Godfrey Emsworth and James Dodd. During the "morning fight at Buffelsspruit, outside Pretoria, on the Eastern railway line," however, Emsworth, Anderson, and one Baldy Simpson had gotten separated from their mates, and the latter two were killed. *The Adventure of the Blanched Soldier*, II, 718.

ANDERSON: The village constable of Fulworth, he had been called to investigate the murder of Fitzroy McPherson, and he quickly showed his "good sense" by soliciting the advice of Sherlock Holmes. *The Adventure of the Lion's Mane*, II, 779.

ANDERSON MURDERS: The Anderson murders, in North Carolina, were similar to the case that Holmes investigated in *The Hound of the Baskervilles*. *The Hound of the Baskervilles*, II, 96.

ANDOVER: A case similar to the one that Mary Sutherland brought to Sherlock Holmes occurred in Andover, in 1877. *A Case of Identity*, I, 411.

ANDREWS: "Little more than a boy, frank-faced and cheerful, with the breezy manner of one who is out for a holiday, and means to enjoy every minute of it." He was sent by the Scowrers' county delegate, Evans Pott, to murder the manager of the Crow Hill Mine. He lodged with Jack McMurdo. *The Valley of Fear*, I, 555.

ANERLEY ARMS: The hotel at which John Hector McFarlane stayed, after, he insisted, leaving Jonas Oldacre alive and well. The police opinion, however, was that McFarlane had stayed there after killing Oldacre. *The Adventure of the Norwood Builder*, II, 419.

ANGEL, HOSMER: Mary Sutherland's fiancé, whom she met at the gasfitters' ball. He mysteriously disappeared from his cab on their way to the church to be married. Supposedly, he was a cashier in an office in Leadenhall Street, and he always typed his letters to Miss Sutherland. Said she, "He was a very shy man, Mr. Holmes. He would rather walk with me in the evening than in the daylight, for he said that he hated to be conspicuous. Very retiring and gentlemanly he was. Even his voice was gentle." *A Case of Identity*, I, 409, 412.

ANGLO-INDIAN CLUB: One of Colonel Sebastian Moran's clubs. *The Adventure of the Empty House*, II, 347.

ANNA: A onetime Russian Nihilist. "There was a certain nobility in the woman's bearing... which compelled something of respect and admiration." She and her husband had belonged to a revolutionary group known both as The Brotherhood and as The Order. Another member of that group was a "noble, unselfish, loving" man named Alexis, who was "the friend of [Anna's] heart." "Then there came a time of trouble ... and in order to save his own life and to earn a great reward," her husband had betrayed his wife and other comrades. What was worse, he had withheld certain letters and a diary which would have proved Alexis's innocence. Thus, after she had completed her term of servitude in Siberia, Anna came to England to steal the letters and the diary so that Alexis might also be set free. *The Adventure of the Golden Pince-Nez*, II, *passim*.

ANSTRUTHER: When Watson hesitated to join Holmes in investigating the murder of Charles McCarthy because of his heavy case load, Watson's wife suggested that Anstruther would be willing to do his medical work for him. *The Boscombe Valley Mystery*, II, 134.

ANTHONY: Manservant at Merripit House, home of the Stapletons, in Devonshire. *The Hound of the Baskervilles*, II, 49, 109-10.

APPLEDORE, SIR CHARLES: His daughter, Edith, married the Duke of Holdernesse in 1888. *The Adventure of the Priory School*, II, 608.

APPLEDORE, EDITH: Daughter of Sir Charles Appledore. She married the Duke of Holdernesse in 1888. She had one son, who was abducted from the Priory School. At about the same time as his abduction, she became estranged from the Duke and took up residence in the south of France. *The Adventure of the Priory School*, II, 608-9.

APPLEDORE TOWERS: Charles Augustus Milverton's residence, in Hampstead. *The Adventure of Charles Augustus Milverton*, II, 564, 565.

ARCADIA MIXTURE: When Holmes called on Watson at the time of the adventure of the Crooked Man, Watson was still smoking the Arcadia mixture of his bachelor days, as Holmes could tell by the fluffy ash on his friend's coat. *The Crooked Man*, II, 225.

ARCHIE: John Clay's companion in the attempted robbery of the cellar of the Coburg branch of the City and Suburban Bank. *The Red-Headed League*, I, 436.

ARIZONA: Francis Hay Moulton prospected there after leaving San Francisco. *The Adventure of the Noble Bachelor*, I, 296.

ARMITAGE, JAMES: A young bank employee convicted of embezzlement and sentenced to transportation to Australia in 1855 aboard the barque *Gloria Scott*. He participated in a successful convict uprising aboard ship and, upon arriving in Sydney, changed his name. He prospered, and eventually returned to England under the assumed name. *The "Gloria Scott"*, 1, 116ff.

ARMITAGE, MR.: Father of Percy Armitage, who was engaged to Helen Stoner. *The Adventure of the Speckled Band*, 1, 249.

ARMITAGE, PERCY: Second son of Mr. Armitage, of Crane Water, near Reading, he was engaged to be married to Helen Stoner, stepdaughter of Dr. Grimesby Roylott, of Stoke Moran, in western Surrey. *The Adventure of the Speckled Band*, 1, 249.

ARMSTRONG, DR. LESLIE: Holmes thought Dr. Armstrong "a man of energy and character." Indeed, the detective was so impressed with Armstrong that he claimed never to have "seen a man who, if he turned his talents that way, was more calculated to fill the gap left by the illustrious Moriarty." Like Moriarty, Armstrong was "a thinker of European reputation in more than one branch of science"; unlike the infamous Professor, however, Armstrong battled Holmes with a noble objective in mind. Once Armstrong understood that Holmes intended no harm, he "wrung Holmes by the hand." *The Adventure of the Missing Three-Quarter*, 11, 483, 484, 490.

ARNSWORTH CASTLE BUSINESS: "When a woman thinks that her house is on fire, her instinct is at once to rush to the thing that she values most. It is a perfectly overpowering impulse, and I have more than once taken advantage of it. In the case of the Darlington Substitution Scandal it was of use to me, and also in the Arnsworth Castle business." *A Scandal in Bohemia*, 1, 364.

ART: Holmes, who was descended from the French artist, Vernet, felt that "art in the blood is liable to take the strangest forms," and that heredity was the one source of his faculty of observation and his facility at deduction. *The Greek Interpreter*, 1, 590; see also *The Adventure of the Copper Beeches*, 11, 114.

ASHES, TOBACCO: "He had even smoked there. I found the ash of a cigar, which my special knowledge of tobacco ashes enabled me to pronounce as an Indian cigar. I have, as you know, devoted some attention to this, and written a little monograph on the ashes of 140 different varieties of pipe, cigar, and cigarette tobacco." *The Boscombe Valley Mystery*, II, 148; see also *The Crooked Man*, II, 225; *A Study in Scarlet*, I, 173.

ASTON: The man who called himself John Garrideb excitedly displayed a marked newspaper advertisement to Nathan Garrideb. Both men believed that they could attain great wealth by finding another Garrideb, and the newspaper advertisement had supposedly been placed by one "Howard Garrideb, Constructor of Agricultural Machinery," who could be reached at the Grosvenor Buildings, Aston. *The Adventure of the Three Garridebs*, II, 649.

ASTRONOMY: In Watson's famous catalogue of "Sherlock Holmes—his limits," he rated the Great Detective's knowledge of astronomy as "Nil." *A Study in Scarlet*, I, 156.

ATHENS: Both Sophy and Paul Kratides were from Athens. *The Greek Interpreter*, I, 598.

ATKINSON: At the time of *A Scandal in Bohemia*, Watson had from time to time heard some vague account of Holmes's doings, such as his clearing up of the singular tragedy of the Atkinson brothers at Trincomalee. *A Scandal in Bohemia*, I, 347.

ATLANTA: Mr. and Mrs. John Hebron and their child lived there. Mr. Hebron and the child supposedly died there of the yellow fever. *The Yellow Face*, I, 579.

ATWOOD: He sold his Vermissa Valley ironworks to the West Wilmerton General Mining Company. *The Valley of Fear*, I, 543.

AUGUST 1914: The word "August" and the numbers "1914" were the keys to Von Bork's double (letter/number) combination lock. *His Last Bow*, II, 797.

THE AURORA: Mordecai Smith's steam launch, chartered by Jonathan Small. *The Sign of the Four*, I, 651.

AUSTRALIA: John Turner had made his fortune in Australia, and then had come back to England. Later, Charles McCarthy joined him, and obtained a fine farm on his estate. *The Boscombe Valley Mystery*, II, 135; see also *The "Gloria Scott"*, I, 117; *The Adventure of the Empty House*, II, 330; *The Adventure of the Priory School*, II, 629; *The Disappearance of Lady Frances Carfax*, II, 662.

AVELING: The mathematical master at the Priory School, he was sure that Heidegger, the missing German master, had had Palmer's tyres on his bicycle. *The Adventure of the Priory School*, II, 617.

AVENGING ANGELS, THE: This Mormon group, also known as the Danite Band, terrorized John Ferrier and ultimately destroyed his daughter, Lucy. "Its invisibility, and the mystery which was attached to it, made this organization doubly terrible. It appeared to be omniscient and omnipotent, and yet was neither seen nor heard. The man who held out against the Church vanished away, and none knew whither he had gone or what had befallen him." *A Study in Scarlet*, I, 207–8.

B

BABOON: One of the exotic pets Dr. Grimesby Roylott kept on his ancestral estate at Stoke Moran, in western Surrey. *The Adventure of the Speckled Band*, I, 258.

BACKWATER, LORD: He recommended Holmes to Lord St. Simon in *The Adventure of the Noble Bachelor*. "Lord Backwater tells me that I may place implicit reliance upon your judgment and discretion." *The Adventure of the Noble Bachelor*, I, 282.

BACKWATER, LORD: He owned Capleton Stables, in Dartmoor, where Desborough, the second favorite in the running of the Wessex Cup, was trained. *Silver Blaze*, II, 264.

BADEN: Watson traced the vanished Lady Frances Carfax to the Englischer Hof in Baden, whence she had left in the company of a Dr. and Mrs. Shlessinger. *The Disappearance of Lady Frances Carfax*, II, 659.

BAGATELLE CARD CLUB: One of the three clubs of which Ronald Adair was a member. "It was shown that after dinner on the day of his death he had played a rubber of whist" at the Bagatelle Card Club. Colonel Sebastian Moran was also a member of the club. *The Adventure of the Empty House*, II, 330, 347.

Pierce Library
Eastern Oregon University
1410 L Avenue
La Grande, OR 97850

BAIN, SANDY: Jockey at Shoscombe Park, Berkshire. Sir Robert Norberton instructed him to give Lady Beatrice Falder's favorite spaniel to Josiah Barnes of the Green Dragon inn. *The Adventure of Shoscombe Old Place*, II, 635.

BAKER, HENRY: "He was a large man, with rounded shoulders, a massive head, and a broad, intelligent face, sloping down to a pointed beard of grizzled brown. A touch of red in nose and cheeks, with a slight tremor of his extended hand, recalled Holmes' surmise as to his habits." His misplaced goose and battered felt hat led Holmes to investigate *The Adventure of the Blue Carbuncle*. *The Adventure of the Blue Carbuncle*, I, 458.

BAKER STREET: Both Holmes and Watson found themselves in the same position on their first meeting, that of searching for cheaper lodgings. Holmes offered: "I have my eye on a suite in Baker Street which would suit us down to the ground." Watson relates the sequel to their mutual agreement, "We met the next day as he had arranged, and inspected the rooms at NO. 221B Baker Street, of which he had spoken at our meeting. They consisted of a couple of comfortable bedrooms and a single large airy sitting-room, cheerfully furnished, and illuminated by two broad windows. So desirable in every way were the apartments, and so moderate did the terms seem when divided between us, that the bargain was concluded upon the spot, and we at once entered into possession." *A Study in Scarlet*, I, 151–53; see also *A Scandal in Bohemia*, I, 347; *The Five Orange Pips*, I, 390; *The Adventure of the Engineer's Thumb*, II, 211; *The Adventure of the Beryl Coronet*, II, 282; *The Adventure of the Copper Beeches*, II, 115; *The Adventure of the Golden Pince-Nez*, II, 350–51; *The Cardboard Box*, II, 193; *The Adventure of the Bruce-Partington Plans*, II, 432; *The Adventure of the Mazarin Stone*, II, 735, 737.

BAKER STREET IRREGULARS: Holmes employed the Baker Street Irregulars in the mystery surrounding the lonely death of Enoch J. Drebber. "'It's the Baker Street division of the detective police force,' said my companion gravely; and as he spoke there rushed into the room half a dozen of the dirtiest and most ragged street arabs that ever I clapped eyes on."

After dismissing the Irregulars, Holmes commented, "There's more work to be got out of one of those little beggars than out of a dozen of the force. The mere sight of an official-looking person seals men's lips.

These youngsters, however, go everywhere, and hear everything. They are as sharp as needles, too; all they want is organization." *A Study in Scarlet*, I, 185; see also *The Sign of the Four*, I, 653.

BALDWIN CARD CLUB: One of the three card clubs of which Ronald Adair was a member. *The Adventure of the Empty House*, II, 330.

BALDWIN, TED: "A Boss of Scowrers," he later assumed the name Hargrave. "He was a handsome, dashing young man of about the same age and build as McMurdo himself." He competed with McMurdo for the affections of Ettie Shafter. *The Valley of Fear*, I, 528, 530.

BALLARAT: The holes which had been dug in the grounds of Pondicherry Lodge in search of the great Agra treasure reminded Watson of the side of a hill near Ballarat, Australia, where prospectors had been at work. *The Sign of the Four*, I, 633.

Charles McCarthy's last dying word to his son was "Ballarat." His son misunderstood, however, and thought that the elder McCarthy had made some delirious allusion to a rat. *The Boscombe Valley Mystery*, II, 139ff.

BALMORAL, DUKE OF: Onetime Secretary for Foreign Affairs, Plantagenet blood by direct descent, Tudor on the distaff side, he was the father of Robert Walsingham de Vere St. Simon, who sought Holmes's aid in *The Adventure of the Noble Bachelor*. *The Adventure of the Noble Bachelor*, I, 282.

BALMORAL, DUKE OF: Ran Iris for the Wessex Cup. The Duke's horse made a bad third. *Silver Blaze*, II, 278.

BALMORAL, LORD: With Godfrey Milner, he had lost as much as £420 in a sitting of cards to Ronald Adair and Colonel Sebastian Moran some weeks before Adair's murder. *The Adventure of the Empty House*, II, 330.

BALZAC, HONORE DE: There was nothing remarkable contained in the text of Mr. Hosmer Angel's letters to Mary Sutherland, save that he quoted Balzac once. *A Case of Identity*, I, 412.

BANNISTER: He had been the servant of Mr. Hilton Soames, of the College of St. Luke's, for over ten years, and was thought absolutely above suspicion in the affair of the disturbed examination papers. Ban-

23

nister "was a little, white-faced, clean-shaven, grizzly haired fellow of fifty." *The Adventure of the Three Students*, II, 369, 375, 382.

BAR OF GOLD, THE: An opium den in Upper Swandam Lane. Watson went there to retrieve Isa Whitney. To his surprise, he also found Sherlock Holmes there. The Bar of Gold was located "between a slop shop and a gin shop, approached by a steep flight of steps leading down to a black gap like the mouth of a cave." *The Man with the Twisted Lip*, I, 369.

BARBERTON: Philip Green, who had found it judicious to go to South Africa, made his fortune there, at Barberton. *The Disappearance of Lady Frances Carfax*, II, 662.

BARCLAY, COLONEL JAMES: He commanded the Royal Mallows regiment, stationed at Aldershot. He was found dead in the locked morning room of his villa, Lachine, alone with his wife, who had fainted. "Barclay's devotion to his wife was greater than his wife's to Barclay. He was acutely uneasy if he were absent from her for a day.... He was a dashing, jovial old soldier in his usual mood, but there were occasions on which he seemed to show himself capable of considerable violence and vindictiveness... [and] the singular sort of depression which came upon him at times." *The Crooked Man*, II, 227.

BARDLE, INSPECTOR: An Inspector of the Sussex Constabulary, he was "a steady, solid, bovine man with thoughtful eyes" who solicited Sherlock Holmes's advice concerning the arrest of Ian Murdoch for the murder of Fitzroy McPherson. *The Adventure of the Lion's Mane*, II, 784.

BARELLI, AUGUSTO: Father of Emilia Barelli Lucca, he was the chief lawyer and once the deputy of the part of Italy around Posilippo, near Naples. He forbade the match between his daughter and Gennaro Lucca, one of his employees; but Emilia's love for Gennaro outweighed her father's argument that her suitor had neither money nor position — thus, she and Gennaro fled together, and were married at Bari. *The Adventure of the Red Circle*, II, 702.

BARITSU: "The Japanese system of wrestling" which, more than once, had proved very useful to Sherlock Holmes. Holmes found his knowledge of baritsu most useful when Professor Moriarty "threw his long arms around" the detective upon the brink of the Reichenbach Fall. *The Adventure of the Empty House*, II, 334.

BARKER: Watson noticed a strange lounger in the street in front of Josiah Amberley's house. "He was a tall, dark, heavily-moustached, rather military-looking man." Holmes later identified the lounger as Barker, a detective and his "hated rival upon the Surrey shore." He had been employed by the family of Dr. Ray Ernest, who had been accused by Amberley of running away with his wife and his fortune. *The Adventure of the Retired Colourman*, II, 547, 549, 553.

BARKER, CECIL JAMES: Of Hales Lodge, Hampstead. A close friend of the Douglas family, of Birlstone Manor, in Sussex, he was under suspicion for a short time in the murder of Jack Douglas, whose body he had discovered. *The Valley of Fear*, I, 485.

BARNES, JOSIAH: The sporting keeper of the Green Dragon Inn, three miles from Shoscombe Old Place, at Crendall. Sir Robert Norberton had strangely given him Lady Beatrice Falder's favorite spaniel. *The Adventure of Shoscombe Old Place*, II, 632.

BARNICOT, DR.: A well-known London medical practitioner, both his residence and principal consulting-room at Kennington Road and his branch surgery and dispensary at Lower Brixton Road contained plaster busts of Napoleon, which were mysteriously dashed into fragments. *The Adventure of the Six Napoleons*, II, 573.

BARRETT, POLICE CONSTABLE: "Passing along Godolphin Street, [he] observed that the door of NO. 16 was ajar." After knocking but receiving no answer, Barrett passed into the front room of the house, where he saw "the unfortunate tenant of the house," international spy Eduardo Lucas, "stabbed to the heart" with a curved Indian dagger. *The Adventure of the Second Stain*, I, 308.

BARRYMORE, ELIZA: A servant at Baskerville Hall, married to the butler. Her brother was Selden, the Notting Hill murderer. *The Hound of the Baskervilles*, II, 43.

BARRYMORE, JOHN: The butler at Baskerville Hall, his family had served the Baskervilles for a hundred years, but a dark secret prompted him to secretly signal to the moor in the dead of night with a candle. *The Hound of the Baskervilles*, II, 41.

BARTON, DR. HILL: Watson, in the guise of Dr. Hill Barton, went to the house of Baron Adelbert Gruner to distract his attention while

Holmes searched his inner study. *The Adventure of the Illustrious Client*, II, 685.

BARTON, INSPECTOR: He took charge of the investigation concerning the sudden disappearance of Neville St. Clair into the squalid room of the wretched beggar, Hugh Boone. *The Man with the Twisted Lip*, I, 376.

BASIL, CAPTAIN: "The fact that several rough-looking men called during that time and inquired for Captain Basil made me understand that Holmes was working somewhere under one of the numerous disguises and names with which he concealed his own formidable identity." *The Adventure of Black Peter*, II, 398.

BASKERVILLE, SIR CHARLES: He had made his fortune in South African speculation, and had returned to the family estate, Baskerville Hall, in Devonshire. His death, although attributed to heart failure, was surrounded by mysterious events that, when brought to Holmes's attention, were successfully investigated. *The Hound of the Baskervilles*, II, II.

BASKERVILLE, ELIZABETH: Daughter of the Hugo Baskerville who set down the legend of the Hound of the Baskervilles in writing in 1742. Hugo's sons were instructed to say nothing of it to her. *The Hound of the Baskervilles*, II, 10.

BASKERVILLE, SIR HENRY: A Canadian farmer, he was the heir to both the Baskerville estate and fortune and also to the menacing legend of the Hound of the Baskervilles. On arriving in London to claim his inheritance, he was confronted by a number of mysterious events. He accepted the aid and advice of Sherlock Holmes, but wound up losing his love and, nearly, his life. He "was a small, alert, dark-eyed man about thirty years of age, very sturdily built, with thick black eyebrows, and a strong, pugnacious face." *The Hound of the Baskervilles*, II, 21.

BASKERVILLE, HUGO: A man "most wild, profane, and godless," he lived at the time of the Great Rebellion. His death at the jaws of a huge hound started the legend of the Hound of the Baskervilles. *The Hound of the Baskervilles*, II, 8–10.

BASKERVILLE, HUGO (18TH CENTURY): Descendant of the original Hugo Baskerville, he set down the legend of the Hound of the Baskervilles in writing for his two sons, John and Roger, in the year 1742. *The Hound of the Baskervilles*, II, 8–10.

BASKERVILLE, REAR-ADMIRAL: His portrait was in the family gallery that Holmes admired while dining with Sir Henry Baskerville. He had served under Rodney in the West Indies. *The Hound of the Baskervilles*, II, 92.

BASKERVILLE, RODGER (DIED 1876): Youngest brother of Sir Charles Baskerville, he was the black sheep of the family at that time. He fled England to South or Central America. He married there, and had one son, also named Rodger. He died of yellow fever in 1876. *The Hound of the Baskervilles*, II, 16, 106.

BASKERVILLE, RODGER (19TH CENTURY): The son of Rodger Baskerville, of South or Central America. He married Beryl Garcia, one of the beauties of Costa Rica, and, "having purloined a considerable sum of public money, he fled to England." *The Hound of the Baskervilles*, II, 106.

BASKERVILLE, SIR WILLIAM: Holmes admired his portrait, which hung in the family gallery at Baskerville Hall. He had been Chairman of Committees of the House of Commons under Pitt. *The Hound of the Baskervilles*, II, 92.

BASKERVILLE HALL: Ancestral estate of the Baskervilles, on the moor in Devonshire; the site of the horrible events detailed in *The Hound of the Baskervilles*. "Two high, narrow towers rose over the trees.... The lodge gates, a maze of fantastic tracery in wrought iron, [the house had] weather-beaten pillars on either side, blotched with lichens, and surmounted by the boars' heads of the Baskervilles. The lodge was a ruin of black granite and bared ribs of rafters, but facing it was a new building, half constructed, the first-fruit of Sir Charles's South African gold. ... The avenue opened into a broad expanse of turf, and the house lay before us. In the fading light I could see that the centre was a heavy block of building from which a porch projected. The whole front was draped in ivy, with a patch clipped bare here and there where a window or a coat-of-arms broke through the dark veil. From this central block rose the twin towers, ancient, crenellated, and pierced with many loopholes. To right and left of the turrets were more modern wings of black granite." *The Hound of the Baskervilles*, II, 39–41.

BASEL: On their Continental journey into Switzerland, Holmes and Watson made their leisurely way, via Luxembourg and Basel. *The Final Problem*, II, 310.

BASS ROCK: The new ship of the Adelaide-Southampton line, it was to be captained by Jack Croker. *The Adventure of the Abbey Grange*, II, 502.

BATES, MR. MARLOW: Manager of Neil Gibson's estate in Hampshire, Bates came to Holmes before his master's own appointment with the detective to warn Holmes of Gibson's cunning and cruelty toward his wife, who had been found shot to death. *The Problem of the Thor Bridge*, II, 591.

BAXTER: Holmes philosophized at the conclusion of his investigation of the brutal slaying of Charles McCarthy: "Why does Fate play such tricks with poor helpless worms? I never hear of such a case as this that I do not think of Baxter's words, and say: 'There, but for the grace of God, goes Sherlock Holmes.'" *The Boscombe Valley Mystery*, II, 152.

BAXTER, EDITH: A maid at King's Pyland stables, in Dartmoor, she carried supper to Ned Hunter, a stable boy. It turned out that there was opium in his curried mutton. *Silver Blaze*, II, 265.

BAYARD: King's Pyland stables were running two horses in the Wessex Cup, Bayard and Silver Blaze. Silver Blaze was a strong favorite, but Fitzroy Simpson queried the stable boy: "Is it a fact that at the weights Bayard could give the other a hundred yards in five furlongs, and that the stable have put their money on him?" That very night, Silver Blaze disappeared. *Silver Blaze*, II, 266.

BAYNES, INSPECTOR: Of the Surrey Constabulary, he sought Holmes's client, John Scott Eccles, in connection with the horrible murder of Mr. Aloysius Garcia. Holmes was most impressed with Baynes's attention to detail and thought that he had proceeded in such a "very prompt and business-like" manner that "you will rise high in your profession. You have instinct and intuition." *The Adventure of Wisteria Lodge*, II, 242, 244, 255.

BEAUCHAMP ARRIANCE: Dr. Leon Sterndale, who loved and was loved only once in his life, spent his time, while in England, in a small bungalow buried in the lonely wood of Beauchamp Arriance, on the Cornish Peninsula. *The Adventure of the Devil's Foot*, II, 516.

BECHER, DR.: He lived in the house in Eyford in which Victor Hatherley was to repair Colonel Lysander Stark's hydraulic press. He was "an Englishman, and there isn't a man in the parish who has a better lined waistcoat." He also went under the name of Mr. Ferguson. *The Adventure of the Engineer's Thumb*, ii, 223.

BEDDINGTON: The famous forger and cracksman, he impersonated clerk Hall Pycroft in a desperate attempt at robbery of Mawson & Williams, the famous financial house. *The Stockbroker's Clerk*, ii, 165.

BEDDOES, MR.: Of Hampshire, he was an old friend of the senior Trevor. Both men shared a checkered past, which caused them to change their names (Beddoes's real surname was Evans) and to endure blackmailing by a certain Hudson. When it appeared that Hudson had "told all," however, the two old friends reacted in drastically different ways. *The "Gloria Scott"*, i, 113.

BEECHER, HENRY WARD: As Holmes observed his friend Watson, the other's "eyes flashed across to the unframed portait of Henry Ward Beecher which stands upon the top of your books." *The Cardboard Box*, ii, 194.

BEES: Watson said, "But you had retired, Holmes. We heard of you as living the life of a hermit among your bees and your books in a small farm upon the South Downs.

"'Exactly, Watson. Here is the fruit of my leisured ease, the *magnum opus* of my latter years!' He picked up the volume from the table and read out the whole title, *Practical Handbook of Bee Culture, with some Observations upon the Segregation of the Queen*. 'Alone I did it. Behold the fruit of pensive nights and laborious days, when I watched the little working gangs as once I watched the criminal world of London.'" *His Last Bow*, ii, 800-1.

BELFAST: The cardboard box that Miss Susan Cushing received containing two severed human ears was posted from Belfast. *The Cardboard Box*, ii, 195, 204.

BELLAMY, MAUD: Fiancée of the murdered Fitzroy McPherson, she was "the beauty of the neighbourhood" around Fulworth, Sussex. Even Sherlock Holmes, for whom women had seldom been an attraction, realized "that no young man would cross her path unscathed." Maud listened to the particulars of her fiancé's death "with a composed concentration which showed [Holmes] that she possessed strong character as well as great beauty." *The Adventure of the Lion's Mane*, ii, 780, 781.

BELLAMY, TOM: The father of William and Maud Bellamy, he had been a fisherman to start with, but he had built up his business to such a degree that he owned "all the boats and bathing-cots at Fulworth." Physically, he was "a middle-aged man with a flaming red beard." *The Adventure of the Lion's Mane*, II, 780–81.

BELLAMY, WILLIAM: The son and business partner of Tom Bellamy and the brother of Maud Bellamy. When Sherlock Holmes visited the Bellamy home after the murder of Maud's fiancé, Fitzroy McPherson, William struck the detective as being "a powerful young man, with a heavy, sullen face." *The Adventure of the Lion's Mane*, II, 780–81.

BELLINGER, LORD: "Twice Premier of Britain," he was "austere, high-nosed, eagle-eyed, and dominant." Lord Bellinger asked Sherlock Holmes to find a stolen State document, but Holmes balked when the Premier refused to confide the contents of the document to him. Lord Bellinger eventually did, and, needless to say, Holmes more than justified the Premier's faith in him. *The Adventure of the Second Stain*, I, 301, 321.

BELLIVER TOR: This was the tor where Watson stalked the hidden lair of the mysterious man. *The Hound of the Baskervilles*, II, 80.

BELMINSTER, DUKE OF: His "youngest daughter," Lady Hilda Trelawney Hope, was, in Watson's opinion, "the most lovely woman in London." *The Adventure of the Second Stain*, I, 309.

BENDER, MR.: The first of an ill-fated expedition of twenty-one people to die on the Great Alkali Plain. Only John and Lucy Ferrier survived. *A Study in Scarlet*, I, 198.

BENGALORE PIONEERS, FIRST: Colonel Sebastian Moran was formerly of the First Bengalore Pioneers. *The Adventure of the Empty House*, II, 346.

BENNETT, TREVOR ("JACK"): "A tall, handsome youth about thirty," he was "well dressed and elegant, but with something in his bearing which suggested the shyness of the student rather than the self-possession of the man of the world." He was "professional assistant to the great scientist," Professor Presbury, and was "engaged to [Presbury's] only daughter." Thus, it was only natural that Bennett should have been concerned about the professor's bizarre behavior — so concerned, in fact, that he sought out the advice of Sherlock Holmes. *The Adventure of the Creeping Man*, II, 753.

BENTINCK STREET: As Holmes passed the corner which leads from Bentinck Street on to the Welbeck Street crossing, a two-horse van, furiously driven, whizzed round and was on him like a flash. This was the first of Professor Moriarty's promised attacks on his life. *The Final Problem*, 11, 306.

BENTLEY'S PRIVATE HOTEL: Two days prior to their important match with Oxford, the rugger team of Cambridge varsity settled at Bentley's private hotel in London. *The Adventure of the Missing Three-Quarter*, 11, 477.

BEPPO: He had worked in Morse Hudson's shop and at the Gelder & Co. sculptor works. Holmes traced to him an ingenious plot to hide the famous black pearl of the Borgias, which had been stolen. Also, he was "a well-known ne'er-do-well among the Italian colony. He had once been a skilful sculptor and had earned an honest living, but he had taken to evil courses, and had twice already been in gaol." *The Adventure of the Six Napoleons*, 11, 576, 584.

BERKELEY SQUARE: The home of General and Miss Violet de Merville, at 104 Berkeley Square, was "one of those awful grey London castles which would make a church seem frivolous." *The Adventure of the Illustrious Client*, 11, 679–80.

BERKSHIRE: Colonel Lysander Stark, who had hired Victor Hatherley to repair his hydraulic press, lived in Eyford, in Berkshire. *The Adventure of the Engineer's Thumb*, 11, 213; see also *The Adventure of the Speckled Band*, 1, 245; *The Adventure of the Veiled Lodger*, 11, 455; *The Adventure of Shoscombe Old Place*, 11, 635.

BERKSHIRES (ROYAL BERKSHIRE REGIMENT): Originally attached to the Fifth Northumberland Fusiliers as an Assistant Surgeon, the young Dr. Watson, after having joined them in India during the second Afghan War, was removed from his brigade and attached to the Berkshires, with whom he served at the "fatal battle of Maiwand," in which he was seriously wounded. *A Study in Scarlet*, 1, 143.

BERNSTONE, MRS.: The housekeeper at Pondicherry Lodge, Upper Norwood. *The Sign of the Four*, 1, 633.

BERTILLON, ALPHONSE: On the way down to Woking to investigate the case of Percy Phelps, Holmes's conversation turned to "the Bertillon system of measurements, and he expressed his enthusiastic admiration of the French savant." *The Naval Treaty*, ii, 183; see also *The Hound of the Baskervilles*, ii, 7.

BEVINGTON'S: A silver-and-brilliant pendant of old Spanish design, belonging to the vanished Lady Frances Carfax, was pawned by Henry Peters at Bevington's, in Westminster Road. *The Disappearance of Lady Frances Carfax*, ii, 663.

BHURTEE: The place where the 117th Foot (later the Royal Mallows) were surrounded during the Indian Mutiny. Here commenced a love triangle of James Barclay, Nancy Devoy, and Henry Wood. *The Crooked Man*, ii, 235.

BIBLE: Holmes said to Watson, "You remember the small affair of Uriah and Bathsheba? My Biblical knowledge is a trifle rusty, I fear, but you will find the story in the first or second of Samuel." *The Crooked Man*, ii, 237; see also *The Valley of Fear*, i, 474.

BIDDLE: A member of the Worthingdon bank gang. They pulled their heist in 1875, but were caught, and Biddle was sentenced to fifteen years. They swore revenge on their erstwhile partner, Sutton, who had testified against them. *The Resident Patient*, i, 279, 280.

BILL: The young assistant to Mr. Breckinridge, who owned a meat seller's stall in the Covent Garden Market. The goose that figured in *The Adventure of the Blue Carbuncle* was sold from there. *The Adventure of the Blue Carbuncle*, i, 461.

BILLY THE PAGE: "The young but very wise and tactful page, who had helped a little to fill up the gap of loneliness and isolation which surrounded the saturnine figure of the great detective." Billy and Dr. Watson discussed old times in *The Adventure of the Mazarin Stone*, and Billy played a significant part in the action of the adventure. In fact, Holmes worried, "that boy is a problem, Watson. How far am I justified in allowing him to be in danger?" *The Adventure of the Mazarin Stone*, ii, 735, 736; see also *The Valley of Fear*, i, 473; *The Problem of Thor Bridge*, ii, 591.

BINOMIAL THEOREM: At the age of twenty-one, Professor Moriarty wrote a treatise upon the binomial theorem which had a European vogue. On the strength of it, he won the Mathematical Chair at one of Britain's smaller universities. *The Final Problem*, ii, 303.

BIRD, SIMON: He was murdered by the Scowrers. *The Valley of Fear*, i, 556.

BIRLSTONE, MANOR HOUSE OF: "About half a mile from the town, standing in an old park famous for its huge beech trees, is the ancient Manor House of Birlstone.... The Manor House, with its many gables and its small, diamond-paned windows, was still much as the builder had left it in the early seventeenth century." Here lived the ill-fated John Douglas. *The Valley of Fear*, I, 482–83.

BIRLSTONE, VILLAGE OF: "A small and very ancient cluster of half-timbered cottages on the northern border of the county of Sussex," it was the site of Holmes's investigation. *The Valley of Fear*, I, 482.

BIRMINGHAM: Holmes and Watson journeyed to Birmingham to investigate Hall Pycroft's strange tale of his employment there with the Franco-Midland Hardware Company, Limited. *The Stockbroker's Clerk*, II, 153; see also *The Adventure of the Three Gables*, II, 723; *The Adventure of the Three Garridebs*, II, 649.

BISHOPGATE JEWEL CASE: Holmes had lectured Athelney Jones and others on causes, inferences, and effects in the Bishopgate jewel case. He set them on the right track. Holmes described it as "a piece of very simple reasoning." *The Sign of the Four*, I, 640.

BLACK FORMOSA CORRUPTION: Holmes: "What do you know, pray, of Tapanuli fever? What do you know of the black Formosa corruption?" Watson: "I have never heard of either." *The Adventure of the Dying Detective*, I, 441.

BLACK JACK OF BALLARAT: He made his fortune by highway robbery in Australia. "There were six of us, and we had a wild, free life of it, sticking up a station from time to time, or stopping the wagons on the road to the diggings. Black Jack of Ballarat was the name I went under, and our party is still remembered in the colony as the Ballarat Gang." *The Boscombe Valley Mystery*, II, 150.

BLACK PETER: The name given to Captain Peter Carey of the *Sea Unicorn*, "not only on account of his swarthy features and the colour of his huge beard, but for the humours which were the terror of all around him." *The Adventure of Black Peter*, II, 400.

BLACK TOR: On the moor in Devonshire. Watson spied a mysterious man standing on it. *The Hound of the Baskervilles*, II, 71.

BLACKHEATH: A London suburb. John Hector McFarlane, the accused murderer of Jonas Oldacre, lived at Torrington Lodge, Blackheath, with his parents. *The Adventure of the Norwood Builder*, II, 417; see also *The Adventure of the Missing Three-Quarter*, II, 476; *The Adventure of the Sussex Vampire*, II, 465.

BLACKHEATH STATION: Watson caught his train there on returning from Josiah Amberley's house in Lewisham. A detective, Barker, took the carriage next to Watson's, hoping for concealment, but the Doctor recognized him from a previous encounter. *The Adventure of the Retired Colourman*, II, 549.

BLACKWATER, EARL OF: He had entrusted his son to Dr. Thorneycroft Huxtable's care at the Priory School, in Hallamshire. *The Adventure of the Priory School*, II, 609.

BLAIR ISLAND: In the Andaman Islands. Jonathan Small was sent to the prison colony there to serve his life sentence for the murder of one Achmet. *The Sign of the Four*, I, 682,

BLAKER, FOREMAN: He earned the enmity of the Scowrers of Vermissa Valley by firing three of their members. *The Valley of Fear*, I, 541.

BLANDFORD STREET: Holmes and Watson, stalking the savage hunter who planned to assassinate the Great Detective, came out into Manchester Street, and so to Blandford Street, where they turned swiftly down a narrow passage. *The Adventure of the Empty House*, II, 338.

BLESSINGTON, MR.: He provided Dr. Percy Trevelyan with the capital to set up his Brook Street practice in return for three quarters of the earnings, the Doctor's care, and live-in quarters in the house. Blessington's habits were retiring, but the strange events that began to take place in the house prompted Dr. Trevelyan to ask Holmes's advice. *The Resident Patient*, I, *passim*.

BLOOMSBURY: The mysterious lodger of Bloomsbury was Emilia Lucca. *The Adventure of the Red Circle*, II, 701.

BLOUNT: A student at "Harold Stackhurst's well-known coaching establishment, The Gables," he was one of the persons who discovered the carcass of Fitzroy McPherson's Airedale terrier "on the very edge of the pool" where its master had received a killing blow. *The Adventure of the Lion's Mane*, II, 776, 784.

BLUE CARBUNCLE: A precious stone belonging to the Countess of

Morcar. "A brilliantly scintillating blue stone, rather smaller than a bean in size, but of such purity and radiance that it twinkled like an electric point in the dark hollow of his [the commissionaire's] hand.... This stone is not yet twenty years old. It was found in the banks of the Amoy River in Southern China, and is remarkable in having every characteristic of the carbuncle, save that it is blue in shade, instead of ruby red. In spite of its youth, it has already a sinister history. There have been two murders, a vitriol-throwing, a suicide, and several robberies brought about for the sake of this forty-grain weight of crystallized charcoal. Who would think that so pretty a toy would be a purveyor to the gallows and the prison?" *The Adventure of the Blue Carbuncle*, I, 455, 457.

BLYMER ESTATE: Holmes had in a squat notebook all of the facts concerning the death of old Mrs. Harold, who had left Count Negretto Sylvius the Blymer estate, which he rapidly gambled away. *The Adventure of the Mazarin Stone*, II, 741.

BOB: Lucy Ferrier's brother, who died on an ill-fated expedition across the Great Alkali Plain. *A Study in Scarlet*, I, 198.

BOCCACCIO: Among other things in the pockets of Enoch J. Drebber, found dead in a lonely suburban London apartment, was a pocket edition of Boccaccio's *Decameron*, with the name of Joseph Stangerson on the fly-leaf. *A Study in Scarlet*, I, 169.

BOER WAR: James M. Dodd, who sought Holmes's help in ascertaining the fate of his old companion in the South African war, was a veteran of the Boer War. *The Adventure of the Blanched Soldier*, II, 707, 712.

BOGUS LAUNDRY AFFAIR: Aldridge, who was something like Jim Browner, big, clean-shaven, swarthy, and powerful, had helped Lestrade and Holmes in the bogus laundry affair. *The Cardboard Box*, II, 204.

BOHEMIA, KING OF: The note that Holmes received anonymously bore the watermark of the Egria Papier Gesellschaft. Egria was a town in Bohemia, not far from Carlsbad. Later, Holmes was confronted with the august person of Wilhelm Gottsreich Sigismond von Ormstein, Grand Duke of Cassel-Falstein and hereditary King of Bohemia. *A Scandal in Bohemia*, I, 350, 353; see also *A Case of Identity*, I, 405; *His Last Bow*, II, 802.

BOMBAY: The young Dr. Watson, recently attached as Assistant Surgeon to the Fifth Northumberland Fusiliers, who were stationed in India, arrived in that country at Bombay, where he "learned that my corps had advanced through the passes, and was already deep in the enemy's country." *A Study in Scarlet*, I, 143.

BOND STREET: Madame Lesurier's millinery shop was in Bond Street. One of her accounts, made out to a William Darbyshire, was found on John Straker's dead body. *Silver Blaze*, II, 272; see also *The Hound of the Baskervilles*, II, 28.

BOOK OF LIFE, THE: Watson perused a magazine article entitled *The Book of Life*, which Holmes had marked in pencil. The author outlined how the observant man might, through the science of deduction and analysis, infer the existence of the Atlantic through a single drop of water, or deduce a man's occupation through the slightest detail of his appearance or dress. Watson thought the article was "ineffable twaddle," little knowing that its author, Sherlock Holmes, sat across from him at the breakfast table. *A Study in Scarlet*, I, 159–60.

BOONE, HUGH: A crippled beggar of hideous aspect, he made his home in the upper room of the Bar of Gold opium den into which Neville St. Clair was seen to suddenly disappear. Boone "is a professional beggar, though in order to avoid the police regulations he pretends to a small trade in wax vestas.... His appearance, you see, is so remarkable that no one can pass him without observing him. A shock of orange hair, a pale face disfigured by a horrible scar, which by its contraction, has turned up the outer edge of his upper lip, a bull-dog chin, and a pair of very penetrating dark eyes, which present a singular contrast to the colour of his hair, all mark him out from amid the common crowd of mendicants, and so, too, does his wit, for he is ever ready with a reply to any piece of chaff which may be thrown at him by the passers-by." *The Man with the Twisted Lip*, I, 376.

BORDEAUX: Westhouse & Marbank, the great claret importers, had their French offices in Bordeaux. Supposedly James Windibank was there when his stepdaughter, Mary Sutherland, wrote him to ask permission to marry Hosmer Angel. *A Case of Identity*, I, 409.

BORGIAS: The black pearl of the Borgias was stolen from the Prince of Colonna's bedroom at the Dacre Hotel. *The Adventure of the Six Napoleons*, II, 585.

BOSCOMBE POOL: Charles McCarthy was brutally slain on the moist, grassy edge of the Boscombe Pool. *The Boscombe Valley Mystery*, II, 135, 145.

BOSCOMBE VALLEY: Boscombe Valley, site of the brutal murder of Charles McCarthy, is a country district, not very far from Ross, in Herefordshire. *The Boscombe Valley Mystery*, II, 135.

BOSWELL, JAMES: As Holmes noted the approach of the august author of the anonymous note he had received at the outset of his encounter with *the* woman, Watson offered to go, but Holmes replied, "Stay where you are. I am lost without my Boswell. And this promises to be interesting. It would be a pity to miss it." *A Scandal in Bohemia*, I, 351.

BOTANY: In Watson's famous catalogue of "Sherlock Holmes—his limits," he rated the Great Detective's knowledge of botany as "Variable. Well up in belladonna, opium, and poisons generally. Knows nothing of practical gardening." *A Study in Scarlet*, I, 156.

BOUGUEREAU, ADOLPHE WILLIAM: No doubt could have been thrown on the authenticity of the Bouguereau that hung in Thaddeus Sholto's house. *The Sign of the Four*, I, 626.

BOWERY, THE: The dangerous section of New York City in which Gennaro Lucca saved Tito Castalotte from some ruffians. By doing so, Lucca made "a powerful friend." *The Adventure of the Red Circle*, II, 702.

BOXER CARTRIDGES: "When Holmes in one of his queer humours would sit in an arm-chair, with his hair-trigger and a hundred Boxer cartridges, and proceed to adorn the opposite wall with a patriotic V.R. done in bullet-pocks," the good Dr. Watson felt "strongly that neither the atmosphere nor the appearance of our room was improved by it." *The Musgrave Ritual*, I, 123.

BOXING: In Watson's famous catalogue of "Sherlock Holmes—his limits," he noted that the Great Detective was "an expert singlestick player, boxer, and swordsman." *A Study in Scarlet*, I, 156; see also *The Yellow Face*, I, 575; *The "Gloria Scott"*, I, 108–9; *The Adventure of the Solitary Cyclist*, II, 390–91.

BRACKENSTALL, SIR EUSTACE: One of the richest men in Kent, Sir Eustace was a tall, well-made man about forty years old. Though a decent chap when sober, he turned into a fiend when under the influence of alcohol—for example, once he drenched his wife's dog with petroleum and set it afire! He was killed by a blow to the head with a heavy poker, and Stanley Hopkins thought the case would be "something quite in [Sherlock Holmes's] line." *The Adventure of the Abbey Grange*, II, 496.

BRACKENSTALL, LADY MARY: Née Miss Mary Fraser in Adelaide, Australia, Lady Brackenstall was a beautiful blonde, golden-haired and blue-eyed. After arriving in England with her maid, Theresa Wright, she was won over by Sir Eustace Brackenstall's title, money, and "London ways." Their relationship quickly deteriorated during their several months of marriage. *The Adventure of the Abbey Grange*, II, 493ff.

BRACKWELL, LADY EVA: "The most beautiful *débutante* of last season," Lady Eva found her planned marriage to the Earl of Dovercourt threatened by Charles Augustus Milverton. Milverton had gained possession of several imprudent letters Lady Eva had once written to "an impecunious young squire in the country," and Milverton intended to dispatch the letters to the Earl, thus breaking off the match, unless seven thousand pounds were paid him. *The Adventure of Charles Augustus Milverton*, II, 560.

BRADFORD: Holmes was jubilant over his discovery of "an infallible test for blood stains." He felt it would have been decisive in the case of Mason of Bradford. *A Study in Scarlet*, I, 150, 151.

BRADLEY'S: Holmes asked Watson, as the latter went out, to ask Bradley's to send up a pound of the strongest shag tobacco to help the Great Detective mull over the salient points of the mysterious death of Sir Charles Baskerville. *The Hound of the Baskervilles*, II, 17.

BRADSHAW (RAILWAY GUIDE): Holmes asked Watson to look up the trains in Bradshaw when he contemplated meeting with Miss Violet Hunter at the Black Swan Hotel in Winchester. *The Adventure of the Copper Beeches*, II, 120; see also *The Valley of Fear*, I, 474.

BRADSTREET, INSPECTOR: He was in charge of the Bow Street police station when Holmes and Watson wished to interview the wretched beggar Hugh Boone in the matter of the sudden disappearance of Neville St. Clair. *The Man with the Twisted Lip*, I, 382.

Bradstreet also gave evidence as to the arrest of one John Horner, who was taken into custody in the disappearance of the Countess of Morcar's fabulous jewel, the blue carbuncle. *The Adventure of the Blue Carbuncle*, I, 456.

Bradstreet accompanied Holmes, Watson, Victor Hatherley, and a plainclothesman to Eyford in Berkshire to investigate the brutal severing of Mr. Hatherley's thumb. *The Adventure of the Engineer's Thumb*, II, 221.

BRAMBLETYE HOTEL: In Forest Row, Sussex. Inspector Stanley Hopkins had arranged for rooms for Holmes and Watson there after their investigation of the scene of the bloody death of Captain Peter Carey at Woodman's Lee. John Hopley Neligan had also stayed there. *The Adventure of Black Peter*, II, 408.

BRAZIL: Jonathan Small and Tonga had booked passage on the *Esmeralda*, at Gravesend, bound for the Brazils, in their attempt to escape England after the murder of Bartholomew Sholto. *The Sign of the Four*, I, 670; see also *The Problem of Thor Bridge*, II, 591.

BRECKINRIDGE, MR.: Proprietor of a meat market in Covent Garden, he sold a goose to Mr. Windigate of the Alpha Inn, whose Christmas goose club then allotted it to Mr. Henry Baker. *The Adventure of the Blue Carbuncle*, I, 460.

BREWER, SAM: A well-known Curzon Street moneylender. He was the chief creditor of Sir Robert Norberton. Norberton had once almost come to Holmes's attention when he nearly horsewhipped Brewer to death on Newmarket Heath. *The Adventure of Shoscombe Old Place*, II, 630.

BRIARBRAE: Percy Phelps's residence, in Woking. *The Naval Treaty*, II, 169.

BRICKFALL & AMBERLEY: Manufacturers of artistic materials. "You will see their names upon paint-boxes." Josiah Amberley, the retired junior partner of the firm, came to Holmes with the tragic story of his wife's elopement with a neighbor — and with Amberley's fortune. *The Adventure of the Retired Colourman*, II, 546.

BRIONY LODGE: Irene Adler's residence was Briony Lodge, Serpentine Avenue, St. John's Wood. *A Scandal in Bohemia*, I, 355-56.

BRITISH GOVERNMENT: Holmes said that Watson was correct in thinking that his brother Mycroft was under the British Government. "You would also be right in a sense if you said that occasionally he *is* the British Government." *The Adventure of the Bruce-Partington Plans*, II, 433.

BRITISH MUSEUM: Holmes spent one morning in the British Museum reading Eckermann's *Voodooism and the Negroid Religions*, among other works, in order to determine the significance of the torn bird, the pail of blood, and the charred bones found in the "weird kitchen" of Wisteria Lodge. *The Adventure of Wisteria Lodge*, II, 250, 259; see also *The Adventure of the Blue Carbuncle*, I, 459; *The Musgrave Ritual*, I, 125–26; *The Hound of the Baskervilles*, II, 107; *The Adventure of the Red Circle*, II, 696, 701.

BRIXTON: The Tangeys, the commissionaire and charwoman at the Foreign Office on the night that the top-secret naval treaty disappeared from Percy Phelps's office there, lived at NO. 16 Ivy Lane, Brixton. *The Naval Treaty*, II, 174; see also *The Adventure of Black Peter*, II, 408; *The Disappearance of Lady Frances Carfax*, II, 664; *The Adventure of the Three Garridebs*, II, 654; *The Adventure of the Red Circle*, II, 694.

BRODERICK AND NELSON: The dog Toby followed the scent of creosote to Broderick and Nelson's large timber yard. *The Sign of the Four*, I, 649.

BROOK STREET: Dr. Percy Trevelyan had his headquarters at 403 Brook Street. Mr. Blessington, his benefactor, shared the residence with him. *The Resident Patient*, I, 268, 273.

BROOKLYN: The borough of New York City in which Gennaro and Emilia Lucca had taken and furnished a little house. *The Adventure of the Red Circle*, II, 702.

BROOKS: According to Holmes, this criminal was one of the "fifty men" who had good reason for taking Holmes's life. *The Adventure of the Bruce-Partington Plans*, II, 432.

THE BROTHERHOOD: One of the two names used by the Russian Nihilist group of which Anna, her estranged husband, and "the friend of her heart," Alexis, had been members. *The Adventure of the Golden Pince-Nez*, II, 365.

BROWN, LIEUTENANT BROMLEY: One of the three men in command of the native troops at the Blair Island penal colony in the Andaman Islands. *The Sign of the Four*, I, 682.

BROWN, JOSIAH: Of Laburnum Lodge, Laburnum Vale, Chiswick. Holmes knew that his might be the next of the plaster casts of Devine's bust of Napoleon to be smashed. *The Adventure of the Six Napoleons*, II, 583.

BROWN, SAM: One of the burly police inspectors who accompanied Athelney Jones, Holmes, and Watson on board the police launch in pursuit of the steam launch *Aurora*. *The Sign of the Four*, I, 672.

BROWN, SILAS: Trainer and manager at Capleton Stables, in Dartmoor, where Desborough, the second favorite for the Wessex Cup, was kept. Holmes said of him, "A more perfect compound of the bully, coward and sneak than Master Silas Brown I have seldom met with." *Silver Blaze*, II, 274, 275.

BROWNER, JIM: Married Mary Cushing in Liverpool. He first worked as a steward on a South American line, but later transferred to the Liverpool, Dublin, and London Steam Packet Company aboard the *May Day*. He was involved with two of the Cushing sisters. *The Cardboard Box*, II, 199, 202, 204.

BRUCE-PARTINGTON SUBMARINE: A weapon so powerful that it was said that "naval warfare becomes impossible within the radius of a Bruce-Partington's operation." Once Holmes learned of the theft of the submarine's plans, he had to figure out why seven of the ten stolen papers ended up "in the pockets of a dead junior clerk in the heart of London." *The Adventure of the Bruce-Partington Plans*, II, 435–36.

BRUCE PINKERTON PRIZE: Dr. Percy Trevelyan, while at King's College Hospital, won the Bruce Pinkerton prize and medal for his monograph upon obscure nervous lesions. *The Resident Patient*, I, 268, 269.

BRUNTON, RICHARD: The butler at Hurlstone, the ancestral home of a branch of the Musgrave family, in Sussex. His mysterious disappearance, after he had been caught going through the Musgrave family papers, brought Holmes into the case. *The Musgrave Ritual*, I, 128.

BRUSSELS: On their Continental journey into Switzerland, Holmes and Watson landed at Dieppe, and made their way by nightfall to Brussels. *The Final Problem*, II, 310; see also *The Stockbroker's Clerk*, II, 157.

BUDAPEST: A newspaper clipping from Budapest told of the fate of Wilson Kemp, Harold Latimer, and Sophy Kratides. *The Greek Interpreter*, I, 605; see also *The Adventure of the Devil's Foot*, II, 516, 524.

BUDDHA: After receiving a summons from Eugenia Ronder at the beginning of *The Adventure of the Veiled Lodger*, "Sherlock Holmes threw himself with fierce energy upon the pile of commonplace books in the corner [of his sitting-room].... So excited was he that he did not rise, but sat upon the floor like some strange Buddha, with crossed legs, the huge books all round him, and one open upon his knees." *The Adventure of the Veiled Lodger*, II, 455; see also *The Sign of the Four*, I, 662.

BUFFALO: Holmes, in the disguise of Altamont, the Irish-American spy, graduated in an Irish secret society at Buffalo. *His Last Bow*, II, 801.

BULL, THE: Holmes and Watson took rooms at The Bull inn in Esher, Surrey, when they traveled there to investigate a mystery. *The Adventure of Wisteria Lodge*, II, 246.

BULL PUP: Watson confessed to Holmes, upon their first meeting, that one of his shortcomings was that he kept a bull pup. *A Study in Scarlet*, I, 151.

BULL-TERRIER: Holmes's sole friend during his two years at college was Victor Trevor, whom he met "only through the accident of his bull-terrier freezing on my ankle one morning as I went down to chapel." *The "Gloria Scott"*, I, 108.

BURNETT, MISS: An Englishwoman of about forty, she possessed an "aquiline and emaciated face." She served as governess for Mr. Henderson's children. She was part of a plot to murder Don Juan Murillo, the Tiger of San Pedro. *The Adventure of Wisteria Lodge*, II, 254.

BURNWELL, SIR GEORGE: The friend of Arthur Holder, he secretly courted Arthur's cousin, Mary Holder. Alexander Holder, Arthur's father, said of Burnwell: "He is older than Arthur, a man of the world to his finger-tips, one who has been everywhere, seen everything, a brilliant talker, and a man of great personal beauty. Yet when I think of him in cold blood...I am convinced...that he is one who should be deeply distrusted." Holmes seconded this latter opinion, "He is one of the most dangerous men in England—a ruined gambler, an absolutely desperate villain; a man without heart or conscience." *The Adventure of the Beryl Coronet*, II, 287, 296–97.

C

CAIRNS, PATRICK: "A fierce, bull-dog face was framed in a tangle of hair and beard, and two bold dark eyes gleamed behind the cover of thick, tufted, overhung eyebrows." Captain Basil (Sherlock Holmes in disguise) hired him as harpooner for his exploring expedition. He had been a harpooner for twenty-six years, and had sailed out of Dundee aboard the *Sea Unicorn*. *The Adventure of Black Peter*, II, 410–11.

CALCUTTA: Dr. Grimesby Roylott had, by his professional skill and force of character, established a large practice in Calcutta. *The Adventure of the Speckled Band*, I, 245.

CALHOUN, CAPTAIN JAMES: Of the barque *Lone Star*, Savannah, Georgia. He was the leader of the gang that pursued two generations of Openshaws to their deaths. *The Five Orange Pips*, I, 402, 403.

CAMBERWELL: Madame Charpentier's boarding-house, where the late Enoch J. Drebber had stayed, was in Torquay Terrace, Camberwell. *A Study in Scarlet*, I, 184; see also *A Case of Identity*, I, 410; *The Valley of Fear*, I, 477; *The Disappearance of Lady Frances Carfax*, II, 657.

CAMBERWELL POISONING CASE: "The year '87 furnished us with a long series of cases of greater or less interest, of which I retain the records." One of the cases during this twelve-month period was the Camberwell poisoning case. "In the latter, as may be remembered, Sherlock Holmes was able, by winding up the dead man's watch, to prove that it had been wound up two hours ago, and that therefore the deceased had gone to bed within that time—a deduction which was of the greatest importance in clearing up the case." *The Five Orange Pips*, I, 389.

CAMBERWELL ROAD: The hat found beside the dead body of Enoch J. Drebber was made by John Underwood and Sons, 129 Camberwell Road. *A Study in Scarlet*, I, 187.

CAMBRIDGE: Sherlock Holmes, who traveled to Cambridge to investigate the mysterious disappearance of the athletic Godfrey Staunton, thought of Cambridge as an "inhospitable town." *The Adventure of the Missing Three-Quarter*, II, 484, 486; see also *The Naval Treaty*, II, 167; *The Adventure of the Golden Pince-Nez*, II, 353.

CAMDEN HOUSE: The house opposite Holmes's and Watson's quarters at 221B Baker Street. It was empty, with "bare planking" and wallpaper "hanging in ribbons." *The Adventure of the Empty House*, II, 338, 340.

CAMFORD: The name both of a "famous University [composed of] . . . ancient colleges" and of the "charming town" in which the university was located. *The Adventure of the Creeping Man*, II, 752.

CAMPDEN HOUSE ROAD: Horace Harker's plaster cast of Devine's bust of Napoleon was found smashed to pieces in the front garden of an empty house in Campden House Road. *The Adventure of the Six Napoleons*, II, 576.

CAMPDEN MANSIONS: Louis La Rothière, of Campden Mansions, Notting Hill, was one of three foreign agents in England capable of handling as large an affair as the stealing of the Bruce-Partington submarine plans. *The Adventure of the Bruce-Partington Plans*, II, 445.

CANDAHAR: The young Dr. Watson, newly attached to the Fifth Northumberland Fusiliers as Assistant Surgeon, joined his regiment at Candahar, in Afghanistan. *A Study in Scarlet*, I, 143.

CANTERBURY: The Continental Express that carried Holmes and Watson stopped at Canterbury. There, they left the train and made a cross-country journey to Newhaven, and from there to Dieppe by boat. *The Final Problem*, II, 309-10.

CANTLEMERE, LORD: He was helping to manage the recovery of the stolen Mazarin stone and was opposed to Holmes's involvement in the case. Holmes flippantly "discovered" the stolen property on Lord Cantlemere's person. *The Adventure of the Mazarin Stone*, II, 745.

CAPITAL AND COUNTIES BANK: Holmes's financial agents were the Capital and Counties Bank, Oxford Street branch. *The Adventure of the Priory School*, II, 625; see also *The Man with the Twisted Lip*, I, 373; *The Adventure of the Bruce-Partington Plans*, II, 435.

CAPLETON STABLES: Located on the moor, about two miles from the King's Pyland Stables, Capleton Stables was owned by Lord Backwater and managed by Silas Brown. *Silver Blaze*, II, 264.

CARBONARI: The "old" Italian organization, to which the Neapolitan terrorist society, the Red Circle, was allied. *The Adventure of the Red Circle*, II, 703; see also *A Study in Scarlet*, I, 184.

CARERE, MLLE: The full explanation of the adventure of *The Hound of the Baskervilles* had to wait until Holmes had concluded two cases of "the utmost importance... in the second he had defended the unfortunate Mme Montpensier from the charge of murder which hung over her in connection with the death of her step-daughter, Mlle Carère, the young lady who, as it will be remembered, was found six months later alive and married in New York." *The Hound of the Baskervilles*, II, 105.

CAREY, MISS: Daughter of the murdered Captain Peter Carey; "a pale fair-haired girl, whose eyes blazed defiantly at us as she told us that she was glad that her father was dead, and that she blessed the hand which had struck him down." *The Adventure of Black Peter*, II, 404.

CAREY, MRS.: Wife of the murdered Captain Peter Carey; "a haggard grey-haired woman, the widow of the murdered man, whose gaunt and deep-lined face, with the furtive look of terror in the depths of her red-rimmed eyes, told of the years of hardship and ill-usage which she had endured." *The Adventure of Black Peter*, II, 404.

CAREY, CAPTAIN PETER: Of Woodman's Lee, Sussex. The very obscure circumstances surrounding his death led Inspector Stanley Hopkins to call Holmes into the case. Peter Carey "was born in '45.... He was a most daring and successful seal and whale fisher. In 1883 he commanded the steam sealer *Sea Unicorn*, of Dundee.... His household consisted of his wife, his daughter, aged twenty, and two female servants.... The man was an intermittent drunkard, and when he had the fit on him he was a perfect fiend...you would go far before you found a more dangerous man than Peter Carey." *The Adventure of Black Peter*, II, 400.

CARFAX, THE LADY FRANCES: Holmes believed that "one of the most dangerous classes in the world is the drifting and friendless woman. She is the most harmless, and often the most useful of mortals, but she is the inevitable inciter of crime in others." Lady Frances was one such, being the sole survivor of the direct family of the late Earl of Rufton. When her old governess had not heard from her for several weeks, Holmes was called in. *The Disappearance of Lady Frances Carfax*, II, 657, 669.

CARINA: Holmes suggested to Watson, "Let us escape from this weary workaday world by the side door of music. Carina sings to-night at the Albert Hall, and we still have time to dress, dine and enjoy." *The Adventure of the Retired Colourman*, II, 550.

CARLO: The mastiff guard-dog at the Copper Beeches in Hampshire. Only Toller, the groom, could handle him. *The Adventure of the Copper Beeches*, II, 125, 126.

CARLO: A spaniel owned by Robert Ferguson, Carlo walked with difficulty. Its hind legs moved irregularly and its tail was on the ground. Though a veterinarian had diagnosed Carlo's malady as spinal meningitis, Holmes understood that the beast's infirmity had been brought about by unnatural causes. *The Adventure of the Sussex Vampire*, ii, 468, 473.

CARLTON: Mycroft Holmes's club, the Diogenes, lay "some little distance from the Carlton," in Pall Mall. *The Greek Interpreter*, i, 593.

Holmes received a note from Sir James Damery asking to see the detective. The note was sent from the Carlton Club. *The Adventure of the Illustrious Client*, ii, 671.

CARLYLE, THOMAS: Watson felt that Holmes's "ignorance was as remarkable as his knowledge. Of contemporary literature, philosophy and politics he appeared to know next to nothing. Upon my quoting Thomas Carlyle, he inquired in the naivest way who he might be and what he had done." *A Study in Scarlet*, i, 154; see also *The Sign of the Four*, i, 648.

CARNAWAY, JIM: A Scowrer killed in an attempt to murder Chester Wilcox. His widow received a pension from the Vermissa Valley Lodge. *The Valley of Fear*, i, 542.

CARRUTHERS, BOB: "He was a dark, sallow, clean-shaven, silent person; but he had polite manners and a pleasant smile." When he invited the very poor Violet Smith to accept a good-paying position as music teacher to his only daughter, Miss Smith accepted. Carruthers was a good friend of the bully, Jack Woodley; they had ulterior motives for involving Miss Smith in the household. Carruthers fell in love with Violet, and his strange behavior stemming from this romance prompted Miss Smith to consult with Sherlock Holmes. *The Adventure of the Solitary Cyclist*, ii, 385ff.

CARRUTHERS, COLONEL: At the time Holmes received the interesting telegram from Scott Eccles concerning a "most incredible and grotesque experience" about which he wished to consult Holmes, the Great Detective had been bored "since we locked up Colonel Carruthers," and thus, was more than eager to take up any case that held some promise of interest. *The Adventure of Wisteria Lodge*, ii, 238.

CARTER: Treasurer of the Vermissa Valley Lodge of the Ancient Order of Freemen. "He was a capable organizer, and the actual details of nearly every outrage had sprung from his plotting brain." *The Valley of Fear*, i, 569.

CARTWRIGHT: A member of the Worthingdon bank gang. On the evidence of his deceitful confederate, Sutton, he was hanged. *The Resident Patient*, I, 279.

CARTWRIGHT: "A lad of fourteen, with a bright, keen face," he had shown some ability during the investigation of the case which had saved the good name, and perhaps the life, of Wilson, the manager of the district messenger station where Cartwright worked. Holmes employed Cartwright to search for the newspaper from which the message of warning to Sir Henry Baskerville had been clipped. Later, disguised as a country lad, Cartwright brought food and supplies to Holmes. Cartwright also kept track of Dr. Watson's activities at Baskerville Hall. *The Hound of the Baskervilles*, II, 28.

CASTALOTTE, TITO: An Italian gentleman, he was "saved...from some ruffians in a place called the Bowery" by Gennaro Lucca. Castalotte was the senior partner in the firm of Castalotte & Zamba, the chief fruit importers of New York. Moreover, he had all power within the firm; so, as a reward, he "made [Lucca] head of a department, and showed his goodwill towards him in every way." Indeed, as Castalotte was a bachelor, and felt as if Gennaro was his son, both Gennaro and his wife loved him as if he were their father. Thus, it was certainly understandable that Gennaro balked when the Red Circle, a Neapolitan terrorist society of which he was no longer a willing member, ordered him to blow up both Castalotte and Castalotte's house with dynamite because Castalotte refused to yield to their violent threats. *The Adventure of the Red Circle*, II, 702–3.

CATULLUS: One of the three books which Sherlock Holmes, in the guise of an elderly, deformed bibliophile, offered to sell Watson, shortly after the two had collided outside the house in which Ronald Adair had been murdered. *The Adventure of the Empty House*, II, 332.

CAUNTER: The elder of the two boys occupying the inner room attached to Lord Saltire's bedroom at the Priory School. He was a light sleeper but heard no disturbance on the night that Lord Saltire mysteriously disappeared. *The Adventure of the Priory School*, II, 610.

CAVENDISH CARD CLUB: One of the three card clubs of which Ronald Adair was a member. *The Adventure of the Empty House*, II, 330.

CAVENDISH SQUARE: Dr. Percy Trevelyan noted that "a specialist who aims high is compelled to start in one of a dozen streets in the Cavendish Square quarter, all of which entail enormous rents and furnishing expenses." He was able to meet those costs through the windfall of Mr. Blessington's investment in his practice. *The Resident Patient*, I, 269; see also *The Adventure of the Empty House*, II, 337.

CEDARS, THE: Near Lee, in Kent, it was the residence of Neville St. Clair, who mysteriously disappeared into the room of the wretched beggar, Hugh Boone. Watson and Holmes stayed at The Cedars during their investigation of the case. *The Man with the Twisted Lip*, I, 372, 378.

CENTRAL PRESS SYNDICATE: Mr. Horace Harker, on whose doorstep a man was brutally slain, was so agitated by the event that he felt he could not write up the story for his news service, the Central Press Syndicate. *The Adventure of the Six Napoleons*, II, 575.

CHALDEAN: Sherlock Holmes made a "study of those Chaldean roots which," in his opinion, "are surely to be traced in the Cornish branch of the great Celtic speech." *The Adventure of the Devil's Foot*, II, 526.

CHANDOS, SIR CHARLES: Ames, the butler of Birlstone Manor, in Sussex, had been in service with Sir Charles Chandos for ten years before being employed by John Douglas. *The Valley of Fear*, I, 490.

CHARING CROSS: Somewhere in the vaults of the bank of Cox & Co., at Charing Cross, there was a "battered tin dispatch-box" of Watson's, crammed full of his records of Holmes's cases. *The Problem of Thor Bridge*, II, 588; see also *The Man with the Twisted Lip*, I, 382; *The Greek Interpreter*, I, 596.

CHARING CROSS HOSPITAL: James Mortimer had been house surgeon at Charing Cross Hospital from 1882 to 1884. He left his commemorative walking stick—which had the inscription, "To James Mortimer, M.R.C.S., from his friends of the C.C.H.," engraved upon it—at 221B. *The Hound of the Baskervilles*, II, 5.

Holmes was first carried to the Charing Cross Hospital and then taken to his rooms in Baker Street after the murderous attack made upon him at the direction of the notorious Baron Adelbert Gruner. *The Adventure of the Illustrious Client*, II, 682.

CHARING CROSS HOTEL: Holmes laid a trap for a certain international agent in the smoking-room of the Charing Cross Hotel. *The Adventure of the Bruce-Partington Plans*, II, 452.

CHARING CROSS POST OFFICE: Scott Eccles sent Holmes a telegram from the Charing Cross Post Office describing his "most incredible and grotesque experience" at the hands of Aloysius Garcia. *The Adventure of Wisteria Lodge*, 11, 238.

CHARING CROSS STATION: A woman, who was later learned to have been the unfortunate Mme. Henri Fournaye, "attracted much attention at Charing Cross Station on Tuesday morning by the wildness of her appearance and the violence of her gestures." *The Adventure of the Second Stain*, 1, 312.

One of the villains who gave the letter "M" such luster in Holmes's scrapbook was Mathews, who "knocked out my left canine in the waiting-room at Charing Cross." *The Adventure of the Empty House*, 11, 346; see also *The Adventure of the Abbey Grange*, 11, 491; *The Adventure of the Illustrious Client*, 11, 682.

CHARLES I: He entrusted his crown to the Musgrave family so that they could pass it on to Charles II when he ascended to the throne. *The Musgrave Ritual*, 1, 140.

CHARLES II: Sir Ralph Musgrave had been "a prominent Cavalier, and the right-hand man of Charles 11 in his wanderings." *The Musgrave Ritual*, 1, 138, 140.

CHARLINGTON HALL: Located between the village of Farnham and Chiltern Grange, "the house was invisible from the road, but the surroundings all spoke of gloom and decay." An unfrocked clergyman named Williamson lived alone with a small staff of servants at the hall, and a permanent houseguest was Jack Woodley, of South African infamy. *The Adventure of the Solitary Cyclist*, 11, 388.

CHARPENTIER, ALICE: Her brother thrashed Enoch J. Drebber following Drebber's improper advances toward her. Tobias Gregson thought she was "an uncommonly fine girl." *A Study in Scarlet*, 1, 187, 188.

CHARPENTIER, ARTHUR: A sub-lieutenant in the Royal Navy, he gave Enoch J. Drebber a sound thrashing after Drebber had made improper advances towards Charpentier's sister. This occurred on the very night that Drebber was found murdered. Tobias Gregson took him into custody for the murder. *A Study in Scarlet*, 1, 185.

CHARPENTIER, MADAME: The late Enoch J. Drebber and his secretary, Joseph Stangerson, had stayed at Madame Charpentier's boarding-house, in Torquay Terrace, Camberwell. *A Study in Scarlet*, 1, 184.

CHEESEMAN'S: Robert Ferguson's home near Lamberley, Sussex, was an isolated and ancient farm-house. "The ancient tiles which lined the porch were marked with the rebus of a cheese and a man, after the original builder." *The Adventure of the Sussex Vampire*, 11, 463, 468.

CHEETAH: One of the exotic pets Dr. Grimesby Roylott kept on his ancestral estate at Stoke Moran, in western Surrey. *The Adventure of the Speckled Band*, 1, 258–59.

CHEMISTRY: Young Stamford, Watson's former dresser at Barts, felt that Sherlock Holmes was "a first-class chemist." Watson, too, felt that Holmes's knowledge of chemistry was "profound." But later, Watson changed his opinion to "eccentric." *A Study in Scarlet*, 1, 148, 156; see also *The Five Orange Pips*, 1, 399; *The Sign of the Four*, 1, 657.

CHEQUERS: The inn in Lamberley, Sussex, at which Holmes and Watson stayed while investigating a mother's strange behavior. *The Adventure of the Sussex Vampire*, 11, 468.

CHEQUERS: The ancient hostel in Camford at which Holmes and Watson stayed while involved in *The Adventure of the Creeping Man*. Holmes recalled that "the port [at the inn] used to be above mediocrity, and the linen above reproach." *The Adventure of the Creeping Man*, 11, 757.

CHESS: "Amberley excelled at chess—one mark, Watson, of a scheming mind." *The Adventure of the Retired Colourman*, 11, 554.

CHESTERFIELD: Neville St. Clair's father had been a schoolmaster in Chesterfield. One day, Neville had suddenly disappeared into the beggar Hugh Boone's room, and not a trace of his body had been found. *The Man with the Twisted Lip*, 1, 385; see also *The Adventure of the Priory School*, 11, 616, 626.

CHESTERTON: One of the villages on the north side of Cambridge, it had been explored and found disappointing by Sherlock Holmes in his search for Godfrey Staunton, the missing star of Cambridge University's rugger team. *The Adventure of the Missing Three-Quarter*, 11, 487.

CHICAGO: Abe Slaney was known as "the most dangerous crook in Chicago." Though Holmes claimed knowledge of Chicago criminals, he relied on a friend in the New York Police Bureau to provide him with this information about Slaney. *The Adventure of the Dancing Men*, II, 542.

Holmes, in the disguise of Altamont, the Irish-American spy, started in Chicago the long trek that was to culminate in his capture of the German spy Von Bork. *His Last Bow*, II, 801; see also *The Adventure of the Three Garridebs*, II, 645, 651–52.

CHILTERN GRANGE: About six miles from the village of Farnham, Chiltern Grange was the residence of Bob Carruthers. *The Adventure of the Solitary Cyclist*, II, 385.

CHINA: Holmes deduced that Jabez Wilson, the man with the fiery red hair, had been to China, by the tattoo immediately above Wilson's right wrist. "That trick of staining the fishes' scales of a delicate pink is quite peculiar to China. When, in addition, I see a Chinese coin hanging from your watch-chain, the matter becomes even more simple." *The Red-Headed League*, I, 420.

CHISWICK: Josiah Brown, whose plaster cast of Napoleon's head was smashed, resided at Laburnum Lodge, Laburnum Vale, Chiswick. *The Adventure of the Six Napoleons*, II, 580.

CHOPIN, FREDERIC: Holmes looked forward to spending his afternoon at Hallé's listening to Norman-Neruda play. Said he to Watson, "Her attack and her bowing are splendid. What's that little thing of Chopin's she plays so magnificently: Tra-la-la-lira-lira-lay." *A Study in Scarlet*, I, 178.

CHOWDAR, LAL: The faithful servant of Major John Sholto. *The Sign of the Four*, I, 628.

CHRISTIE'S: Reclusive collector Nathan Garrideb seldom went out, except to "drive down to Sotheby's or Christie's [sales room]." *The Adventure of the Three Garridebs*, II, 648; see also *The Adventure of the Illustrious Client*, II, 685.

CHURCH STREET: Sherlock Holmes, while posing as an elderly, deformed bibliophile, claimed to Watson that he kept a little bookshop at the corner of Church Street, quite near Watson's Kensington digs. *The Adventure of the Empty House*, II, 332; see also *The Adventure of the Six Napoleons*, II, 578.

CIGAR: Holmes reasoned that the murderer of Enoch J. Drebber had smoked a Trichinopoly cigar. "I gathered up some scattered ash from the floor. It was dark in colour and flakey — such an ash as is only made by a Trichinopoly. I have made a special study of cigar ashes — in fact, I have written a monograph upon the subject. I flatter myself that I can distinguish at a glance the ash of any known brand either of cigar or of tobacco." *A Study in Scarlet*, I, 173.

CITY AND SUBURBAN BANK, COBURG BRANCH: It lay just around the corner from Jabez Wilson's Coburg Square pawnshop. *The Red-Headed League*, I, 431.

CLAPHAM JUNCTION: As Holmes, Watson, and Colonel Ross returned to London following the successful conclusion of *Silver Blaze*, their train passed through Clapham Junction on its way to Victoria Station. *Silver Blaze*, II, 281; see also *The Greek Interpreter*, I, 600; *The Naval Treaty*, II, 179.

CLARIDGE'S HOTEL: Von Bork's servant Martha was to meet Holmes at Claridge's Hotel on the day following the capture of the German spy. *His Last Bow*, II, 800; see also *The Problem of Thor Bridge*, II, 589.

CLAY, JOHN: Vincent Spaulding, the "bright-looking, clean-shaven young fellow" who was Jabez Wilson's assistant, was actually John Clay. Holmes observed: "He is, in my judgment, the fourth smartest man in London, and for daring I am not sure that he has not a claim to be third. I have known something of him before." Peter Jones, the official police investigator, assessed the man thus: "John Clay, the murderer, thief, smasher, and forger. He's a young man...but he is at the head of his profession, and I would rather have my bracelets on him than on any criminal in London. He's a remarkable man, is young John Clay. His grandfather was a Royal Duke, and he himself has been to Eton and Oxford. His brain is as cunning as his fingers, and though we meet signs of him at every turn, we never know where to find the man himself." *The Red-Headed League*, I, 430, 433.

CLAYTON, JOHN: Of 3 Turpey Street, the Borough, he was a rough-looking man. His cab, number 2704, out of Shipley's Yard, near Waterloo Station, picked up a fare in Trafalgar Square who offered him two guineas to do what he said all day. *The Hound of the Baskervilles*, II, 34.

CLEFT TOR: John Barrymore, the butler at Baskerville Hall, got late-night signals from the Cleft Tor. *The Hound of the Baskervilles*, II, 64.

CLEVELAND: In the pocket of Enoch J. Drebber, found dead under mysterious circumstances in an empty house on the Brixton Road, were cards bearing his name and onetime residence, Cleveland, Ohio. *A Study in Scarlet*, I, 165, 222.

COAL AND IRON POLICE, THE: A special body of police raised by the railways and colliery owners in the Vermissa Valley to supplement the efforts of the ordinary civil police, helpless in the face of the Scowrers, who terrorized the district. *The Valley of Fear*, I, 537.

COBB, JOHN: A groom at Charles McCarthy's Hatherley Farm, he accompanied McCarthy to Ross on the day McCarthy's son returned from Bristol. *The Boscombe Valley Mystery*, II, 138.

COBURG SQUARE: Jabez Wilson had a small pawnbroker's business at Coburg Square, near the City. *The Red-Headed League*, I, 422.

COCAINE: "Sherlock Holmes took his bottle from the corner of the mantelpiece, and his hypodermic syringe from its neat morocco case. With his long, white, nervous fingers he adjusted the delicate needle, and rolled back his left shirt-cuff. For some little time his eyes rested thoughtfully upon the sinewy forearm and wrist, all dotted and scarred with innumerable puncture marks. Finally, he thrust the sharp point home, pressed down the tiny piston, and sank back into the velvet-lined armchair with a long sigh of satisfaction.

"Three times a day for many months I had witnessed this performance, but custom had not reconciled my mind to it. On the contrary, from day to day I had become more irritable at the sight, and my conscience swelled nightly within me at the thought that I had lacked the courage to protest...

"'Which is it today,' I asked, 'morphine or cocaine?'

"'It is cocaine,' he said, 'a seven-per-cent. solution. Would you care to try it?'" *The Sign of the Four*, I, 610; see also *The Yellow Face*, I, 575.

COLONNA, PRINCE OF: The famous black pearl of the Borgias had been stolen from his bedroom at the Dacre Hotel. *The Adventure of the Six Napoleons*, II, 585.

CONDUIT STREET: The notorious Colonel Sebastian Moran's address was in Conduit Street. *The Adventure of the Empty House*, II, 347.

CONK-SINGLETON FORGERY CASE: After the successful conclusion to *The Adventure of the Six Napoleons*, Holmes instructed Watson to get out the papers of the Conk-Singleton forgery case. *The Adventure of the Six Napoleons*, II, 587.

COOK, POLICE CONSTABLE: Of the H Division. While "on duty near Waterloo Bridge, [he] heard a cry for help and a splash in the water. The night, however, was extremely dark and stormy, so that, in spite of the help of several passers-by, it was quite impossible to effect a rescue." *The Five Orange Pips*, I, 401.

COOK'S (THOMAS COOK): Lady Frances Carfax had booked her journey from Lausanne to Baden through the local Cook's office. It was from the manager there that Watson learned where she had gone after leaving Lausanne. *The Disappearance of Lady Frances Carfax*, II, 659.

COOMBE TRACEY: The town in Devonshire in which Laura Lyons lived. When Inspector Lestrade came to assist Holmes, his train arrived there. It was also from there that Sherlock Holmes got his supplies while in the area. *The Hound of the Baskervilles*, II, 71, 96, 110.

COPERNICAN THEORY: Watson felt that Holmes's "ignorance was as remarkable as his knowledge. Of contemporary literature, philosophy and politics he appeared to know next to nothing.... My surprise reached a climax, however, when I found incidentally that he was ignorant of the Copernican Theory and of the composition of the Solar System." *A Study in Scarlet*, I, 154.

COPPER BEECHES, THE: Home of the Rucastles, five miles on the far side of Winchester, in Hampshire. *The Adventure of the Copper Beeches*, II, 117, 123.

COPTIC MONASTERIES: Professor Coram's *magnum opus* was an analysis of the documents found in the Coptic monasteries of Syria and Egypt, a work which, he believed, would "cut deep at the very foundations of revealed religion." *The Adventure of the Golden Pince-Nez*, II, 360.

COPTIC PATRIARCHS: At the time of *The Adventure of the Retired Colourman*, Holmes was "preoccupied with this case of the two Coptic Patriarchs, which should come to a head to-day." *The Adventure of the Retired Colourman*, II, 547.

CORAM, PROFESSOR: An elderly man, he was the resident of Yoxley Old Place in Kent. An invalid, he spent half his time in bed, "and the other half hobbling around the house with a stick, or being pushed about the grounds…in a bath-chair." Coram was a very heavy smoker, consuming a thousand Alexandrian cigarettes per fortnight, and his addiction proved to be his downfall. *The Adventure of the Golden Pince-Nez*, II, *passim*.

CORMAC, TIGER: "A thick-set, dark-faced, brutal-looking young man," he was one of the murderers connected with the Scowrers. *The Valley of Fear*, I, 541.

CORNELIUS, MR.: Another name used by Jonas Oldacre for the purpose of swindling his creditors. *The Adventure of the Norwood Builder*, II, 430.

CORNISH LANGUAGE: Sherlock Holmes "had…conceived the idea that [the ancient Cornish language] was akin to the Chaldean, and had been largely derived from the Phoenician traders in tin." *The Adventure of the Devil's Foot*, II, 509.

CORNISH PENINSULA: It was to a small cottage near Poldhu Bay, at the farthest extremity of the Cornish Peninsula, that Holmes and Watson traveled so that the Great Detective might recuperate from his "constant hard work and occasional indiscretions." *The Adventure of the Devil's Foot*, II, 509.

CORNWALL: The failure of the West Country banking firm, Dawson & Neligan, was the ruin of half the families of Cornwall. *The Adventure of Black Peter*, II, 406; see also *The Red-Headed League*, I, 433.

COROT, JEAN BAPTISTE: Thaddeus Sholto called himself "a patron of the arts. It is my weakness. The landscape is a genuine Corot…." *The Sign of the Four*, I, 626.

CORPORATION STREET: The temporary offices of the Franco-Midland Hardware Company were at 126B Corporation Street, in Birmingham. *The Stockbroker's Clerk*, II, 156, 159.

COSTA RICA: Beryl Garcia was from Costa Rica. Her husband purloined a large sum of public money, and the couple was forced to flee to England. *The Hound of the Baskervilles*, II, 106; see also *The Adventure of Black Peter*, II, 402.

COVENT GARDEN: At the conclusion of *The Adventure of the Red Circle*, Sherlock Holmes asked Watson to accompany him to a Wagner night at Covent Garden. *The Adventure of the Red Circle*, II, 704.

COVENT GARDEN MARKET: Mr. Breckinridge had his meat stall in Covent Garden Market. The goose that figures in the ensuing adventure was sold there. *The Adventure of the Blue Carbuncle*, I, 460.

COVENTRY: At the time of *The Adventure of the Solitary Cyclist*, Violet Smith's fiancé, Cyril Morton, was employed by the Midland Electric Company, at Coventry. *The Adventure of the Solitary Cyclist*, II, 387; see also *The Five Orange Pips*, I, 392.

COVENTRY, SERGEANT: Of the local Hampshire police, he was examining the affair surrounding the death of Maria Pinto Gibson, wife of Neil Gibson, the Gold King, who was found shot to death on Thor Bridge. *The Problem of Thor Bridge*, II, 597.

COWPER: Jefferson Hope learned from a Mormon named Cowper, to whom he had rendered services at different times, the news that Lucy Ferrier had been forced to marry Enoch Drebber. *A Study in Scarlet*, I, 220.

COX & CO.: "Somewhere in the vaults of the bank of Cox & Co., at Charing Cross, there is a travel-worn and battered tin dispatch-box with my name, John H. Watson, M.D., Late Indian Army, painted upon the lid. It is crammed with papers, nearly all of which are records of cases to illustrate the curious problems which Mr. Sherlock Holmes had at various times to examine." *The Problem of Thor Bridge*, II, 588.

COXON & WOODHOUSE: Hall Pycroft used to have a job at Coxon & Woodhouse, of Drapers' Gardens, but "they were let in early in the spring through the Venezuelan loan, as no doubt you remember, and came a nasty cropper." Mr. Pycroft eventually found a seemingly good job through Mr. Coxon's testimonial, but the strange circumstances surrounding it prompted him to seek Holmes's advice. *The Stockbroker's Clerk*, II, 155.

CRABBE, OLD MAN: Two Scowrers, Lander and Egan, claimed the head-money for the shooting of old man Crabbe at Stylestown. *The Valley of Fear*, I, 564.

CRANE WATER: Near Reading, it was the home of the Armitages. Percy Armitage was engaged to Helen Stoner. *The Adventure of the Speckled Band*, I, 249.

CRAVEN STREET: Site of the Mexborough Private Hotel, where Jack and Beryl Stapleton lodged while in London. *The Hound of the Baskervilles*, II, 108.

CREDIT LYONNAIS: A cheque to Miss Marie Devine from the vanished Lady Frances Carfax had been cashed at the Crédit Lyonnais at Montpelier some weeks after Lady Frances Carfax's disappearance. *The Disappearance of Lady Frances Carfax*, II, 658; see also *The Adventure of the Mazarin Stone*, II, 741.

CREMONA VIOLINS: As Holmes and Watson journeyed to NO. 3, Lauriston Gardens to investigate the mysterious death of Enoch J. Drebber in an empty house, the Great Detective "was in the best of spirits, and prattled away about Cremona fiddles, and the difference between a Stradivarius and an Amati." *A Study in Scarlet*, I, 166.

CRENDALL: Three miles from Shoscombe Old Place in Berkshire. Holmes and Watson stayed at the Green Dragon Inn located there. *The Adventure of Shoscombe Old Place*, II, 632, 636.

CREWE: Mrs. Stoner, who had married the fierce Dr. Grimesby Roylott, died some years later in a railway accident near Crewe. *The Adventure of the Speckled Band*, I, 246.

CRIMEAN WAR: The ill-fated barque *Gloria Scott* left England from Falmouth, bound for Australia with her cargo of criminals, at the height of the Crimean War. *The "Gloria Scott"*, I, 117; see also *The Crooked Man*, II, 227; *The Adventure of the Golden Pince-Nez*, II, 353; *The Disappearance of Lady Frances Carfax*, II, 663; *The Adventure of the Blanched Soldier*, II, 708.

CRITERION BAR: Dr. John H. Watson, recently returned from the second Afghan War, fortuitously ran into young Stamford, his former dresser at Barts, in the Criterion Bar. Watson was looking for lodgings cheaper than his hotel room in the Strand, and Stamford introduced him to Sherlock Holmes, who needed someone with whom to share a suite in Baker Street. *A Study in Scarlet*, I, 145, 151.

CROCKFORD (CHURCH OF ENGLAND DIRECTORY): Holmes looked up Vicar J. C. Elman's name in his Crockford. *The Adventure of the Retired Colourman*, II, 551.

CROKER, JACK (CAPTAIN): A very tall young man, with blue eyes and a golden mustache, he was remarkably quick-witted, strong as a lion, and active as a squirrel. Formerly first officer of the *Rock of Gibraltar*, he had fallen in love with Mary Fraser, when she was traveling from her native Adelaide, Australia, to England on board that ship, though Mary returned his love with only friendship. *The Adventure of the Abbey Grange*, II, *passim.*

CROSBY: A banker, he met a "terrible death" in 1894. Watson connected this death with "the repulsive story of the red leech." *The Adventure of the Golden Pince-Nez*, II, 350.

CROWDER, WILLIAM: A gamekeeper at John Turner's Boscombe Valley estate, he saw Charles McCarthy, followed by his son, walking down to the Boscombe Pool. Later, Charles McCarthy was found murdered. *The Boscombe Valley Mystery*, II, 135.

CROWN INN: Opposite Dr. Grimesby Roylott's ancestral home, in Stoke Moran, in western Surrey. Holmes and Watson took rooms there on the night concluding their investigation. *The Adventure of the Speckled Band*, I, 250, 256.

CROYDON: Miss Susan Cushing, who received a parcel containing two severed human ears, lived in Cross Street, Croydon. *The Cardboard Box*, II, 195.

CUBITT, HILTON: Of Ridling Thorpe Manor, Norfolk. He came to Holmes with a problem involving his wife's reticence over the significance of some curiously drawn stick figures. *The Adventure of the Dancing Men*, II, 528.

CUBITT, MRS. HILTON: Her maiden name was Elsie Patrick. She made her husband promise not to inquire into her previous life in America. *The Adventure of the Dancing Men*, II, 529.

CUMMINGS, MR. JOYCE: The barrister hired to defend Grace Dunbar in the matter of the shooting death of her employer's wife, Maria Pinto Gibson. *The Problem of Thor Bridge*, II, 600.

CUNNINGHAM, ALEC: "A dashing young fellow, whose bright, smiling expression and showy dress were in strange contrast with the business which had brought us there," he was the son of Mr. Cunningham, and also one of the Reigate Squires. Alec nearly succeeded in finishing the Great Detective's illustrious career. *The Reigate Squires*, I, 337.

CUNNINGHAM, MR.: "An elderly man, with a strong, deep-lined, heavy-eyed face," he was one of the Reigate Squires. William Kirwan, his coachman, was killed in the robbery of Cunningham's house. *The Reigate Squires*, I, 337.

CUSACK, CATHERINE: The maid to the Countess of Morcar, whose fabulous jewel, the blue carbuncle, was stolen from her dressing room. *The Adventure of the Blue Carbuncle*, I, 456.

CUSHING, MARY: Youngest sister of Susan Cushing, she married Jim Browner. She had been missing for some three days when her sister received a gruesome package in the mail. *The Cardboard Box*, II, *passim*.

CUSHING, SARAH: The younger sister of Susan Cushing, she had lived for a time with her married sister in Liverpool, and later, with her older sister in Croydon. She moved out of Susan Cushing's house, after some disagreement, to live in New Street, Wallington. When Holmes called on her there, she could not see him because of brain fever. *The Cardboard Box*, II, 200, 205.

CUSHING, MISS SUSAN: She lived in Cross Street, Croydon, and received a cardboard box which contained two severed human ears. Inspector Lestrade brought Holmes into the case. She was "a maiden lady of fifty, has led a most retired life, and has so few acquaintances or correspondents that it is a rare event for her to receive anything through the post." *The Cardboard Box*, II, 195–96.

CYANEA CAPILLATA: "A curious waving, vibrating, hairy creature with streaks of silver among its yellow tresses," its bite is "as dangerous to life as, and far more painful than, the bite of the cobra." A *Cyanea capillata* was responsible for the deaths of both Fitzroy McPherson and his Airedale terrier. *The Adventure of the Lion's Mane*, II, 788.

D

DACRE HOTEL: The famous black pearl of the Borgias had been stolen from the Prince of Colonna's bedroom at the Dacre Hotel. *The Adventure of the Six Napoleons*, II, 585.

DAILY GAZETTE: One of several popular London journals whose "agony columns" were filed by Sherlock Holmes in a great book. Holmes's compilation proved useful to him on many occasions, not the least of which was *The Adventure of the Red Circle*, as the detective was able to use the *Daily*

Gazette's agony column to lead him to a monstrous killer. *The Adventure of the Red Circle*, II, 694.

DAILY TELEGRAPH: Concerning the murder of Enoch J. Drebber, "the *Daily Telegraph* remarked that in the history of crime there had seldom been a tragedy which presented stranger features." *A Study in Scarlet*, I, 184; see also *The Adventure of the Norwood Builder*, II, 414, 416; *The Adventure of the Second Stain*, I, 312; *The Adventure of the Bruce-Partington Plans*, II, 449.

D'ALBERT, THE COUNTESS: Charles Augustus Milverton thought that one of the Countess's servants had come to sell him five compromising letters about her. *The Adventure of Charles Augustus Milverton*, II, 568.

DAMERY, COLONEL SIR JAMES: He consulted Holmes for his illustrious client in the Baron Adelbert Gruner affair. "He has rather a reputation for arranging delicate matters which are to be kept out of the papers." *The Adventure of the Illustrious Client*, II, 671.

DANITE BAND: "To this day, in the lonely ranches of the West, the name of the Danite Band, or the Avenging Angels, is a sinister and ill-omened one." *A Study in Scarlet*, I, 208.

DANZIG: Watson retained an almost verbatim report of Holmes's interview with Monsieur Dubuque, of the Paris police, and Fritz von Waldbaum, the well-known specialist of Danzig, in the matter of the Adventure of the Second Stain. *The Naval Treaty*, II, 167.

DARBYSHIRE, WILLIAM: An account for thirty-seven pounds fifteen from Madame Lesurier's millinery shop in Bond Street was found on John Straker's dead body. Holmes said, "When I returned to London I called upon the milliner, who at once recognized Straker [from a photo] as an excellent customer, of the name Darbyshire." *Silver Blaze*, II, 272, 281.

DARLINGTON SUBSTITUTION SCANDAL: "When a woman thinks that her house is on fire, her instinct is at once to rush to the thing that she values most. It is a perfectly overpowering impulse, and I have more than once taken advantage of it. In the case of the Darlington Substitution Scandal it was of use to me...." *A Scandal in Bohemia*, I, 364.

DARTMOOR: Site of the mysterious events surrounding the disappearance of the racehorse, Silver Blaze, and the murder of its trainer, John Straker. *Silver Blaze*, II, 261.

DARWIN, CHARLES: Holmes remembered his afternoon at Hallé's, listening to Norman-Neruda play. "Do you remember what Darwin says about music? He claims that the power of producing and appreciating it existed among the human race long before the power of speech was arrived at. Perhaps that is why we are so subtly influenced by it. There are vague memories in our souls of those misty centuries when the world was in its childhood." *A Study in Scarlet*, I, 178–79, 184.

DAUBENSEE: As Holmes and Watson passed over the Gemmi Pass along the border of the melancholy Daubensee, "a large rock which had been dislodged from the ridge upon our right clattered down and roared into the lake behind us." *The Final Problem*, II, 312.

DAVENPORT, J.: He answered Mycroft Holmes's newspaper advertisement requesting information about Sophy Kratides's whereabouts. *The Greek Interpreter*, I, 602.

DAWSON: A bookkeeper on Abel White's indigo plantation. Jonathan Small was overseer there. Both Dawson and his wife were killed in the Indian Mutiny. *The Sign of the Four*, I, 674.

DAWSON: Groom at the Capleton stables, in Dartmoor, where Desborough, the second favorite for the Wessex Cup, was trained. *Silver Blaze*, II, 274.

DAWSON & NELIGAN: West Country bankers whose failure ruined half the families of Cornwall. After the failure, Neligan disappeared. Dawson had retired some time before. *The Adventure of Black Peter*, II, 406.

DE BRINVILLIERS, MARCHIONESS: In attributing the death of Enoch J. Drebber to political refugees and revolutionists, the *Daily Telegraph* included mention of the Marchioness de Brinvilliers. *A Study in Scarlet*, I, 184.

DE CROY, PHILIPPE: As Holmes sat down to await the expected arrival of the murderer of Enoch J. Drebber, he took up a curious old book he had bought at a stall the day before—*De Jure inter Gentes*, published in Latin at Liège in the Lowlands, in 1642.

"Who is the printer?" asked Watson.

"Philippe de Croy, whoever he may have been." *A Study in Scarlet*, I, 180.

DE MERVILLE, GENERAL: Of Khyber fame. His daughter had been

enthralled by love for the notorious Baron Adelbert Gruner, and the General could do nothing about it. "De Merville is a broken man. The strong soldier has been utterly demoralized by this incident. He has lost the nerve which never failed him on the battlefield and has become a weak, doddering old man, utterly incapable of contending with a brilliant, forceful rascal like this Austrian." *The Adventure of the Illustrious Client*, II, 673, 674.

DE MERVILLE, VIOLET: She wished to marry the notorious Baron Adelbert Gruner. She was "young, rich, beautiful, accomplished, a wonder-woman in every way." Holmes described her beauty thus: "She is beautiful, but with the ethereal other-world beauty of some fanatic whose thoughts are set on high. I have seen such faces in the pictures of the old masters of the Middle Ages." *The Adventure of the Illustrious Client*, II, 673, 680.

DE QUINCEY, THOMAS: Isa Whitney "was much addicted to opium. The habit grew upon him...from some foolish freak when he was at college, for having read De Quincey's description of his dreams and sensations, he had drenched his tobacco with laudanum in an attempt to produce the same effects." *The Man with the Twisted Lip*, I, 368.

DE RESZKE (JEAN, EDOUARD; OPERA SINGERS): Starred in *Les Huguenots*, to which Holmes invited Watson after wrapping up the case. *The Hound of the Baskervilles*, II, 112.

DEEP DENE HOUSE: The residence of one Jonas Oldacre, Deep Dene House was located at the Sydenham end of the road of that name in the London suburb of Lower Norwood. *The Adventure of the Norwood Builder*, II, 416, 423.

DENNIS, SALLY: Someone posing as a Mrs. Sawyer picked up the wedding ring that Holmes had advertised as having been found in the roadway between the White Hart Tavern and Holland Grove on the night that Enoch J. Drebber was murdered. Mrs. Sawyer claimed that the ring belonged to her daughter, Sally, who had been married to Tom Dennis only a year before. *A Study in Scarlet*, I, 181.

DENNIS, TOM: Supposedly a steward aboard a Union ship. He had purportedly married Sally Sawyer. *A Study in Scarlet*, I, 181.

DESBOROUGH: Lord Backwater's racehorse, quartered at the Capleton stables, in Dartmoor, was the second favorite in the running of the Wessex Cup. *Silver Blaze*, ii, 268.

DESMOND, JAMES: An elderly clergyman in Westmorland. It was thought that he would inherit the Baskerville estate upon the death of Sir Henry Baskerville. *The Hound of the Baskervilles*, ii, 31–32.

DETECTIVE, CONSULTING: Holmes explained his profession to his new companion, Dr. Watson, "Well, I have a trade of my own. I suppose I am the only one in the world. I'm a consulting detective, if you can understand what that is. Here in London we have lots of Government detectives and lots of private ones. When these fellows are at fault, they come to me, and I manage to put them on the right scent." *A Study in Scarlet*, i, 160.

DEVINE: A French sculptor. Casts of his head of Napoleon were being smashed systematically in London. *The Adventure of the Six Napoleons*, ii, 573.

DEVINE, MISS MARIE: The Lady Frances Carfax's maid. Watson pursued her to Montpelier in hopes of finding some trace of the vanished Lady. *The Disappearance of Lady Frances Carfax*, ii, 660.

DEVONSHIRE: Site of Baskerville Hall. *The Hound of the Baskervilles*, ii, 36.

DEVOY, NANCY: Daughter of a colour-sergeant of the Royal Mallows regiment, she later married James Barclay of the same regiment. *The Crooked Man*, ii, 227.

DIEPPE: Having left the Continental Express at Canterbury, Holmes and Watson traveled overland to Newhaven, and from there to Dieppe, on their way to Switzerland. *The Final Problem*, ii, 309.

DIOGENES CLUB: Mycroft Holmes, who had "better powers of observation" than Sherlock himself, was a member of the Diogenes Club. Sherlock said, "The Diogenes Club is the queerest club in London, and Mycroft one of the queerest men.... There are many men in London, you know, who, some from shyness, some from misanthropy, have no wish for the company of their fellows. Yet they are not averse to comfortable chairs and the latest periodicals. It is for the convenience of these that the Diogenes Club was started, and it now contains the most unsociable and unclubbable men in town. No member is permitted to take the least notice of any other one. Save in the Strangers' Room, no talking is, under any circumstances, permitted, and three offences, if brought to the notice of the committee, render the talker liable to expulsion." *The Greek Interpreter*, I, 591, 593; see also *The Adventure of the Bruce-Partington Plans*, II, 433.

DIXIE, STEVE: Black fighter and member of the Spencer John gang, he burst into Holmes's rooms to try to bully him into staying out of the Harrow Weald case. *The Adventure of the Three Gables*, II, 722.

DIXON, JEREMY: A resident of Trinity College, Cambridge University, he was the owner of the canine detective Pompey, whom Sherlock Holmes considered "a very eminent specialist in the [art of tracking]." *The Adventure of the Missing Three-Quarter*, II, 487–88.

DIXON, MRS.: A lady-housekeeper who had been engaged by Bob Carruthers to look after his establishment, Chiltern Grange. *The Adventure of the Solitary Cyclist*, II, 385.

DOBNEY, SUSAN: "Old Susan Dobney with the mob cap!" was the Lady Frances Carfax's former governess, to whom the Lady had had occasion to write regularly every two weeks. When Miss Dobney had not heard from her former mistress for nearly five weeks, she called on Holmes to discover her whereabouts. *The Disappearance of Lady Frances Carfax*, II, 657, 661.

DODD, JAMES M.: He had recently returned to England from South Africa, where he had served with the Imperial Yeomanry, Middlesex Corps. He wore a short beard, and his card told Holmes that he was currently employed as a stockbroker. While in the Army, Dodd had had one Godfrey Emsworth as his best friend. Thus, he was understandably upset when he received no word from his "closest pal" for more than six months. *The Adventure of the Blanched Soldier*, II, 707ff.

DOGS: "I have serious thoughts of writing a small monograph upon the uses of dogs in the work of the detective."

"But surely, Holmes, this has been explored. Bloodhounds — sleuth-hounds —"

"No, no, Watson; that side of the matter is, of course, obvious. But there is another which is far more subtle.... A dog reflects the family life. Whoever saw a frisky dog in a gloomy family, or a sad dog in a happy one? Snarling people have snarling dogs, dangerous people have dangerous ones. And their passing moods may reflect the passing moods of others." *The Adventure of the Creeping Man*, II, 752.

Poor Fitzroy McPherson's faithful Airedale terrier suffered the same fate as his master. Holmes mused, "That the dog should die was after the beautiful, faithful nature of dogs." *The Adventure of the Lion's Mane*, II, 783.

DOLORES: A maid who had been with Mrs. Robert Ferguson before the latter's marriage — "a friend rather than a servant." Because of her longer association, Dolores had a better understanding of her mistress's character than did Mr. Ferguson. *The Adventure of the Sussex Vampire*, II, 466, 469.

DOLSKY: "The forcible administration of poison," said Holmes, "is by no means a new thing in criminal annals. The cases of Dolsky in Odessa, and of Leturier in Montpellier, will occur at once to any toxicologist." *A Study in Scarlet*, I, 232.

DONNITHORPE: A little hamlet, just to the north of Langmere, in Norfolk. It was the site of Holmes's first case, *The "Gloria Scott"*. *The "Gloria Scott"*, I, 108.

DORAK: Kept a large general store in London, and also acted as agent, for one Lowenstein of Prague, to the two clients Lowenstein had in England. *The Adventure of the Creeping Man*, II, 760.

DORAN, ALOYSIUS, ESQ.: A San Francisco millionaire, he had made his fortune in mining in the Rockies. He had one daughter, Miss Hatty Doran, who mysteriously disappeared from her wedding breakfast. *The Adventure of the Noble Bachelor*, I, 284.

DORAN, MISS HATTY: Only daughter of Aloysius Doran, the California millionaire, she mysteriously disappeared from her wedding breakfast, much to the consternation of her newly acquired spouse, Lord St. Simon, who sought Holmes's aid in solving the case. *The Adventure of the Noble Bachelor*, I, 284.

DORKING, COLONEL: A victim of Charles Augustus Milverton's machinations, he saw his wedding to the Honourable Miss Miles called off only two days before it was to take place. *The Adventure of Charles Augustus Milverton*, II, 561.

DOUGLAS, JOHN ("JACK"): "Douglas was a remarkable man both in character and in person; in age he may have been about fifty, with a strong-jawed, rugged face, a grizzling moustache, peculiarly keen grey eyes, and a wiry, vigorous figure which had lost nothing of the strength and activity of youth." *The Valley of Fear*, I, 483.

DOUGLAS, MRS. IVY: Of Birlstone Manor, in Sussex. "It was known that she was an English lady who had met Mr. Douglas in London, he being at that time a widower. She was a beautiful woman, tall, dark, and slender, some twenty years younger than her husband, a disparity which seemed in no way to mar the contentment of their family life." *The Valley of Fear*, I, 484.

DOVERCOURT, EARL OF: He was engaged to marry Lady Eva Brackwell, but Charles Augustus Milverton felt quite certain that the Earl was the sort of man who would call off the wedding if he learned of the "imprudent... sprightly" letters Lady Eva had once written another man. *The Adventure of Charles Augustus Milverton*, II, 560.

DOWNING, CONSTABLE: Of the Surrey Constabulary, he was badly bitten on the thumb in the struggle to capture the mulatto cook of Wisteria Lodge. *The Adventure of Wisteria Lodge*, II, 251.

DOWSON, BARON: Holmes noted to Count Negretto Sylvius, "Old Baron Dowson said the night before he was hanged that in my case what the law had gained the stage had lost." *The Adventure of the Mazarin Stone*, II, 740.

DREBBER: One of the four principal Mormon Elders. *A Study in Scarlet*, I, 203.

DREBBER, ENOCH J.: The body of a gentleman, well dressed, and having cards in his pocket bearing the name of Enoch J. Drebber, was found by a constable in a lonely house at 3 Lauriston Gardens. On the wall the word RACHE was found scrawled in blood.

As a younger man, when he vied with Joseph Stangerson for the hand of Lucy Ferrier, Drebber was "a bull-necked youth with coarse, bloated features." His father had given his mills over to him, and he eventually forced Lucy's hand in marriage. *A Study in Scarlet*, I, 167–68, 211.

DUBUQUE, MONSIEUR: Watson retained an almost verbatim report of Holmes's interview with Monsieur Dubuque, of the Paris police, and Fritz von Waldbaum, the well-known specialist of Danzig, in the matter of the Adventure of the Second Stain. *The Naval Treaty*, II, 167.

DUNBAR, GRACE: Governess to Neil and Maria Pinto Gibson's two children. Gibson pressed his affections upon her, but she refused. She had a strange influence over the tycoon's mind for the good use of his fortune, and so stayed on in his service. But when Gibson's wife was found shot to death, and the murder pistol found on the floor of Grace Dunbar's wardrobe, suspicion naturally fell heavily upon her. *The Problem of Thor Bridge*, II, 600-I.

DUNDAS SEPARATION CASE: Watson, in his discussion with Holmes as to whether commonplace occurrences held any interest for the reasoner, brought forward an article entitled, "'A husband's cruelty to his wife.' There is half a column of print, but I know without reading it that it is all perfectly familiar to me. There is, of course, the other woman, the drink, the push, the blow, the bruise, the sympathetic sister or landlady. The crudest of writers could invent nothing more crude."

"Indeed, your example is an unfortunate one for your argument," said Holmes. "This is the Dundas separation case, and, as it happens, I was engaged in clearing up some small points in connection with it. The husband was a teetotaller, there was no other woman, and the conduct complained of was that he had drifted into the habit of winding up every meal by taking out his false teeth and hurling them at his wife, which you will allow is not an action likely to occur to the imagination of the average story-teller." *A Case of Identity*, I, 404-5.

DUNDEE: Joseph Openshaw received a letter, postmarked from Dundee, in which there were five dried orange seeds and a message from the K.K.K. to "Put the papers on the sundial." *The Five Orange Pips*, I, 395, 403.

The steam sealer *Sea Unicorn*, which Captain Peter Carey commanded, sailed out of Dundee. *The Adventure of Black Peter*, II, 400.

DUNN, JOSIAH H.: Manager of the Crow Hill mine in Vermissa Valley, he was murdered by the Scowrers. *The Valley of Fear*, I, 557.

DUPIN: Watson told the Great Detective that he reminded him of Edgar Allan Poe's Dupin. Holmes replied, "Now, in my opinion, Dupin was a very inferior fellow. That trick of his of breaking in on his friends' thoughts with an apropos remark after a quarter of an hour's silence is really very showy and superficial. He had some analytical genius, no doubt; but he was by no means such a phenomenon as Poe appeared to imagine." *A Study in Scarlet*, I, 162.

DURONDO, VICTOR: The San Pedro Minister in London, he met and married his wife there. She said: "A nobler man never lived upon earth. Unhappily, Murillo [dictator of San Pedro] heard of his excellence, recalled him on some pretext, and had him shot. With a premonition of his fate he had refused to take me with him. His estates were confiscated, and I was left with a pittance and a broken heart." *The Adventure of Wisteria Lodge*, II, 256.

DURONDO, SIGNORA VICTOR: The true name of Miss Burnett, who served as governess for the two daughters of Mr. Henderson of High Gable, in Surrey. *The Adventure of Wisteria Lodge*, II, 256.

DYNAMICS OF AN ASTEROID, THE: Holmes said of Moriarty: "Is he not the celebrated author of *The Dynamics of an Asteroid* — a book which ascends to such rarefied heights of pure mathematics that it is said that there was no man in the scientific press capable of criticizing it?" *The Valley of Fear*, I, 472.

E

EAGLE COMMERCIAL, THE: A hotel in Tunbridge Wells in which a man named Hargrave, a suspected murderer, had stayed. *The Valley of Fear*, I, 508.

EAR: "As a medical man, you are aware, Watson, that there is no part of the body which varies so much as the human ear. Each ear is as a rule quite distinctive, and differs from all other ones. In last year's *Anthropological Journal* you will find two short monographs from my pen upon the subject." *The Cardboard Box*, II, 202.

EAR-FLAPPED TRAVELLING-CAP: It was worn by Holmes on his way down to Dartmoor to investigate the disappearance of the racehorse, Silver Blaze, and the murder of his trainer, John Straker. *Silver Blaze*, II, 262.

EARLY ENGLISH CHARTERS: At the time that Mr. Hilton Soames came to Holmes with the problem of the three students, Holmes and

Watson were residing in furnished lodgings in one of the great university towns where Holmes was doing library research "in Early English charters — researches which led to results so striking that they may be the subject of one of my future narratives." *The Adventure of the Three Students*, II, 368.

ECCLES, JOHN SCOTT: "A stout, tall, grey-whiskered and solemnly respectable person ... his life history was written in his heavy features and pompous manner. From his spats to his gold-rimmed spectacles he was a Conservative, a Churchman, a good citizen, orthodox and conventional to the last degree." This paragon of respectability consulted Holmes about a "most incredible and grotesque experience." *The Adventure of Wisteria Lodge*, II, 238–39.

EDGWARE ROAD: The Church of St. Monica, where Godfrey Norton and Irene Adler were married, with the disguised Sherlock Holmes as a witness, was in the Edgware Road. *A Scandal in Bohemia*, I, 358, 364.

Nathan Garrideb lived in Little Ryder Street, one of the smaller offshoots from the Edgware Road, and his house agents, Holloway and Steele, kept offices in the Edgware Road. *The Adventure of the Three Garridebs*, II, 647, 650.

EDMUNDS, MR.: Of the Berkshire Constabulary, he was a thin, yellow-haired young man. Some time after he had concluded his investigation of the Abbas Parva tragedy, he was sent to Allahabad. Sherlock Holmes considered Edmunds "a smart lad" because he remained uncertain about one or two points regarding the tragedy — points which also baffled Holmes, after the younger man "dropped in and smoked a pipe or two" over the case. *The Adventure of the Veiled Lodger*, II, 456, 458.

EDWARDS, BIRDY: Pinkerton's "best man," he was instrumental in breaking up the dread Scowrers in the Vermissa Valley. *The Valley of Fear*, I, *passim*.

EGAN: A Scowrer, he and one Lander claimed the head-money for the shooting of old man Crabbe at Stylestown. *The Valley of Fear*, I, 564.

EGRIA: German-speaking country, not far from Carlsbad, in Bohemia. "Remarkable as being the scene of the death of Wallenstein, and for its numerous glass factories and paper mills." The mysterious note that Holmes received anonymously had Eg P Gt woven into the texture of the paper. It stood for Egria Papier Gesellschaft. *A Scandal in Bohemia*, I, 350.

ELEY'S NO. 2: Holmes said to Watson, "I should be very much obliged if you would slip your revolver into your pocket. An Eley's No. 2 is an excellent argument with gentlemen who can twist steel pokers into knots." *The Adventure of the Speckled Band*, I, 252.

ELISE: The woman at Colonel Lysander Stark's house who warned Victor Hatherley to flee the strange assignment, and who later was probably instrumental in saving his life. *The Adventure of the Engineer's Thumb*, II, 216, 220.

ELMAN, J.C.: M.A., of Little Purlington, Essex, Vicar of Mossmoor-cum-Little Purlington, he was "a big, solemn, rather pompous clergyman." Josiah Amberley received a telegram that supposedly came from him, reading, "Come at once without fail. Can give you information as to your recent loss. — ELMAN. The Vicarage." After Amberley and Dr. Watson had hastened to Little Purlington to interview him, Elman denied ever sending such a message. *The Adventure of the Retired Colourman*, II, 551.

ELRIGE: He owned the isolated farmhouse in Norfolk where Abe Slaney stayed while communicating with Elsie Patrick. *The Adventure of the Dancing Men*, II, 539.

EMSWORTH, COLONEL: A "huge, bow-backed man with a smoky skin and a straggling grey beard," he had won the Victoria Cross in the Crimean War. He had a red-veined nose jutting out like a vulture's beak and two fierce grey eyes glaring out from under tufted brows. His hot temper, coupled with his still prodigious physical attributes, cowed nearly everyone, but Sherlock Holmes was able to force the old warrior's hand with but a single word scrawled upon a loose sheet of notebook paper. *The Adventure of the Blanched Soldier*, II, 708–9.

EMSWORTH, GODFREY: The only son of a famous warrior, Godfrey "had the fighting blood in him" and had volunteered for service in the Boer War. It was said that Godfrey had been the finest lad in his regiment; so it was hardly surprising that an "upstanding Briton" like James Dodd was attracted to him. The two were mates for a rough year, until Godfrey was hit with a bullet from an elephant gun in the action near

Diamond Hill outside Pretoria. *The Adventure of the Blanched Soldier*, II, *passim*.

EMSWORTH, MRS. COLONEL: "A gentle little white mouse of a woman," she responded eagerly to James Dodd's description of her son's bravery in the Boer War. *The Adventure of the Blanched Soldier*, II, 709.

ENGLISCHER HOF: On May the 3rd, 1891, Holmes and Watson put up at the Englischer Hof, run by Peter Steiler the elder, in the small Swiss village of Meiringen. *The Final Problem*, II, 312.

Lady Frances Carfax had stayed a fortnight at the Englischer Hof in Baden, where she had made the acquaintance of a Dr. and Mrs. Shlessinger. She had left there in their company. *The Disappearance of Lady Frances Carfax*, II, 659.

ERNEST, DR. RAY: Chess-playing neighbor of Josiah Amberley, accused by Amberley of running away with his wife and fortune. Ernest's family hired the detective, Barker, to seek out the truth of the matter. *The Adventure of the Retired Colourman*, II, 547.

ESCOTT: One of Holmes's disguises: that of a goateed, swaggering plumber with a rising business. In this disguise, Holmes got himself engaged to Charles Augustus Milverton's housemaid, Agatha, in order to gain information about her master. *The Adventure of Charles Augustus Milverton*, II, 563.

ESSEX: Little Purlington, site of Vicar J. C. Elman's church, was in Essex. *The Adventure of the Retired Colourman*, II, 551.

ETHEREGE, MRS: She advised Mary Sutherland to consult Sherlock Holmes in the matter of the disappearance of her fiancé, almost on the church steps. Mrs. Etherege's husband had once been very easily found by Holmes when everyone else had given him up for dead. *A Case of Identity*, I, 406.

ETON: John Clay, grandson of a duke, and who was himself a "murderer, thief, smasher, and forger," had been to school at Eton. *The Red-Headed League*, I, 433.

Colonel Sebastian Moran, whom Holmes finally bagged with Oscar Meunier's waxen image, was educated at Eton and Oxford. *The Adventure of the Empty House*, II, 346.

EUSTON STATION: Enoch J. Drebber and Joseph Stangerson had departed for Euston Station with the intention of catching the Liverpool express, on the night that Drebber was murdered. *A Study in Scarlet*, I, 184; see also *The Adventure of the Priory School*, II, 612; *The Adventure of the Blanched Soldier*, II, 715.

EVANS: Convicted of forgery, he was sentenced to transportation to the Australian colonies in 1855. He participated in the convict uprising aboard the barque *Gloria Scott*, made his way to Australia, prospered there under the assumed name of Beddoes, and eventually returned to England a wealthy man. *The "Gloria Scott"*, I, 119.

EVANS: A police officer who was shot because he had ventured to arrest two members of the Scowrers. *The Valley of Fear*, I, 560.

EVANS, CARRIE: Also known as Carrie Norlett, she was the personal maid of Lady Beatrice Falder at Shoscombe Old Place. *The Adventure of Shoscombe Old Place*, II, 638.

EVANS, "KILLER": His Scotland Yard dossier revealed the following about "Killer" Evans, of sinister and murderous reputation: "Aged forty-four. Native of Chicago. Known to have shot three men in the States. Escaped from penitentiary through political influence. Came to London in 1893. Shot a man over cards in a night club in the Waterloo Road in January, 1895. Man died, but he was shown to have been the aggressor in the row. Dead man was identified as Rodger Prescott, famous as forger and coiner in Chicago. Killer Evans released in 1901. Has been under police supervision since, but so far as known has led an honest life." If Evans had, in fact, been leading "an honest life" up until the time of *The Adventure of the Three Garridebs*, it was then that he returned to his criminal ways. *The Adventure of the Three Garridebs*, II, 651ff.

EYFORD: A little place in Berkshire near the borders of Oxfordshire, within seven miles of Reading. Colonel Lysander Stark asked the hydraulic engineer, Victor Hatherley, to come down to Eyford to fix the hydraulic press that Stark had installed in his house. *The Adventure of the Engineer's Thumb*, II, 213.

F

FAIRBAIRN, ALEC: "He was a man with winning ways, and he made friends wherever he went. He was a dashing, swaggering chap, smart and curled, who had seen half the world and could talk of what he had seen." He paid a very high price for the love of Mary Browner. *The Cardboard Box*, II, 206.

FAIRBANK: The "modest residence" of Alexander Holder in the southern suburb of Streatham. The Beryl coronet, one of the most precious public possessions of the Empire, was stolen from his house. *The Adventure of the Beryl Coronet*, II, 291.

FALDER, LADY BEATRICE: Sister of Sir Robert Norberton, with whom she lived on her deceased husband's estate, Shoscombe Old Place. She was especially fond of the famous Shoscombe spaniels and also took an interest in Sir Robert's Shoscombe Park Stables. Sir Robert's strange and cruel attitude toward her aroused the suspicion of John Mason, who came to Holmes with the problem. *The Adventure of Shoscombe Old Place*, II, 631ff.

FALDER, SIR DENIS (18TH CENTURY): Buried in the crypt of the ruined chapel on the grounds of Shoscombe Park. *The Adventure of Shoscombe Old Place*, II, 639.

FALDER, SIR JAMES: Of Shoscombe Old Place. He left his estate to his widow, Lady Beatrice, as a life interest, to revert to his brother upon her death. *The Adventure of Shoscombe Old Place*, II, 631.

FALDER, SIR WILLIAM (18TH CENTURY): Buried in the crypt of the ruined chapel on the grounds of Shoscombe Park. *The Adventure of Shoscombe Old Place*, II, 639.

FAREHAM: Joseph Openshaw had left home to visit his old friend Major Freebody. He had been "returning from Fareham in the twilight, and as the country was unknown to him, and the chalk-pit unfenced, the jury had no hesitation in bringing in a verdict of 'Death from accidental causes.'" *The Five Orange Pips*, I, 396.

FARINTOSH, MRS: She had consulted Holmes concerning an opal tiara, and later recommended his services to Helen Stoner, who sought his advice in the tragic death of her sister. *The Adventure of the Speckled Band*, I, 244-45.

FARNHAM: A village on the borders of Surrey. Sherlock Holmes felt that the area around Farnham was "a beautiful neighbourhood, and full of the most interesting associations." At the beginning of *The Adventure of the Solitary Cyclist*, Holmes cited, as one of those associations, the fact that it was near Farnham that he and Watson took Archie Stamford, the forger. *The Adventure of the Solitary Cyclist*, II, 383–84.

FARQUHAR, MR.: Watson purchased his medical practice in the Paddington district from old Mr. Farquhar, who had "had at one time an excellent general practice, but his age, and an affliction of the nature of St. Vitus' dance from which he suffered, had very much thinned it." *The Stockbroker's Clerk*, II, 153.

FATE: At the conclusion of his investigation of the brutal slaying of Charles McCarthy, Holmes philosophized: "Why does Fate play such tricks with poor helpless worms? I never hear of such a case as this that I do not think of Baxter's words, and say: 'There, but for the grace of God, goes Sherlock Holmes.'" *The Boscombe Valley Mystery*, II, 152.

The Great Detective showed to the once-beautiful Eugenia Ronder such sympathy as he was seldom known to exhibit. "Poor girl! Poor girl! The ways of Fate are indeed hard to understand. If there is not some compensation hereafter, then the world is a cruel jest." *The Adventure of the Veiled Lodger*, II, 460.

FENCING: Apart from fencing and boxing, Holmes had few athletic tastes during his two years at college. *The "Gloria Scott"*, I, 108.

FERGUSON: The retired sea captain who had owned The Three Gables before the Maberleys. Holmes speculated that Ferguson might have buried his treasure there. *The Adventure of the Three Gables*, II, 727.

FERGUSON, JACK: Elder son of Robert Ferguson, by the latter's first marriage, "he was a remarkable lad, pale-eyed and fair-haired, with excitable blue eyes which blazed into a sudden flame of emotion and joy [whenever] they rested upon his father." "A fall in childhood and a twisted spine" had caused the fifteen-year-old Jack's body to be "circumscribed in action," but he was "very developed in mind." *The Adventure of the Sussex Vampire*, II, 466, 470ff.

FERGUSON, MR.: Partner of Colonel Lysander Stark in his clandestine project. Also known as Dr. Becher, he was probably instrumental in saving Victor Hatherley's life. *The Adventure of the Engineer's Thumb*, II, 217.

FERGUSON, MR.: Secretary to Mr. Neil Gibson, the Gold King. *The Problem of Thor Bridge*, II, 591.

FERGUSON, ROBERT: In younger days, Big Bob Ferguson had been the finest three-quarter Richmond ever had—indeed, when that rugby team had played the Blackheath squad of which Watson was a member, Ferguson's strength was such that he was able to throw the robust Watson over the ropes into the crowd. In later years, however, Ferguson's "great frame had fallen in, his hair was scanty, and his shoulders were bowed." In his opinion, he had been especially aged by the bizarre events which had taken place in his household. His second wife, a Peruvian lady, had twice assaulted Ferguson's son by his first marriage, and worse, had twice been caught sucking at a small wound in the neck of "her own child, a dear boy just under one year of age." *The Adventure of the Sussex Vampire*, II, *passim*.

FERGUSON & MUIRHEAD: Tea brokers, of Mincing Lane; and one of them—Ferguson—solicited Sherlock Holmes's aid concerning his wife's strange behavior. *The Adventure of the Sussex Vampire*, II, 462, 474.

FERRERS DOCUMENTS: Holmes initially felt that he and Watson were too busy, having been retained in the case of the Ferrers Documents, and with the Abergavenny murder coming up for trial, to investigate the problem that Dr. Thorneycroft Huxtable brought to them. *The Adventure of the Priory School*, II, 608.

FERRIER, DR.: He lived near the unfortunate Percy Phelps in Woking, and kindly took charge of him on his return there after the mysterious disappearance of a top-secret naval treaty from Phelps's office. At the time, Phelps, by his own admission, was "practically a raving maniac." *The Naval Treaty*, II, 176.

FERRIER, JOHN: "His face was lean and haggard, and the brown parchment-like skin was drawn tightly over the projecting bones; his long, brown hair and beard were all flecked and dashed with white; his eyes were sunken in his head, and burned with an unnatural lustre; while the hand which grasped his rifle was hardly more fleshy than that of a skeleton." Thus was John Ferrier's appearance before his rescue from the Great Alkali Plain by the migrating Mormon band. He prospered greatly in Utah, but saw everything taken from him by the Avenging Angels. *A Study in Scarlet*, I, 197.

FERRIER, LUCY: John Ferrier's adopted daughter. Upon her rescue by the migrating Mormon band in the Great Alkali Plain, she was "a little child, with her round, white arms encircling [Ferrier's] brown, sinewy neck, and her golden-haired head resting upon the breast of his velveteen tunic." She prospered, as did her adoptive father, and grew more beautiful each day. Indeed, she was the flower of Utah. Lucy fell in love with Jefferson Hope, and suffered the affections of Drebber and Stangerson. Finally, the Ferriers were forced to flee. *A Study in Scarlet*, I, 201.

FIGHTING COCK INN: On the Chesterfield High Road, in Hallamshire. Its owner was Mr. Reuben Hayes, and Watson described it as a "forbidding and squalid inn." *The Adventure of the Priory School*, II, 620.

FISHER, PENROSE: According to Watson, he was one of the best medical practitioners in London. Watson proposed to consult Fisher for Sherlock Holmes in light of his strange malady. *The Adventure of the Dying Detective*, I, 441.

FLAUBERT, GUSTAVE: Holmes, drifting into ennui after unraveling the mystery surrounding Jabez Wilson's partial employment, found some solace in Gustave Flaubert's comment to George Sand, "*L'homme c'est rien — l'oeuvre c'est tout* [The man is nothing, the work is everything]." *The Red-Headed League*, I, 438.

FLEET STREET: The offices of the Red-Headed League were at 7 Pope's Court, Fleet Street. *The Red-Headed League*, I, 421, 423; see also *The Resident Patient*, I, 267.

FLORENCE, ITALY: A week after his supposed death at the Reichenbach Fall, Sherlock Holmes "found [himself] in Florence, with the certainty that no one in the world knew what had become of [him]." *The Adventure of the Empty House*, II, 336.

FLORIDA: Elias Openshaw had emigrated to America when he was a young man, and had become a planter in Florida, where he was reported to have done very well. *The Five Orange Pips*, I, 392.

FOLKESTONE COURT: With hindsight, Sherlock Holmes noted, concerning Jack Stapleton, "It is suggestive that during the last three years there have been four considerable burglaries in the West country, for none of which was any criminal ever arrested. The last of these, at Folkestone Court, in May, was remarkable for the cold-blooded pistolling of the page, who surprised the masked and solitary burglar." *The Hound of the Baskervilles*, II, 109.

FOLLIOTT, SIR GEORGE: His large house, Oxshott Towers, was near Aloysius Garcia's Wisteria Lodge, in Surrey. *The Adventure of Wisteria Lodge*, II, 246.

FOOTSTEPS: Holmes mentioned that he had "been guilty of several monographs," among which was one "upon the tracing of footsteps, with some remarks upon the uses of plaster of Paris as a preserver of impresses." *The Sign of the Four*, I, 612; see also *A Study in Scarlet*, I, 232.

FORBES, MR.: The detective in charge of the investigation of the disappearance of the top-secret naval treaty from Percy Phelps's office, he was at first somewhat hostile concerning Holmes's interest in the case, but later welcomed the Great Detective's advice. *The Naval Treaty*, II, 177–78.

FORDHAM: A Horsham lawyer, he prepared the will which left Elias Openshaw's estate "with all its advantages and all its disadvantages" to his brother, Joseph. *The Five Orange Pips*, I, 393, 394.

FORDHAM, DR.: The senior Trevor's physician. *The "Gloria Scott"*, I, 114.

FORDINGBRIDGE: The mysterious letter that led to the death of Justice of the Peace Trevor was postmarked at Fordingbridge. Trevor's old friend, Beddoes, was from this Hampshire town. *The "Gloria Scott"*, I, 114.

FORRESTER, INSPECTOR: "A smart, keen-faced young fellow," he carried out the official investigations of both the burglary of Mr. Acton's home and the murder of William Kirwan. He sought Holmes's help in these cases. *The Reigate Squires*, I, 333.

FORRESTER, MRS. CECIL: Mary Morstan was employed by her as a governess, and it was on Mrs. Forrester's recommendation that Mary sought out Holmes's aid in *The Sign of the Four*. Holmes had been of some slight service to Mrs. Forrester in a previous case that consisted of unraveling a little domestic complication. *The Sign of the Four*, I, 616, 643.

FOULMIRE: A moorland farmhouse in Devonshire, near Baskerville Hall, site of the mysterious death of Sir Charles Baskerville. *The Hound of the Baskervilles*, II, 18.

FOURNAYE, HENRI: A certain international spy "lived a double life": when in London, he was Eduardo Lucas, an unmarried man; when in

Paris, he was Henri Fournaye. He met an untimely demise during the time that Holmes sought a letter missing from Trelawney Hope's dispatch box. *The Adventure of the Second Stain*, I, 308, 312.

FOURNAYE, MME. HENRI: The woman to whom Eduardo Lucas, the international spy, was secretly married in Paris, she was "of creole origin, [was] of an extremely excitable nature, and [had] suffered in the past from attacks of jealousy which amounted to frenzy." One such attack caused her to follow her husband, who lived a double life, to London. *The Adventure of the Second Stain*, I, 312.

FOWLER, MR.: Alice Rucastle met Mr. Fowler at a friend's and had fallen in love with him. When she mysteriously disappeared, he proved a faithful lover. *The Adventure of the Copper Beeches*, II, 131–32.

FRANCE: The naval treaty which disappeared mysteriously from Percy Phelps's office was one which, he knew, "the French or Russian embassies would pay an immense sum to learn the contents of...." The treaty "foreshadowed the policy which this country would pursue in the event of the French fleet gaining a complete ascendancy over that of Italy in the Mediterranean." *The Naval Treaty*, II, 171, 172.

During his wanderings after his supposed death above the Fall of Reichenbach, Holmes traveled in France and "spent some months in a research into the coal-tar derivatives, which [he] conducted in a laboratory at Montpellier." *The Adventure of the Empty House*, II, 337; see also *A Case of Identity*, I, 408; *The Stockbroker's Clerk*, II, 157, 159; *The Final Problem*, II, 303.

FRANCO-MIDLAND HARDWARE COMPANY LIMITED: Supposedly, it had 134 branches in the towns and villages of France, not counting one in Brussels and one in San Remo. *The Stockbroker's Clerk*, II, 157.

FRANKFORT: Holmes was jubilant over his discovery of "an infallible test for blood stains.... There was the case of Von Bischoff at Frankfort last year. He would certainly have been hung had this test been in existence." *A Study in Scarlet*, I, 150, 151.

FRANKLAND, MR.: Of Lafter Hall, Devonshire. "He is an elderly man, red-faced, white-haired, and choleric. His passion is for British law, and he has spent a large fortune in litigation." He also kept close tabs on activity on the moor, with his high-power telescope. His daughter was Laura Lyons, of Coombe Tracey. *The Hound of the Baskervilles*, II, 54.

FRASER: He formed a shipboard friendship with a Mr. Vandeleur on a voyage from Central America to England, and joined with him in establishing a successful school in the east of Yorkshire. Later, Fraser died of consumption. *The Hound of the Baskervilles*, II, 106.

FRASER, ANNIE: She posed as the bogus Dr. Shlessinger's wife. "A tall, pale woman, with ferret eyes," she was an Englishwoman who was his companion in crime. *The Disappearance of Lady Frances Carfax*, II, 662, 664, 666.

FRASER, MISS MARY: The maiden name of Lady Brackenstall. Physically beautiful, she was also—by her own admission—"sensitive and high spirited." She felt that her upbringing in Adelaide, Australia, had ill prepared her for "English life, with its proprieties and its primness." *The Adventure of the Abbey Grange*, II, 493ff.

FRATTON: Sherlock Holmes, in the guise of Altamont, the Irish-American spy, claimed to have rooms "down Fratton way." *His Last Bow*, II, 798.

FREEBODY, MAJOR: On the day of his death, Joseph Openshaw had left home to visit an old friend of his, Major Freebody, "who is in command of one of the forts upon Portsdown Hill." *The Five Orange Pips*, I, 395, 396.

FREEMASON: Holmes knew that Jabez Wilson, the man with the fiery red hair, was a Freemason because Wilson wore an arc-and-compass breastpin representative of that order. *The Red-Headed League*, I, 419, 420; see also *The Adventure of the Norwood Builder*, II, 415.

FREEMEN, ANCIENT ORDER OF: Lodge 341, Vermissa Valley, housed the dreaded secret society known as the Scowrers. *The Valley of Fear*, I, 522.

FRESNO STREET: The offices of the Aberdeen Shipping Company, where Mrs. Neville St. Clair picked up a small parcel of considerable value, were in Fresno Street. *The Man with the Twisted Lip*, I, 374.

FRIESLAND: Sherlock Holmes felt that his first few months back in London following the death of Professor Moriarty were uneventful. Watson, who had resumed his partnership with Holmes during that period, disagreed, citing, among other cases, "the shocking affair of the Dutch steamship, *Friesland*, which so nearly cost [them] both [their] lives." *The Adventure of the Norwood Builder*, II, 414.

FULWORTH: Sherlock Holmes's retirement villa was near the little cove and village of Fulworth in Sussex. The village of Fulworth lies in a hollow curving in a semicircle round the bay. *The Adventure of the Lion's Mane*, II, 776, 780.

G

GABLES, THE: Half a mile off from Sherlock Holmes's retirement villa was "Harold Stackhurst's well-known coaching establishment, The Gables, quite a large place, which [contained] some score of young fellows preparing for various professions, with a staff of several masters." Two of those masters were Fitzroy McPherson and Ian Murdoch, both of whom fell prey to the monster known as "The Lion's Mane." *The Adventure of the Lion's Mane*, II, 776.

GABORIAU, EMILE: Watson queried his new companion whether he had "read Gaboriau's works. Does Lecoq come up to your idea of a detective?"

Sherlock Holmes sniffed sardonically, "Lecoq was a miserable bungler. He had only one thing to recommend him, and that was his energy. That book made me positively ill." *A Study in Scarlet*, I, 162.

"THE GAME IS AFOOT": "It was on a bitterly cold and frosty morning during the winter of '97 that I was wakened by a tugging at my shoulder. It was Holmes. The candle in his hand shone upon his eager, stooping face, and told me at a glance that something was amiss.

"'Come, Watson, come!' he cried. 'The game is afoot. Not a word! Into your clothes and come!'" *The Adventure of the Abbey Grange*, II, 491.

GARCIA, ALOYSIUS: Of Wisteria Lodge, near Esher, in Surrey. He was "of Spanish descent and connected in some way with the Embassy. He spoke perfect English, was pleasing in his manner, and as good-looking a man as ever I saw in my life," said Scott Eccles. After inviting Eccles to visit him, both Garcia and his house staff disappeared by the time Mr. Eccles awoke in the morning. *The Adventure of Wisteria Lodge*, II, 240, 257.

GARCIA, BERYL: One of the beauties of Costa Rica, she married Rodger Baskerville the younger. *The Hound of the Baskervilles*, II, 106.

GARRIDEB, ALEXANDER HAMILTON: According to "John Garrideb," the wealthy landowner had left a most unusual will, in which his estimated fortune of fifteen million dollars could be dispersed only when three other persons named Garrideb could be found to inherit the monies. *The Adventure of the Three Garridebs*, II, 645, 654.

GARRIDEB, HOWARD: Howard Garrideb was the third person of that unusual surname needed to fulfill the terms of the will left by the wealthy Alexander Hamilton Garrideb. Supposedly, the will stated that its fifteen million dollars could be dispersed only when three male Garridebs stood "in a row." John was first; Nathan, a reclusive London collector, was second; and Howard, reputedly a "constructor of agricultural machinery" from near Birmingham, seemed to be the third. *The Adventure of the Three Garridebs*, II, 649.

GARRIDEB, JOHN: Supposedly a "Counsellor at Law" from Moorville, Kansas, he was "a short, powerful man with the round, fresh, clean-shaven face characteristic of so many American men of affairs." Sherlock Holmes quickly determined that John Garrideb was not what he claimed to be, but "what [was] his game, then?" *The Adventure of the Three Garridebs*, II, 644ff.

GARRIDEB, NATHAN: A recluse with a singularly queer name, he was "a very tall, loose-jointed, round-backed person, gaunt and bald, some sixty-odd years of age.... The general effect, however, was amiable, though eccentric." He was interested in, and knowledgeable about, a wide variety of topics, and he maintained extensive collections pertinent thereto. Thus, he became quite excited when a man calling himself John Garrideb told him that, if they could locate a third man with the same surname, they stood to inherit five million dollars each from the estate of one Alexander Hamilton Garrideb. *The Adventure of the Three Garridebs*, II, 647ff.

GELDER & CO.: A sculptor works in Stepney. They had supplied both Morse Hudson and Harding Brothers with their plaster casts of Devine's head of Napoleon. The Italian piecework man, Beppo, was employed by them at one time. *The Adventure of the Six Napoleons*, II, 578.

GEMMI PASS: Having branched off from the Valley of the Rhône at Leuk, Holmes and Watson made their way over the Gemmi Pass through Interlaken. It was in the pass, along the banks of the Daubensee, that a large rock was dislodged from a ridge upon their right and narrowly missed them. *The Final Problem*, II, 312.

GENEVA: Upon receiving word in Strasbourg that Professor Moriarty had escaped the nets of the London police, Holmes and Watson almost immediately were on their way to Geneva. *The Final Problem*, II, 312.

GEOLOGY: In Watson's famous catalogue of "Sherlock Holmes — his limits," he rated the Great Detective's knowledge of geology as "Practical, but limited. Tells at a glance different soils from each other. After walks has shown me splashes upon his trousers, and told me by their colour and consistence in what part of London he had received them." *A Study in Scarlet*, I, 156; see also *The Five Orange Pips*, I, 399.

GEORGIA: The Ku Klux Klan, which pursued two generations of Openshaws to their deaths, had some of its main branches in Georgia. Significantly, the barque *Lone Star* sailed out of Savannah, Georgia. *The Five Orange Pips*, I, 400, 402.

GHAZIS: Dr. John H. Watson, newly attached to the Berkshires during the second Afghan War, was seriously wounded in the rout of the British at Maiwand. He would "have fallen into the hands of the murderous Ghazis had it not been for the devotion and courage shown by Murray, my orderly, who threw me across a packhorse, and succeeded in bringing me safely to the British lines." *A Study in Scarlet*, I, 143.

GIANT RAT OF SUMATRA, THE: "A story for which the world [was] not yet prepared" at the time Sherlock Holmes undertook *The Adventure of the Sussex Vampire*. *The Adventure of the Sussex Vampire*, II, 462.

GIBSON, J. NEIL: The American senator and Gold King. He had bought a considerable estate in Hampshire, and lived there with his family and servants. When his wife was found shot to death on Thor Bridge, suspicion fell upon his children's governess, whom, it was shown, Gibson had designs upon. He came to Holmes seeking help in clearing up the mystery. Holmes said, "This man is the greatest financial power in the world, and a man, as I understand, of most violent and formidable character." *The Problem of Thor Bridge*, II, 589, 590, 592.

GIBSON, MRS. J. NEIL: The married name of Maria Pinto. *The Problem of Thor Bridge*, II, 594.

GILCHRIST, MR.: A scholar at the College of St. Luke's, in one of England's great university towns, he was a candidate for the Fortescue Scholarship. He is described as "a fine scholar and athlete; plays in the Rugby team and the cricket team for the college, and got his Blue for the hurdles and the long jump. He is a fine, manly fellow...very poor, but he is hard-working and industrious. He will do well." *The Adventure of the Three Students*, II, 374, 376, 379.

GILCHRIST, SIR JABEZ: "The notorious Sir Jabez Gilchrist, who ruined himself on the Turf," was the father of Mr. Gilchrist of the College of St. Luke's. *The Adventure of the Three Students*, II, 374.

GLORIA SCOTT: A barque which, in 1855, was pressed into service as a convict ship bound for the Australian colonies. She "had been in the Chinese tea-trade, but she was an old-fashioned, heavy-bowed, broadbeamed craft, and the new clippers had cut her out. She was a 500-ton boat, and besides her thirty-eight gaol-birds, she carried twenty-six of a crew, eighteen soldiers, a captain, three mates, a doctor, a chaplain, and four warders." The vessel was set down by the Admiralty as being lost at sea in that same year. *The "Gloria Scott"*, I, 117, 121; see also *The Musgrave Ritual*, I, 125; *The Adventure of the Sussex Vampire*, II, 462–63.

GLOUCESTER ROAD STATION: Holmes began his investigation of Hugo Oberstein's house at 13 Caulfield Gardens at the Gloucester Road Station, where a helpful railway official showed him that Caulfield Gardens overlooked the London Underground. *The Adventure of the Bruce-Partington Plans*, II, 446.

GODOLPHIN STREET: "One of the old-fashioned and secluded rows of eighteenth-century houses which [lay] between the [Thames] and the Abbey, almost in the shadow of the great tower of the Houses of Parliament," it was the street in which Eduardo Lucas's house was situated. *The Adventure of the Second Stain*, I, 308, 313.

GOETHE, JOHANN WOLFGANG VON: Holmes quotes Goethe twice in *The Sign of the Four*. *The Sign of the Four*, I, 642, 688.

GOLDONI'S RESTAURANT: A "garish Italian restaurant" to which Holmes summoned Watson during *The Adventure of the Bruce-Partington*

Plans. Holmes asked his old friend to join him in a coffee and curaçao and to try one of the proprietor's cigars, which were "less poisonous than one would expect." *The Adventure of the Bruce-Partington Plans*, II, 446.

GORDON, GENERAL: As Sherlock Holmes observed him, Watson's "eyes fixed themselves upon [his] newly framed picture of General Gordon...." *The Cardboard Box*, II, 194.

GORDON SQUARE: Francis Hay Moulton took lodgings there after he arrived in London. *The Adventure of the Noble Bachelor*, I, 297.

GORGIANO, GIUSEPPE: "Both Italy and America are full of stories of his dreadful powers." Known variously as "Gorgiano of the Red Circle," "Black Gorgiano," and—most simply and ominously—"Death," he "was red to the elbow in murder" in the south of Italy, and was "at the bottom of fifty murders" in America. Born in Posilippo, near Naples, he was "a huge man... [and] everything about him was grotesque, gigantic, and terrifying"; thus, he was an ideal agent for the Red Circle, a Neapolitan terrorist society. Having been forced to flee to New York to avoid the Italian police, he had started "a branch of [this] dreadful society in his new home." *The Adventure of the Red Circle*, II, 699ff.

GOROT, CHARLES: A clerk in the Foreign Office, he was left alone in Percy Phelps's office the very evening that a top-secret naval treaty disappeared. Said Phelps to Holmes, "His people are of Huguenot extraction, but as English in sympathy and tradition as you and I are. Nothing was found to implicate him in any way... and there the matter dropped." *The Naval Treaty*, II, 177.

GOWER: A Scowrer, he participated in the assault upon James Stanger, editor of the Vermissa *Herald*. *The Valley of Fear*, I, 545.

GRAFENSTEIN, COUNT VON UND ZU: Holmes saved from murder, by the Nihilist Klopman, Count Von und Zu Grafenstein, who was uncle of the German spy, Von Bork. *His Last Bow*, II, 802.

GRAHAM & MCFARLANE: The unfortunate John Hector McFarlane was the junior partner in the law firm of Graham & McFarlane of 426 Gresham Buildings, E. C. *The Adventure of the Norwood Builder*, II, 417.

GRAND HOTEL: It was between the Grand Hotel and Charing Cross Station, "where a one-legged newsvendor displayed his evening papers," that Watson saw the headline which struck his very soul with horror: "MURDEROUS ATTACK UPON SHERLOCK HOLMES." *The Adventure of the Illustrious Client*, II, 682.

GRAVESEND: Jonathan Small and Tonga had booked passage on the *Esmeralda*, at Gravesend, bound for the Brazils, in their attempt to escape England. *The Sign of the Four*, I, 670; see also *The Five Orange Pips*, I, 403; *The Man with the Twisted Lip*, I, 379.

GREAT ALKALI PLAIN: "In the central portion of the great North American Continent there lies an arid and repulsive desert, which for many a long year served as a barrier against the advance of civilization. From the Sierra Nevada to Nebraska, and from the Yellowstone River in the north to the Colorado upon the south, is a region of desolation and silence." It was upon this Great Alkali Plain that John Ferrier and his adopted daughter, Lucy, were stranded. They were subsequently rescued by the migrating Mormon band. *A Study in Scarlet*, I, 196.

GREAT MOGUL, THE: Said to be the second largest diamond in existence, it was part of the great Agra treasure stolen by the men bound by the sign of the four. *The Sign of the Four*, I, 680.

GREAT ORME STREET: Mrs. Warren, a landlady who came to Sherlock Holmes complaining about the unusual habits of one of her lodgers, lived in "a high, thin, yellow-brick edifice in Great Orme Street, a narrow thoroughfare at the north-east side of the British Museum." *The Adventure of the Red Circle*, II, 696.

GREEN, ADMIRAL: He commanded the Sea of Azov fleet in the Crimean War. His son, who had been "a wild youngster," went to South Africa, where he made his fortune. *The Disappearance of Lady Frances Carfax*, II, 661, 663.

GREEN DRAGON INN: Run by Josiah Barnes at Crendall, Berkshire, it was a fine old-fashioned tavern. *The Adventure of Shoscombe Old Place*, II, 632.

GREEN, THE HON. PHILIP: Jules Vibart described him as "*Un sauvage — un véritable sauvage!*" and the landlord of the Englischer Hof in Baden called him "a bulky, bearded, sunburned fellow, who looks as if he would be more at home in a farmers' inn than in a fashionable hotel. A hard, fierce man, I should think, and one whom I should be sorry to offend." The son of the famous admiral, he had been following the Lady Frances Carfax, who had suddenly vanished. *The Disappearance of Lady Frances Carfax*, II, 658, 659, 661, 662.

GREGORY, INSPECTOR: He invited Holmes to look into the disappearance of the horse, Silver Blaze, and into the mysterious affair of the death of his trainer. Holmes told Watson: "Inspector Gregory, to whom the case is committed, is an extremely competent officer. Were he but gifted with imagination he might rise to great heights in his profession." *Silver Blaze*, II, 268, 269.

GREGSON, INSPECTOR TOBIAS: He sought Holmes's aid in the case of Enoch J. Drebber, who was found dead under mysterious circumstances in an empty house off the Brixton Road. Holmes remarked, "Gregson is the smartest of the Scotland Yarders; he and Lestrade are the pick of a bad lot. They are both quick and energetic, but conventional—shockingly so. They have their knives into one another, too. They are as jealous as a pair of professional beauties." *A Study in Scarlet*, I, 165, 167.

Holmes said, "I am the last and highest court of appeal in detection. When Gregson, or Lestrade, or Athelney Jones are out of their depth— which, by the way, is their normal state—the matter is laid out before me." *The Sign of the Four*, I, 611.

Gregson accompanied Holmes to Beckenham in the matter of the illegal detention of Paul Kratides. *The Greek Interpreter*, I, 602.

Gregson was "an energetic, gallant, and, within his limitations, a capable officer." He introduced Inspector Baynes of the Surrey Constabulary to Holmes, and joined them in the investigation of the horrible death of Mr. Aloysius Garcia, of Wisteria Lodge, near Esher. *The Adventure of Wisteria Lodge*, II, 240.

In *The Adventure of the Red Circle*, this Scotland Yard detective appeared to Holmes and Watson as "a man, muffled in a cravat and greatcoat... leaning against [a] railing." Gregson's welcome of Holmes at that time was anything but muffled, however: he said that he "was never in a case yet that [he] didn't feel stronger for having [Holmes] on [his] side." Holmes commented: "Our official detectives may blunder in the matter of intelligence, but never in that of courage." Gregson proved in this case that "London dangers were the privilege of the London force." *The Adventure of the Red Circle*, II, 698, 699, 700.

GREUZE, JEAN BAPTISTE: A French artist who flourished between the years 1750 and 1800. According to Holmes, "Modern criticism has more than endorsed the high opinion formed of him by his contemporaries." A portrait by Greuze, "a young woman with her head on her hands, peeking at you sideways," hung on the wall of Professor Moriarty's study. *The Valley of Fear*, I, 478.

GREYMINSTER, DUKE OF: In *The Adventure of the Blanched Soldier*, Holmes speaks of the Duke of Greyminster's deep involvement in the case of the Abbey School. *The Adventure of the Blanched Soldier*, II, 715.

GRICE PATERSONS, THE: "The year '87 furnished us with a long series of cases of greater or less interest, of which I retain the records." One of the cases during this twelve-month period concerned the "singular adventures of the Grice Patersons in the island of Uffa." *The Five Orange Pips*, I, 389.

GRIGGS, JIMMY: The clown employed by Ronder's wild beast show, he "had not much to be funny about [in the days when the show was declining due to Ronder's drunkenness and brutality], but he did what he could to hold things together." Indeed, the little man possessed such a large spirit that, when Mrs. Ronder was attacked by a dangerous lion, he helped to drive the creature off with a pole. *The Adventure of the Veiled Lodger*, II, 456, 459.

GRIMPEN: The village in Devonshire around which the events surrounding *The Hound of the Baskervilles* were played out. *The Hound of the Baskervilles*, II, 44.

GRIMPEN MIRE: It was said that "a false step yonder [into the Mire] means death to man or beast." Watson compared his feelings concerning the events surrounding *The Hound of the Baskervilles* to the Mire, which dominated the countryside around Baskerville Hall: "Ever since I have been here I have been conscious of shadows all round me. Life has become like that great Grimpen Mire, with little green patches everywhere into which one may sink and with no guide to point the track." *The Hound of the Baskervilles*, II, 47, 51.

GRODNO: In Little Russia. Holmes recalled that incidents similar to those played out in *The Hound of the Baskervilles* had occurred in Grodno in the year '66. *The Hound of the Baskervilles*, II, 96.

GROSS & HANKEY'S: Presumably jewelers, in Regent Street. It is thought that Godfrey Norton purchased the ring for his marriage to Irene Adler there. *A Scandal in Bohemia*, I, 358.

GROSVENOR HOTEL: Peter Steiler the elder, Holmes's and Watson's host at the Englischer Hof in Meiringen, had learned his excellent English while serving for three years as a waiter at the Grosvenor Hotel in London. *The Final Problem*, II, 312.

GROSVENOR MANSIONS: Residence of Lord St. Simon. *The Adventure of the Noble Bachelor*, I, 282.

GROSVENOR SQUARE: Isadora Klein's residence was in Grosvenor Square. *The Adventure of the Three Gables*, II, 731.

GROSVENOR SQUARE FURNITURE VAN, THE LITTLE PROBLEM OF THE: At the time of *The Adventure of the Noble Bachelor*, Holmes noted that the little problem of the Grosvenor Square furniture van "is quite cleared up now—though, indeed, it was obvious from the first." *The Adventure of the Noble Bachelor*, I, 284.

GRUNER, BARON ADELBERT: Sir James Damery said of him, "There is no more dangerous man in Europe." He was known as the "Austrian murderer," having apparently engineered the death of his wife in the Splügen Pass. Now, he threatened marriage to an enthralled Violet de Merville. "The fellow is, as you may have heard, extraordinarily handsome, with a most fascinating manner, a gentle voice, and that air of romance and mystery which means so much to a woman. He is said to have the whole sex at his mercy and to have made ample use of the fact." Sir James had come to Holmes for his illustrious client to seek his help in preventing the potentially fatal match. *The Adventure of the Illustrious Client*, II, 672, 673, 676, 686, 688.

H

HAFIZ: In the case of Mary Sutherland, Holmes concluded, "If I tell her she will not believe me. You may remember the old Persian saying, 'There is danger for him who taketh the tiger cub, and danger also for whoso snatches a delusion from a woman.' There is as much sense in Hafiz as in Horace, and as much knowledge of the world." *A Case of Identity*, I, 417.

HAINES-JOHNSON: A dishonest auctioneer and appraiser who offered to purchase The Three Gables and all its furnishings intact at a very good price from Mrs. Mary Maberley. *The Adventure of the Three Gables*, II, 727.

HALES, WILLIAM: Of Stake Royal, he was one of the best-known and most popular mine-owners in the Gilmerton district, and had been marked for death by the Scowrers. He was murdered by Ted Baldwin. *The Valley of Fear*, I, 557.

HALIFAX, NOVA SCOTIA: When Colonel Spence Munro accepted a post here, Violet Hunter, who had been a governess in his family for five years, was forced to seek other employment. *The Adventure of the Copper Beeches*, II, 116.

HALLE, SIR CHARLES: Holmes wanted to speed up his investigation of the lonely death of Enoch J. Drebber in an empty London suburban apartment, for "I want to go to Hallé's to hear Norman Neruda this afternoon." *A Study in Scarlet*, I, 174.

HALLIDAY'S PRIVATE HOTEL: Joseph Stangerson was found stabbed to death in his room in Halliday's Private Hotel, in Little George Street. *A Study in Scarlet*, I, 190, 191.

HAMMERFORD WILL CASE: It was Sir James Damery who managed the delicate negotiations with Sir George Lewis over the Hammerford Will case. *The Adventure of the Illustrious Client*, II, 671.

HAMMERSMITH WONDER: One of the cases docketed under the letter "V" in Holmes's great index volume was that of Vigor, the Hammersmith Wonder. *The Adventure of the Sussex Vampire*, II, 463.

HAMPSHIRE: Site of *The Adventure of the Copper Beeches*. Jephro Rucastle called it a "charming rural place." But Holmes noted ominously: "You look at these scattered houses, and you are impressed by their beauty. I look at them, and the only thought which comes to me is a feeling of their isolation, and of the impunity with which crime may be committed there.... Look at these lonely houses, each in its own fields, filled for the most part with poor ignorant folk who know little of the law. Think of the hellish cruelty, the hidden wickedness which may go on, year in, year out, in such places, and none the wiser." *The Adventure of the Copper Beeches*, II, 117, 121, 122; see also *The Adventure of the Speckled Band*, I, 245; *The "Gloria Scott"*, I, 113, 114; *The Problem of Thor Bridge*, II, 589, 604.

HAMPSTEAD HEATH: Charles Augustus Milverton's residence, Appledore Towers, was in Hampstead Heath. Holmes and Watson ran two miles across the Heath after burglarizing Milverton's house. *The Adventure of Charles Augustus Milverton*, II, 558, 570; see also *The Adventure of the Red Circle*, II, 695.

HANOVER SQUARE: Site of St. George's Church, where Lord St. Simon and Miss Hatty Doran were married. *The Adventure of the Noble Bachelor*, I, 285.

HARDEN, JOHN VINCENT: A well-known tobacco millionaire, he had been subjected to a peculiar persecution which Sherlock Holmes viewed as "a very abstruse and complicated problem." Indeed, the detective was so totally engrossed in the important research connected with the Harden case that he had to postpone his personal involvement in Violet Smith's case. *The Adventure of the Solitary Cyclist*, II, 383, 388.

HARDING, MR.: Founder and manager of Harding Brothers emporium, Kensington. His firm had sold plaster casts of Devine's head of Napoleon to Horace Harker, Josiah Brown, and Mr. Sandeford; each cast was eventually smashed. *The Adventure of the Six Napoleons*, II, 580.

HARDY, MR.: Foreman who carried on Mr. Sutherland's plumbing business with Sutherland's widow until her remarriage to James Windibank. He escorted Mrs. Sutherland and her daughter, Mary, to the gasfitters' ball, where Mary met, and fell in love with, Hosmer Angel. *A Case of Identity*, I, 407, 408.

HARDY, SIR CHARLES: The Right Honourable Trelawney Hope had had a valuable State document taken from among the papers he kept in a locked dispatch-box in his bedroom. Another of those papers was a "report from Sir Charles Hardy." *The Adventure of the Second Stain*, I, 321.

HARDY, SIR JOHN: In the afternoon of March 30, 1894, he had, along with two others, played whist with Ronald Adair. As there had been "a fairly equal fall of the cards," Sir John certainly had no reason to bear Adair any ill will; thus, he must have been shocked when he discovered that Adair was murdered later that same day. *The Adventure of the Empty House*, II, 330.

HARGRAVE: The alias of Ted Baldwin, who traveled to England to attempt to murder John Douglas. *The Valley of Fear*, I, 508.

HARGREAVE, WILSON: Holmes's friend of the New York Police Bureau, "who has more than once made use of my knowledge of London crime," furnished Holmes with important information by cable. *The Adventure of the Dancing Men*, II, 542.

HARKER, MR. HORACE: Of the Central Press Syndicate. A man was found brutally slain on his doorstep at NO. 131 Pitt Street and his plaster cast of Devine's bust of Napoleon was missing. He was further upset because he was so flustered by the horrible event that he could not cover his own story. *The Adventure of the Six Napoleons,* II, 575.

HAROLD, MRS.: Holmes had all the facts, in a squat notebook, concerning the death of old Mrs. Harold, who had left Count Negretto Sylvius the Blymer estate. *The Adventure of the Mazarin Stone,* II, 741.

HARRAWAY: Secretary of the Vermissa Valley branch of the Scowrers, he was "a lean, bitter man, with a long scraggy neck and nervous jerky limbs — a man of incorruptible fidelity where the finances of the Order were concerned, and with no notion of justice or honesty to anyone beyond." *The Valley of Fear,* I, 542, 569.

HARRINGBY, LORD: His large house, The Dingle, was within a mile or two of Oxshott, in Surrey. *The Adventure of Wisteria Lodge,* II, 246.

HARRIS, MR.: Sherlock Holmes posed as an accountant, Mr. Harris, of Bermondsey, in his interview with Hall Pycroft's employer, Mr. Harry Pinner, of the Franco-Midland Hardware Company. *The Stockbroker's Clerk,* II, 162.

HARRISON, ANNIE: The bride-to-be of the unfortunate Percy Phelps. She nursed the young Phelps back to health from a bout of brain fever, after he had suffered a crushing blow to his career one night at the Foreign Office. *The Naval Treaty,* II, 169, 170.

HARRISON, JOSEPH: The brother of Percy Phelps's bride-to-be. Holmes's analysis of him was that he was "an absolutely selfish man" whose "character is a rather deeper and more dangerous one than one might judge from his appearance....I can only say for certain that Mr. Joseph Harrison is a gentleman to whose mercy I would be extremely unwilling to trust." *The Naval Treaty,* II, 170, 191, 192.

HARROW: Miss Honoria Westphail, the aunt of Julia and Helen Stoner, lived near Harrow. It was there that Julia met a half-pay major of the Marines, an event which led to her mysterious death. *The Adventure of the Speckled Band,* I, 247.

HARROW WEALD: The Three Gables was in Harrow Weald. Mrs. Mary Maberley had asked Holmes to come there to investigate the strange events surrounding the desired purchase of her house and almost all of its contents. *The Adventure of the Three Gables,* II, 723.

HARVEY: One of the young stable hands at Shoscombe Park, he ran the central heating furnace at Shoscombe Old Place. One morning, while raking out the cinders, he found the upper condyle of a human femur. *The Adventure of Shoscombe Old Place*, II, 635.

HARWICH: Watson met Holmes at Harwich in his Ford, and thence they proceeded to the German spy Von Bork's country home. One could see the lights of Harwich from the German's residence. *His Last Bow*, II, 796, 800.

HATHERLEY: One of the farms on John Turner's Boscombe Valley estate, it was let to Charles McCarthy. *The Boscombe Valley Mystery*, II, 144.

HATHERLEY, VICTOR: Hydraulic engineer, of 16A Victoria Street, he came to Watson's office near Paddington Station because he had lost his thumb. His tale was so strange that Watson brought him immediately to Baker Street, and Holmes took up the case. *The Adventure of the Engineer's Thumb*, II, 210, 212.

HAVEN, THE: Home of the Bellamy family, in Fulworth, Sussex. *The Adventure of the Lion's Mane*, II, 780.

HAVEN, THE: Mr. Josiah Amberley's residence in Lewisham. *The Adventure of the Retired Colourman*, II, 547.

HAYES, REUBEN: Owner of the Fighting Cock Inn, in Hallamshire. He was "a squat, dark, elderly man," and once had been the head coachman at Holdernesse Hall, but the Duke of Holdernesse had sacked him "without a character on the word of a lying corn-chandler." *The Adventure of the Priory School*, II, 620, 621.

HAYES, MRS. REUBEN: A kindly woman, but entirely under the control of her brutal husband. *The Adventure of the Priory School*, II, 627.

HAYLING, MR. JEREMIAH: This advertisement appeared in the papers about one year prior to Victor Hatherley's employment to fix Colonel Lysander Stark's hydraulic press. "Lost on the 9th inst., Mr. Jeremiah Hayling, aged 26, a hydraulic engineer. Left his lodgings at ten o'clock at night, and has not been heard of since." *The Adventure of the Engineer's Thumb*, II, 221.

HAYTER, COLONEL: He had been under Watson's care in Afghanistan and had a house near Reigate, in Surrey. Holmes and Watson were his guests there during the adventure of *The Reigate Squires*. "Hayter was a fine old soldier, who had seen much of the world, and he soon found, as I had expected, that Holmes and he had plenty in common." *The Reigate Squires*, I, 331, 332.

HAYWARD: A member of the Worthingdon bank gang. They pulled their heist in 1875, but were caught, and Hayward was sentenced to fifteen years. The gang swore, and achieved, revenge on their erstwhile partner, Sutton, who had testified against them. *The Resident Patient*, I, 279, 280.

HEAVY GAME OF THE WESTERN HIMALAYAS: One of Colonel Sebastian Moran's publications. *The Adventure of the Empty House*, II, 346.

HEBRON, LUCY: The daughter of Effie Hebron Munro, who had claimed that Lucy had died of yellow fever in Atlanta. In truth, the child was alive, though weak, and she had been kept in America. *The Yellow Face*, I, 588.

HEBRON, MR. JOHN: An Atlanta lawyer with a good practice, he had died of yellow fever. He was survived by his wife, Effie, and their daughter. *The Yellow Face*, I, 579.

HEBRON, MRS. EFFIE: The wife of Mr. John Hebron of Atlanta, she bore him one child. Widowed, she later married Mr. Grant Munro. *The Yellow Face*, I, 579.

HEIDEGGER, MR.: The German master at the Priory School, in Hallamshire. He mysteriously disappeared on the same night Lord Saltire vanished. Heidegger had been at the school for two years and "came with the best references; but he was a silent, morose man, not very popular either with masters or boys." Later, Heidegger was found brutally murdered. *The Adventure of the Priory School*, II, 610, 618.

HEINRICH: It was Holmes who had brought about the separation between Irene Adler and the late King of Bohemia when the German spy Von Bork's cousin, Heinrich, was the Imperial Envoy. *His Last Bow*, II, 802.

HENDERSON, MR.: Of High Gable, near Oxshott, in Surrey. Holmes determined that Henderson was involved in the death of Aloysius Garcia and the attempted abduction of Miss Burnett. *The Adventure of Wisteria Lodge*, II, 252–53.

HENRIETTA STREET: On the night that Rance discovered the body of Enoch J. Drebber, Constables John Rance and Harry Murcher met at the corner of Henrietta Street and talked for a while. *A Study in Scarlet*, I, 176.

HEREFORD ARMS: Holmes and Watson stayed at the Hereford Arms in Ross while they investigated the facts surrounding the brutal slaying of Charles McCarthy. *The Boscombe Valley Mystery*, II, 140.

HEREFORDSHIRE: Boscombe Valley, site of Charles McCarthy's murder, was a country district, not very far from Ross, in Herefordshire. *The Boscombe Valley Mystery*, II, 135.

HIGGINS, TREASURER: Of the Merton County Lodge of the Ancient Order of Freemen. *The Valley of Fear*, I, 541.

HIGH GABLE: "One house, and only one, riveted my attention. It is the famous old Jacobean grange of High Gable, one mile on the farther side of Oxshott, and less than a half a mile from the scene of the tragedy," said Holmes, while attempting to solve the brutal murder of Aloysius Garcia. *The Adventure of Wisteria Lodge*, II, 252.

HIGH TOR: A moorland farmhouse in Devonshire, near Baskerville Hall, it was the site of the mysterious death of Sir Charles Baskerville. *The Hound of the Baskervilles*, II, 18.

HILL, INSPECTOR: He made a specialty of knowing the prominent criminals of Saffron Hill and the Italian quarter in London. *The Adventure of the Six Napoleons*, II, 581.

HIMALAYAS: One of Colonel Sebastian Moran's publications was *Heavy Game of the Western Himalayas*, 1881. *The Adventure of the Empty House*, II, 346.

The serum of the black-faced langur of the Himalayan slopes was intimately involved in the fate of old Professor Presbury, of Camford. *The Adventure of the Creeping Man*, II, 765.

HISTON: One of the villages on the north side of Cambridge, it had been "explored, and...[found] disappointing" by Sherlock Holmes in his search for Godfrey Staunton, the missing star of Cambridge University's rugger team. *The Adventure of the Missing Three-Quarter*, II, 487.

HOBBS, MR. FAIRDALE: A lodger of Mrs. Warren's, at her house in Great Orme Street, he had brought a simple matter to Sherlock

Holmes's attention in the year immediately prior to his landlady's own request for the detective's services. Though Holmes was reluctant at first to consider the landlady's problem, he was eventually won over when she told him that Hobbs "would never cease talking of...[his] kindness...and the way in which [he had] brought light into the darkness." *The Adventure of the Red Circle*, II, 691, 696.

HOBY, SIR EDWARD: With the senior Trevor, he broke up a poaching gang, whose members then threatened to knife both of them. Sir Edward was even attacked on one occasion. *The "Gloria Scott"*, I, 109.

HOLBORN, THE: Dr. John H. Watson invited young Stamford, his former dresser at Barts, to lunch with him at the Holborn. On their way there in a cab, they discussed Watson's search for cheaper lodgings. *A Study in Scarlet*, I, 145, 148, 149.

HOLBORN BAR: Holmes confronted Steve Dixie, the fighter, with the killing of young Perkins outside the Holborn Bar. *The Adventure of the Three Gables*, II, 723.

HOLDER, ALEXANDER: One of the renowned City bankers, Holder & Stevenson, he accepted a national treasure in return for a short-term loan, and then was thrown into a frenzy when part of it was stolen. *The Adventure of the Beryl Coronet*, II, 282.

HOLDER, ARTHUR: The dissipated son of the great financier, Alexander Holder. Arthur was found by his father holding the Beryl coronet, one of the most precious treasures of the Empire, which had been damaged, with three of its jewels stolen. Alexander immediately suspected his son, and called the police, who arrested him. Although under great suspicion, Arthur remained strangely silent, and later was proved to have been innocent of any wrongdoing. In fact, Holmes said of him, "You owe a very humble apology to that noble lad, your son, who has carried himself in this matter as I should be proud to see my own son do, should I ever chance to have one." *The Adventure of the Beryl Coronet*, II, 296.

HOLDER, JOHN: Jonathan Small's company sergeant in the 3rd Buffs. He saved Small's life by rescuing him from the Ganges after he had been attacked by a crocodile. *The Sign of the Four*, I, 674.

HOLDER, MARY: Niece of Alexander Holder, whom he took into his family after the death of his brother. She mysteriously disappeared after the theft of the Beryl coronet. *The Adventure of the Beryl Coronet*, II, 291.

HOLDER & STEVENSON: The second largest private banking firm in the City, they had their offices in Threadneedle Street. *The Adventure of the Beryl Coronet*, II, 283.

HOLDERNESSE, DUKE OF: His son, Lord Saltire, had disappeared from Dr. Thorneycroft Huxtable's Priory School. The Duke had offered a five-thousand-pound reward for information as to the whereabouts of his son, and an additional one thousand pounds for the identity of the kidnappers. Dr. Huxtable came to Holmes in a state of nervous exhaustion over the disappearance of the young Lord. From his encyclopedia of reference, Holmes learned: "Holdernesse, sixth Duke, K.G., P.C....Baron Beverley, Earl of Carston...Lord-Lieutenant of Hallamshire since 1900. Married Edith, daughter of Sir Charles Appledore, 1888. Heir and only child, Lord Saltire. Owns about two hundred and fifty thousand acres. Minerals in Lancashire and Wales. Address: Carlton House Terrace; Holdernesse Hall, Hallamshire; Carston Castle, Bangor, Wales. Lord of the Admiralty, 1872; Chief Secretary of State for — ." *The Adventure of the Priory School*, II, 608, 612; see also *The Adventure of Black Peter*, II, 398.

HOLDERNESSE HALL: Residence of the Duke of Holdernesse in Hallamshire. *The Adventure of the Priory School*, II, 608.

HOLDHURST, LORD: This great Conservative politician was the uncle of Percy Phelps on Phelps's mother's side. Through Holdhurst's influence and Phelps's skill, the young man obtained a good position at the Foreign Office. Holdhurst was Foreign Minister in the current Administration and perhaps a future Prime Minister. When a naval treaty of vital importance was lost from Phelps's office, Phelps called on his old school friend, Watson, for help. Watson, in turn, involved Sherlock Holmes. *The Naval Treaty*, II, 167, 182.

HOLLAND: At the time of *A Scandal in Bohemia*, Watson had from time to time heard some vague account of Holmes's doings, such as the mission which he had accomplished so delicately and successfully for the reigning family of Holland. *A Scandal in Bohemia*, I, 347; see also *A Case of Identity*, I, 405.

Sherlock Holmes, in the guise of Altamont, the Irish-American spy, said that he was hoping to escape to Holland. *His Last Bow*, II, 798.

HOLLIS: One of the agents of the German spy, Von Bork, he was captured before the outbreak of World War I. Von Bork's comment was that "the man was mad." *His Last Bow*, II, 798.

HOLMES, MYCROFT: Sherlock Holmes said of his elder brother, "If the art of the detective began and ended in reasoning from an arm-chair, my brother would be the greatest criminal agent that ever lived. But he has no ambition and no energy. He would not even go out of his way to verify his own solutions, and would rather be considered wrong than take the trouble to prove himself right. Again and again I have taken a problem to him and have received an explanation which has afterwards proved to be the correct one. And yet he was absolutely incapable of working out the practical points which must be gone into before a case could be laid before a judge or jury."

"It is not his profession, then?" queried Watson.

"By no means. What is to me a means of livelihood is to him the merest hobby of a dilettante. He has an extraordinary faculty for figures, and audits the books in some of the Government departments. Mycroft lodges in Pall Mall, and he walks round the corner into Whitehall every morning and back every evening. From year's end to year's end he takes no other exercise, and is seen nowhere else, except only in the Diogenes Club, which is just opposite his rooms."

Physically, "Mycroft Holmes was a much larger and stouter man than Sherlock. His body was absolutely corpulent, but his face, though massive, had preserved something of the sharpness of expression which was so remarkable in that of his brother. His eyes, which were of a peculiarly light watery grey, seemed to always retain that far-away, introspective look which I had only observed in Sherlock's when he was exerting his full powers." *The Greek Interpreter*, I, 591, 592, 594.

It was Mycroft Holmes who drove the small brougham, waiting close to the curb outside the Lowther Arcade, into which Watson stepped in his mad dash to join Holmes aboard the Continental Express. Mycroft wore a heavy black cloak tipped at the collar with red, and Watson felt that he was "very massive." *The Final Problem*, II, 307-8.

The "one confidant" Sherlock Holmes had during the nearly three years which followed his supposed death at the Reichenbach Fall, Mycroft had preserved Holmes's rooms and papers in Baker Street "exactly as they had always been." *The Adventure of the Empty House*, II, 336, 337.

Mycroft was thought by many to occupy only "some small office under the British Government." In truth, however, he was "the most indispensable man in the country"—indeed, there were times, said Sherlock Holmes, when Mycroft *was* the British Government! He had created his unique governmental position (that of a "central exchange" for incoming data) himself, and it was thought that he was the only man who could ever have performed such a function, for Mycroft's "specialism [was] omniscience." Physically, he was "heavily built and massive, [with] a suggestion of uncouth physical inertia in [his] figure." Sherlock delineated his brother's torpor by saying, "Mycroft has his rails and he runs on them. His Pall Mall lodgings, the Diogenes Club, Whitehall—that is his cycle." Still, Mycroft possessed "a head so masterful in its brow, so alert in its steel-grey, deep-set eyes, so firm in its lips, and so subtle in its play of expression" that there could be no doubting his eminence as an armchair detective, i. e., one who after having been given the details of a particular problem, could "return...an excellent expert opinion ...from [his] armchair." But Mycroft was the first to admit that the often tiresome gathering of such details was "not [his] *metier*." *The Adventure of the Bruce-Partington Plans*, II, 433ff.

HOLMES, SHERLOCK; BIOGRAPHY: Holmes described his investigation of the death of Justice of the Peace Trevor as "the first in which I was ever engaged.... You never heard me talk of Victor Trevor?" he asked. "He was the only friend I made during the two years I was at college. I was never a very sociable fellow, Watson, always rather fond of moping in my rooms and working out my own little methods of thought, so that I never mixed much with the men of my year. Bar fencing and boxing, I had few athletic tastes, and then my line of study was quite distinct from that of the other fellows, so that we had no points of contact at all. Trevor was the only man I knew, and that only through the accident of his bull-terrier freezing on to my ankle one morning as I went down to chapel." *The "Gloria Scott"*, I, 107–8.

"From the years 1894 to 1901 inclusive, Mr. Sherlock Holmes was a very busy man. It is safe to say that there was no public case of any difficulty in which he was not consulted during those eight years, and there were hundreds of private cases, some of them of the most intricate and extraordinary character, in which he played a prominent part." *The Adventure of the Solitary Cyclist*, II, 383.

"I have never known my friend to be in better form, both mental and physical, than in the year '95. His increasing fame had brought with it an immense practice, and I should be guilty of an indiscretion if I were even to hint at the identity of some of the illustrious clients who crossed our humble threshold in Baker Street." *The Adventure of Black Peter*, II, 398.

"It was, then, in the spring of the year 1897 that Holmes' iron constitution showed some symptoms of giving way in the face of constant hard work of a most exacting kind, aggravated, perhaps, by occasional indiscretions of his own." *The Adventure of the Devil's Foot*, II, 508.

It was in the latter part of June, 1902, that "Holmes refused a knighthood for services which may perhaps some day be described." *The Adventure of the Three Garridebs*, II, 643.

Holmes's retirement villa was "situated upon the southern slope of the Downs, commanding a great view of the Channel. At this point the coast-line is entirely of chalk cliffs, which can only be descended by a single, long, tortuous path, which is steep and slippery. At the bottom of the path lie a hundred yards of pebbles and shingle, even when the tide is at full. Here and there, however, there are curves and hollows which make splendid swimming-pools filled afresh with each flow. This admirable beach extends for some miles in each direction, save only at one point where the little cove and village of Fulworth break the line.

"My house is lonely. I, my old housekeeper, and my bees have the estate all to ourselves. Half a mile off, however, is Harold Stackhurst's well-known coaching establishment, The Gables...." *The Adventure of the Lion's Mane*, II, 776.

Watson said, "But you had retired, Holmes. We heard of you as living the life of a hermit among your bees and your books in a small farm upon the South Downs." There, Holmes completed the *magnum opus* of his latter years, *Practical Handbook of Bee Culture, with some Observations upon the Segregation of the Queen*. *His Last Bow*, II, 800.

HOLMES, SHERLOCK; CHARACTER: Young Stamford, Dr. Watson's

former dresser at Barts, was responsible for introducing him to Holmes. Stamford had his own opinion concerning the Great Detective: "You don't know Sherlock Holmes yet, perhaps you would not care for him as a constant companion.... I believe he is well up in anatomy, and he is a first-class chemist; but, as far as I know, he has never taken out any systematic medical classes. His studies are very desultory and eccentric, but he has amassed a lot of out-of-the-way knowledge which would astonish his professors.... Holmes is a little too scientific for my tastes — it approaches to cold-bloodedness. I could imagine his giving a friend a little pinch of the latest vegetable alkaloid, not out of malevolence, you understand, but simply out of a spirit of inquiry in order to have an accurate idea of the effects. To do him justice, I think he would take it himself with the same readiness." Later, Holmes outlined some of his faults to Watson on their first meeting: "Let me see — what are my other shortcomings. I get in the dumps at times, and don't open my mouth for days on end. You must not think I am sulky when I do that. Just let me alone, and I'll soon be right." *A Study in Scarlet*, 1, 148, 149, 151.

Watson had seen little of Holmes at the time of *A Scandal in Bohemia*, for he was absorbed with his new wife, "while Holmes, who loathed every form of society with his whole Bohemian soul, remained in our lodgings in Baker Street, buried among his old books, and alternating from week to week between cocaine and ambition, the drowsiness of the drug, and the fierce energy of his own keen nature. He was still, as ever, deeply attracted by the study of crime, and occupied his immense faculties and extraordinary powers of observation in following out those clues, and clearing up those mysteries, which had been abandoned as hopeless by the official police." *A Scandal in Bohemia*, 1, 346.

Watson wrote, "An anomaly which often struck me in the character of my friend Sherlock Holmes was that, although in his methods of thought he was the neatest and most methodical of mankind, and although he affected a certain quiet primness of dress, he was none the less in his personal habits one of the most untidy men that ever drove a fellow-lodger to distraction. Not that I am in the least conventional in that respect myself .... But with me there is a limit, and when I find a man who keeps his cigars in the coal-scuttle, his tobacco in the toe-end of a Persian slipper, and his unanswered correspondence transfixed by a jack-knife into the very centre of his wooden mantelpiece, then I begin to give myself virtuous airs. I have always held, too, that pistol practice should distinctly be an open-air pastime; and when Holmes in one of his queer humours would sit in an arm-chair, with his hair-trigger and a hundred Boxer cartridges, and proceed to adorn the opposite wall with a patriotic v.r. done in bullet-pocks, I felt strongly that neither the atmosphere nor the appearance of our room was improved by it.

"Our chambers were always full of chemicals and criminal relics, which had a way of wandering into unlikely positions, and of turning up in the butter-dish, or in even less desirable places. But his papers were my great crux. He had a horror of destroying documents, especially those which were connected with his past cases, and yet it was only once in every year or two that he would muster energy to docket and arrange them, for as I have mentioned elsewhere in these incoherent memoirs, the outbursts of passionate energy when he performed the remarkable feats with which his name is associated were followed by reactions of lethargy, during which he would lie about with his violin and his books, hardly moving, save from the sofa to the table." *The Musgrave Ritual*, I, 123–24.

Watson writes, "During my long and intimate acquaintance with Mr. Sherlock Holmes I had never heard him refer to his relations, and hardly ever to his own early life. This reticence upon his part had increased the somewhat inhuman effect which he produced upon me, until sometimes I found myself regarding him as an isolated phenomenon, a brain without a heart, as deficient in human sympathy as he was pre-eminent in intelligence. His aversion to women, and his disinclination to form new friendships, were both typical of his unemotional character, but not more so than his complete suppression of every reference to his own people. I had come to believe that he was an orphan with no relatives living, but one day, to my very great surprise, he began to talk to me about his brother." *The Greek Interpreter*, I, 590.

"Things had indeed been very slow with us, and I had learned to dread such periods of inaction, for I knew by experience that my companion's brain was so abnormally active that it was dangerous to leave it without material upon which to work. For years I had gradually weaned him from that drug mania which had threatened once to check his remarkable career. Now I knew that under ordinary circumstances he no longer craved for this artificial stimulus; but I was well aware that the fiend was not dead, but sleeping; and I have known that the sleep was a light one and the waking near when in periods of idleness I have seen the drawn look upon Holmes' ascetic face, and the brooding of his deep-set and inscrutable eyes." *The Adventure of the Missing Three-Quarter*, II, 475.

"As to my companion, neither the country nor the sea presented the slightest attractions to him. He loved to lie in the very centre of five millions of people, with his filaments stretching out and running through them, responsive to every little rumour or suspicion of unsolved crime. Appreciation of nature found no place among his many gifts, and his only change was when he turned his mind from the evil-doer of the town to track down his brother of the country." *The Cardboard Box*, II, 193.

"Both Holmes and I had a weakness for the Turkish Bath. It was over a smoke in the pleasant lassitude of the drying-room that I have found him less reticent and more human than anywhere else." *The Adventure of the Illustrious Client*, II, 671.

Watson notes that to the once-beautiful Eugenia Ronder, the Great Detective "stretched out his long arm and patted her hand with such a show of sympathy as I had seldom known him to exhibit." *The Adventure of the Veiled Lodger*, II, 460.

HOLMES, SHERLOCK; DESCRIPTION: Watson recorded his first impressions of Holmes upon moving to Baker Street: "His very person and appearance were such as to strike the attention of the most casual observer. In height he was rather over six feet, and so excessively lean that he seemed to be considerably taller. His eyes were sharp and piercing, save during those intervals of torpor to which I have alluded; and his thin, hawk-like nose gave his whole expression an air of alertness and decision. His chin, too, had the prominence and squareness which mark the man of determination. His hands were invariably blotted with ink and stained with chemicals, yet he was possessed of extraordinary delicacy of touch, as I frequently had occasion to observe when I watched him manipulating his fragile philosophical instruments." *A Study in Scarlet*, I, 153.

Watson wrote of Holmes: "As he spoke, he whipped a tape measure and a large round magnifying glass from his pocket. With these two implements he trotted noiselessly about the room, sometimes stopping, occasionally kneeling, and once lying flat upon his face. So engrossed was he with his occupation that he appeared to have forgotten our presence, for he chattered away to himself under his breath the whole time, keeping up a running fire of exclamations, groans, whistles, and little cries suggestive of encouragement and hope. As I watched him I was irresistibly reminded of a pure-blooded, well-trained foxhound as it dashes backwards and forwards through the covert, whining in its eagerness, until it comes across the lost scent. For twenty minutes or more he continued his researches, measuring with the most exact care the distance between marks which were entirely invisible to me, and occasionally applying his tape to the walls in an equally incomprehensible manner." *A Study in Scarlet*, I, 171.

Holmes said to Watson, "'It is quite a three-pipe problem, and I beg that you won't speak to me for fifty minutes.' He curled himself up in his chair, with his thin knees drawn up to his hawk-like nose, and there he sat with his eyes closed and his black clay pipe thrusting out like the bill of some strange bird." *The Red-Headed League*, I, 428.

"Sherlock Holmes was transformed when he was hot upon such a scent as this. Men who had only known the quiet thinker and logician of Baker Street would have failed to recognize him. His face flushed and darkened. His brows were drawn into two hard, black lines, while his eyes shone out from beneath them with a steely glitter. His face was bent downwards, his shoulders bowed, his lips compressed, and the veins stood out like whip-cord in his long, sinewy neck. His nostrils seemed to dilate with a purely animal lust for the chase, and his mind was so absolutely concentrated upon the matter before him, that a question or remark fell unheeded upon his ears, or at the most provoked a quick impatient snarl in reply." *The Boscombe Valley Mystery*, II, 145.

"It was soon evident to me that he [Holmes] was now preparing for an all-night sitting. He took off his coat and waistcoat, put on a large blue dressing-gown, and then wandered about the room collecting pillows from his bed, and cushions from the sofa and arm-chairs. With these he constructed a sort of Eastern divan, upon which he perched himself cross-legged, with an ounce of shag tobacco and a box of matches laid out in front of him. In the dim light of the lamp I saw him sitting there, an old briar pipe between his lips, his eyes fixed vacantly upon the corner of the ceiling, the blue smoke curling up from him, silent, motionless, with the light shining upon his strong-set aquiline features." *The Man with the Twisted Lip*, I, 381.

"Holmes had been seated for some hours in silence, with his long, thin back curved over a chemical vessel in which he was brewing a particularly malodorous product. His head was sunk upon his breast, and he looked from my point of view like a strange, lank bird, with dull grey plumage and a black top-knot." *The Adventure of the Dancing Men*, II, 527.

"His eager face still wore that expression of intense and high-strung energy, which showed me that some novel and suggestive circumstance had opened up a stimulating line of thought. See the foxhound with hanging ears and drooping tail as it lolls about the kennels, and compare it with the same hound as, with gleaming eyes and straining muscles, it runs upon a breast-high scent — such was the change in Holmes since the morning. He was a different man to the limp and lounging figure in the mouse-coloured dressing-gown who had prowled so restlessly only a few hours before round the fog-girt room." *The Adventure of the Bruce-Partington Plans*, II, 440.

When the man who called himself John Garrideb, of Moorville, Kansas, paid a visit on the Great Detective, he identified Holmes at once. He said, "Your pictures are not unlike you, sir, if I may say so." *The Adventure of the Three Garridebs*, II, 644.

HOLMES, SHERLOCK; METHODS AND PSYCHOLOGY OF DETECTION: Holmes countered Watson's astonishment at his professed ignorance of the Copernican Theory and the composition of the Solar System, with his own theory of knowledge: "You see, I consider that a man's brain originally is like a little empty attic, and you have to stock it with such furniture as you choose. A fool takes in all the lumber of every sort that he comes across, so that the knowledge which might be useful to him gets crowded out, or at best is jumbled up with a lot of other things, so that he has a difficulty in laying his hands upon it. Now the skilled workman is very careful indeed as to what he takes into his brain-attic. He will have nothing but the tools which may help him in doing his work, but of these he has a large assortment, and all in the most perfect order. It is a mistake to think that that little room has elastic walls and can distend to any extent. Depend upon it there comes a time when for every addition of knowledge you forget something that you knew before. It is of the highest importance, therefore, not to have useless facts elbowing out the useful ones." *A Study in Scarlet*, I, 153–54.

Peter Jones, who accompanied Holmes down to the cellar of the

Coburg branch of the City and Suburban Bank to unravel the mystery of Jabez Wilson's partial unemployment, said of the Great Detective, "He has his own little methods, which are, if he won't mind my saying so, just a little too theoretical and fantastic, but he has the makings of a detective in him." *The Red-Headed League*, I, 432.

"Sherlock Holmes was a man, however, who when he had an unsolved problem upon his mind would go for days, and even for a week, without rest, turning it over, rearranging his facts, looking at it from every point of view, until he had either fathomed it, or convinced himself that his data were insufficient." *The Crooked Man*, I, 381.

"My dear Watson, I cannot agree with those who rank modesty among the virtues. To the logician all things should be seen exactly as they are, and to under-estimate oneself is as much a departure from truth as to exaggerate one's own powers. When I say, therefore, that Mycroft has better powers of observation than I, you may take it that I am speaking the exact and literal truth." *The Greek Interpreter*, I, 591.

"Perhaps when a man has special knowledge and special powers like my own it rather encourages him to seek a complex explanation when a simpler one is at hand." *The Adventure of the Abbey Grange*, II, 498.

"One of the most remarkable characteristics of Sherlock Holmes was his power of throwing his brain out of action and switching all his thoughts on to lighter things whenever he had convinced himself that he could no longer work to advantage." *The Adventure of the Bruce-Partington Plans*, II, 449.

Holmes felt that tobacco had to take the place of food when he was on the involved case of the stolen Crown diamond. "The faculties become refined when you starve them. Why, surely, as a doctor, my dear Watson, you must admit that what your digestion gains in the way of blood supply is so much lost to the brain. I am a brain, Watson. The rest of me is mere appendix. Therefore, it is the brain I must consider. *The Adventure of the Mazarin Stone*, II, 737.

"It was one of the peculiarities of [Holmes's] proud, self-contained nature that, though he docketed any fresh information very quickly and accurately in his brain, he seldom made any acknowledgment to the giver." *The Adventure of the Sussex Vampire*, II, 463.

"You [the reader] will know, or Watson has written in vain, that I hold a vast store of out-of-the-way knowledge, without scientific system, but very available for the needs of my work. My mind is like a crowded box-room with packets of all sorts stowed away therein — so many that I may well have but a vague perception of what is there." *The Adventure of the Lion's Mane*, II, 784.

HOLMES, SHERLOCK; MUSIC: Watson had the following observations about his newly-acquired companion's skills on the violin: "These were very remarkable, but as eccentric as all his other accomplishments. That he could play pieces, and difficult pieces, I knew well, because at my request he has played me some of Mendelssohn's Lieder, and other favourites. When left to himself, however, he would seldom produce any music or attempt any recognized air. Leaning back in his armchair of an evening, he would close his eyes and scrape carelessly at the fiddle which was thrown across his knee. Sometimes the chords were sonorous and melancholy. Occasionally they were fantastic and cheerful. Clearly they reflected the thoughts which possessed him, but whether the music aided these thoughts, or whether the playing was simply the result of a whim or fancy, was more than I could determine. I might have rebelled against these exasperating solos had it not been that he usually terminated them by playing in quick succession a whole series of my favourite airs as a slight compensation for the trial upon my patience." *A Study in Scarlet*, I, 158.

In describing Holmes at Sarasate's concert at St. James's Hall, Watson said, "My friend was an enthusiastic musician, being himself not only a very capable performer, but a composer of no ordinary merit. All the afternoon he sat in the stalls wrapped in the most perfect happiness, gently waving his long thin fingers in time to the music, while his gently smiling face and his languid, dreamy eyes were as unlike those of Holmes the sleuth-hound, Holmes the relentless, keen-witted, ready-handed criminal agent, as it was possible to conceive. In his singular character the dual nature alternately asserted itself, and his extreme exactness and astuteness represented, as I have often thought, the reaction against the poetic and contemplative mood which occasionally predominated in him.... When I saw him that afternoon so enwrapped in the music of St. James's Hall I felt that an evil time might be coming upon those whom he had set himself to hunt down." *The Red-Headed League*, I, 431.

HOLMES, SHERLOCK; PHILOSOPHY: Holmes spoke of his solution to

Jabez Wilson's problem: "It saved me from ennui. Alas, I already feel it closing in upon me! My life is spent in one long effort to escape the commonplaces of existence. These little problems help me to do so." *The Red-Headed League*, I, 438.

"'My dear fellow,' said Sherlock Holmes, as we sat on either side of the fire in his lodgings at Baker Street, 'life is infinitely stranger than anything which the mind of man could invent. We would not dare to conceive the things which are really mere commonplaces of existence. If we could fly out of that window hand in hand, hover over this great city, gently remove the roofs, and peep in at the queer things which are going on, the strange coincidences, the plannings, the cross-purposes, the wonderful chains of events, working through generations, and leading to the most *outré* results, it would make all fiction with its conventionalities and foreseen conclusions most stale and unprofitable.'" *A Case of Identity*, I, 404.

"There are some trees, Watson, which grow to a certain height and then suddenly develop some unsightly eccentricity. You will see it often in humans. I have a theory that the individual represents in his development the whole procession of his ancestors, and that such a sudden turn to good or evil stands for some strong influence which came into the line of his pedigree. The person becomes, as it were, the epitome of the history of his own family." *The Adventure of the Empty House*, II, 347.

Holmes returned after a not too successful day in searching for the whereabouts of Godfrey Staunton. "A cold supper was ready upon the table, and when his needs were satisfied and his pipe alight he was ready to take that half-comic and wholly philosophic view which was natural to him when his affairs were going awry." *The Adventure of the Missing Three-Quarter*, II, 485.

The Great Detective showed to the once-beautiful Eugenia Ronder such sympathy as he was seldom known to exhibit. "Poor girl! Poor girl! The ways of Fate are indeed hard to understand. If there is not some compensation hereafter, then the world is a cruel jest." He had but stoic advice for her: "The example of patient suffering is in itself the most precious of all lessons to an impatient world." *The Adventure of the Veiled Lodger*, II, 460, 461.

"Sherlock Holmes was in a melancholy and philosophic mood that morning. His alert practical nature was subject to such reactions.

"Did you see him?" he asked.

"You mean the old fellow who has just gone out?" replied Watson.

"Precisely."

"Yes, I met him at the door."

"What did you think of him?"

"A pathetic, futile, broken creature."

"Exactly, Watson. Pathetic and futile. But is not all life pathetic and futile? Is not his story a microcosm of the whole? We reach. We grasp. And what is left in our hands at the end? A shadow. Or worse than a shadow — misery." *The Adventure of the Retired Colourman*, II, 546.

HOLMES, SHERLOCK; PROFESSION: Said Holmes to Watson, "Well, I have a trade of my own. I suppose I am the only one in the world. I'm a consulting detective, if you can understand what that is. Here in London we have lots of Government detectives and lots of private ones. When these fellows are at fault, they come to me, and I manage to put them on the right scent." *A Study in Scarlet*, I, 160.

Watson felt that in Holmes's "position of unofficial adviser and helper to everybody who is absolutely puzzled, throughout three continents, you are brought into contact with all that is strange and bizarre." *A Case of Identity*, I, 404.

Watson said, "In glancing over my notes of the seventy odd cases in which I have during the last eight years studied the methods of my friend Sherlock Holmes, I find many tragic, some comic, a large number merely strange, but none commonplace; for, working as he did rather for the love of his art than for the acquirement of wealth, he refused to associate himself with any investigation which did not tend towards the unusual, and even the fantastic." Later, in discussing the case of Helen Stoner, Holmes noted, "As to reward, my profession is its reward; but you are at liberty to defray whatever expenses I may be put to, at the time which suits you best." *The Adventure of the Speckled Band*, I, 243, 245.

Justice of the Peace Trevor thought highly of the young Sherlock Holmes's powers of observation, saying, "I don't know how you manage this, Mr. Holmes, but it seems to me that all the detectives of fact and of fancy would be children in your hands. That's your life, sir, and you may take the word of a man who has seen something of the world." Holmes recalled later to Watson, "And that recommendation, with the exaggerated estimate of my ability with which he prefaced it, was, if you will believe me, Watson, the very first thing which ever made me feel that a profession might be made out of what had up to that time been the merest hobby." *The "Gloria Scott"*, I, 110.

Holmes said, "In over a thousand cases I am not aware that I have ever used my powers upon the wrong side. Of late I have been tempted to look into the problems furnished by Nature rather than those more superficial ones for which our artificial state of society is responsible. Your memoirs will draw to an end, Watson, upon the day that I crown my career by the capture or extinction of the most dangerous and capable criminal in Europe," Professor Moriarty. *The Final Problem*, II, 312.

"Holmes, however, like all great artists, lived for his art's sake, and, save in the case of the Duke of Holdernesse, I have seldom known him claim any large reward for his inestimable services. So unworldly was he — or so capricious — that he frequently refused his help to the powerful and wealthy where the problem made no appeal to his sympathies, while he would devote weeks of most intense application to the affairs of some humble client whose case presented those strange and dramatic qualities which appealed to his imagination and challenged his ingenuity." *The Adventure of Black Peter*, II, 398; see also *The Adventure of the Priory School*, II, 629.

Said Holmes: "Once or twice in my career I feel that I have done more real harm by my discovery of the criminal than ever he had done by his crime. I have learned caution now, and I had rather play tricks with the law of England than with my own conscience. Let us know a little more before we act." *The Adventure of the Abbey Grange*, II, 503.

"It is my business to know things. That is my trade." *The Adventure of the Blanched Soldier*, II, 717.

Holmes explained to Neil Gibson, the Gold King, that "my professional charges are upon a fixed scale. I do not vary them, save when I remit them altogether." *The Problem of Thor Bridge*, II, 592.

HOLMES, SHERLOCK; AND HIS PUBLIC: Watson was quick to deny Holmes's statement that "'if I show you too much of my method of working, you will come to the conclusion that I am a very ordinary individual after all.'

"'I shall never do that; you have brought detection as near an exact science as it ever will be brought in this world.'

"My companion [Holmes] flushed up with pleasure at my words, and the earnest way in which I uttered them. I had already observed that he was as sensitive to flattery on the score of this art as any girl could be of her beauty." *A Study in Scarlet*, 1, 174.

Holmes, somewhat bitter over the publicity that Lestrade and Gregson hoped to reap after the capture of Jefferson Hope, said, "What you do in this world is a matter of no consequence. The question is, what can you make people believe that you have done." *A Study in Scarlet*, 1, 231.

Watson: "Lestrade and I sat silent for a moment, and then, with a spontaneous impulse, we both broke out clapping as at the well-wrought crisis of a play. A flush of colour sprang to Holmes' pale cheeks, and he bowed to us like the master dramatist who receives the homage of his audience. It was at such moments that for an instant he ceased to be a reasoning machine, and betrayed his human love for admiration and applause. The same singularly proud and reserved nature which turned away with disdain from popular notoriety was capable of being moved to its depths by spontaneous wonder and praise from a friend.... 'Thank you!' said Holmes. 'Thank you!' and as he turned away it seemed to me that he was more nearly moved by the softer human emotions than I had ever seen him." *The Adventure of the Six Napoleons*, 11, 585, 587.

The true reason that Dr. Watson had not published more of the exploits of Sherlock Holmes which were in his possession "lay in the reluctance which Mr. Holmes had shown to the continued publication of his experiences. So long as he was in actual professional practice the records of his successes were of some practical value to him; but since he has definitely retired from London and betaken himself to study and bee-farming on the Sussex Downs, notoriety has become hateful to him, and he has peremptorily requested that his wishes in this matter should be strictly observed." *The Adventure of the Second Stain*, 1, 301.

"To his sombre and cynical spirit all popular applause was always abhorrent, and nothing amused him more at the end of a successful case than to hand over the actual exposure to some orthodox official, and to listen with a mocking smile to the general chorus of misplaced congratulation." *The Adventure of the Devil's Foot*, 11, 508.

HOLMES, SHERLOCK; SKILLS: Holmes requested that Watson again recite the limits of Holmes's knowledge: "Philosophy, astronomy, and politics were marked at zero, I remember. Botany variable, geology profound as regards the mudstains from any region within fifty miles of town, chemistry eccentric, anatomy unsystematic, sensational literature and crime records unique, violin player, boxer, swordsman, lawyer, and self-poisoner by cocaine and tobacco. Those, I think, were the main points of my analysis." *The Five Orange Pips*, I, 399.

As Holmes led Watson unerringly through the back streets of London, Watson marvelled, "Holmes' knowledge of the by-ways of London was extraordinary, and on this occasion he passed rapidly, with an assured step, through a network of mews and stables the very existence of which I had never known." *The Adventure of the Empty House*, II, 338.

"He had at least five small refuges in different parts of London in which he was able to change his personality." *The Adventure of Black Peter*, II, 398.

Holmes always had the idea that he would make a highly efficient criminal. Watson tells us that "Holmes had remarkable powers, carefully cultivated, of seeing in the dark," and that "I knew the opening of safes was a particular hobby with him, and I understood the joy which it gave him to be confronted with this green and gold monster, the dragon which held in its maw the reputations of many fair ladies." *The Adventure of Charles Augustus Milverton*, II, 564, 565, 566.

"Sherlock Holmes was a past master in the art of putting a humble witness at his ease...." *The Adventure of the Missing Three-Quarter*, II, 478; see also *The Adventure of the Red Circle*, II, 691, 692.

HOLMES, SHERLOCK; AND DR. WATSON: "There was a curious secretive streak in the man which led to many dramatic effects, but left even his closest friend guessing as to what his exact plans might be. He pushed to an extreme the axiom that the only safe plotter was he who plotted alone. I was nearer him than anyone else, and yet I was always conscious of the gap between." *The Adventure of the Illustrious Client*, II, 684.

"The ideas of my friend Watson, though limited, are exceedingly pertinacious. For a long time he has worried me to write an experience of my own. Perhaps I have rather invited this persecution, since I have often had occasion to point out to him how superficial are his own accounts and to accuse him of pandering to popular taste instead of confining himself rigidly to facts and figures. 'Try it yourself, Holmes!' he has retorted, and I am compelled to admit that, having taken my pen in hand, I do begin to realize that the matter must be presented in such a way as may interest the reader." *The Adventure of the Blanched Soldier*, II, 707.

"This is a more serious matter than I expected, Watson. It is fair to tell you so, though I know it will only be an additional reason to you for running your head into danger. I should know my Watson by now. But there *is* danger, and you should know it." And so it proved. Holmes concealed a "depth of loyalty and love" for Watson behind a "cold mask," and only this once — when he thought his old comrade seriously injured — did he allow Watson to catch "a glimpse of [his] great heart as well as of [his] great brain." The good Doctor felt that "all [his own] years of humble but single-minded service culminated in that moment of revelation." *The Adventure of the Three Garridebs*, II, 651, 653.

HOLMES, SHERLOCK; AND WOMEN: Of Irene Adler, Watson wrote: "To Sherlock Holmes she is always *the* woman. I have seldom heard him mention her under any other name. In his eyes she eclipses and predominates the whole of her sex. It was not that he felt any emotion akin to love for Irene Adler. All emotions, and that one particularly, were abhorrent to his cold, precise, but admirably balanced mind. He was, I take it, the most perfect reasoning and observing machine that the world has seen: but, as a lover, he would have placed himself in a false position. He never spoke of the softer passions, save with a gibe and a sneer. They were admirable things for the observer — excellent for drawing the veil from men's motives and actions. But for the trained reasoner to admit such intrusions into his own delicate and finely adjusted temperament was to introduce a distracting factor which might throw a doubt upon all his mental results. Grit in a sensitive instrument, or a crack in one of his own high-power lenses, would not be more disturbing than a strong emotion in a nature such as his. And yet there was but one woman to him, and that woman was the late Irene Adler, of dubious and questionable memory." *A Scandal in Bohemia*, I, 346.

Holmes was struck by the great beauty of Maud Bellamy of Fulworth, the village neighboring his retirement villa in Sussex: "Who could have imagined that so rare a flower would grow from such a root and in such an atmosphere? Women have seldom been an attraction to me, for my brain has always governed my heart, but I could not look upon her perfect clear-cut face, with all the freshness of the Downlands in her delicate colouring, without realizing that no young man would cross her path unscathed.... Maud Bellamy will always remain in my memory as a most complete and remarkable woman." *The Adventure of the Lion's Mane*, II, 781–82.

"HOLMES, SHERLOCK": A man using this name hired a cab to shadow Sir Henry Baskerville and Dr. James Mortimer. *The Hound of the Baskervilles*, II, 34.

HOLY LAND: Dr. Shlessinger, while supposedly recuperating at the Englischer Hof in Baden from a disease contracted while carrying out his missionary duties in South America, "was preparing a map of the Holy Land, with special reference to the kingdom of the Midianites, upon which he was writing a monograph." *The Disappearance of Lady Frances Carfax*, II, 659.

HONES, JOHNNY: One of the casualties of the expedition across the Great Alkali Plain, which only John and Lucy Ferrier survived. *A Study in Scarlet*, I, 198.

HOPE, LADY HILDA TRELAWNEY: Youngest daughter of the Duke of Belminster and wife of Britain's Secretary for European Affairs, she was, in Watson's opinion, "the most lovely woman in London." She had come to Sherlock Holmes asking the specifics of the case which her husband had earlier set before the detective; naturally, Holmes refused detailed comment, explaining that he could not violate "professional secrecy." At this, Lady Hilda departed abruptly, leaving Holmes to plumb Watson's supposedly greater knowledge of women's motives. *The Adventure of the Second Stain*, I, *passim*.

HOPE, JEFFERSON, JUNIOR: "He had been a pioneer in California, and could narrate many a strange tale of fortunes made and fortunes lost in those wild, halcyon days. He had been a scout, too, and a trapper, a silver explorer, and a ranchman. Wherever stirring adventures were to be had, Jefferson Hope had been there in search of them." Hope became a favorite of John Ferrier and his adopted daughter, Lucy. When he left for his diggings in the Nevada Mountains, Lucy promised him her hand. *A Study in Scarlet*, I, 206ff.

HOPE, JEFFERSON, SENIOR: He and John Ferrier had been good friends in St. Louis. *A Study in Scarlet*, I, 205.

HOPE, THE RIGHT HONOURABLE TRELAWNEY: Secretary for European Affairs under Lord Bellinger, and a rising statesman in Britain. Behind his "aristocratic mask" lurked a "natural man — impulsive, ardent, keenly sensitive" who showed himself to Holmes and Watson when he lamented the fact than an exceedingly valuable State document had been stolen from his home. In time, Holmes was able to restore the document to the Secretary, and Hope considered the detective "a wizard, a sorcerer" for having been able to do so. *The Adventure of the Second Stain*, I, 301–2.

HOPE TOWN: A small village on the slopes of Mount Harriet on Blair Island in the Andaman Islands. Here, Jonathan Small was given a hut for his good behavior while serving his life sentence for the murder of Achmet the merchant. *The Sign of the Four*, I, 682.

HOPKINS, EZEKIAH: Of Lebanon, Pennsylvania, he was the supposed founder of the Red-Headed League. "He himself was red-headed, and he had a great sympathy for all red-headed men; so, when he died, it was found that he had left his enormous fortune in the hands of trustees, with instructions to apply the interest to the providing of easy berths to men whose hair is of that colour." *The Red-Headed League*, I, 423.

HOPKINS, INSPECTOR STANLEY, OF SCOTLAND YARD: "Our visitor was an exceedingly alert man, thirty years of age, dressed in a quiet tweed suit, but retaining the erect bearing of one who was accustomed to official uniform. I recognized him at once as Stanley Hopkins, a young police inspector for whose future Holmes had high hopes, while he in turn professed the admiration and respect of a pupil for the scientific methods of the famous amateur." Hopkins called Holmes in to help investigate the circumstances surrounding the death of Captain Peter Carey. *The Adventure of Black Peter*, II, 399; see also *The Adventure of the Abbey Grange*, II, 491, 492.

"A promising detective, in whose career Holmes had several times shown a very practical interest," Hopkins believed that the Yoxley case provided him with "a splendid chance of putting [Holmes's] theories into practice." After hearing some of Hopkins's efforts to that end, however, Holmes felt that the other had only "made certain that [he] had made certain of nothing." *The Adventure of the Golden Pince-Nez*, II, 351.

Perceiving that the disappearance of the star of Cambridge's rugger team was a case "more in [Sherlock Holmes's] line than in that of the regular police," Hopkins referred Cyril Overton, captain of the Cambridge team, to the consulting detective. *The Adventure of the Missing Three-Quarter*, II, 476.

HORNER, JOHN: A plumber, aged 26, he was arrested in connection with the disappearance of the Countess of Morcar's fabulous jewel, the blue carbuncle. He had had a previous conviction for robbery. *The Adventure of the Blue Carbuncle*, I, 456.

HORSHAM: A Sussex town north of Lamberley, the village near which Robert Ferguson lived. *The Adventure of the Sussex Vampire*, II, 463; see also *The Five Orange Pips*, I, 390, 392.

HORSOM, DR.: Of 13 Firbank Villas, he had signed the death certificate of Rose Spender, whom Henry Peters and Annie Fraser had brought to their home from the Brixton Workhouse Infirmary. *The Disappearance of Lady Frances Carfax*, II, 667, 668.

HOTEL COSMOPOLITAN: The Countess of Morcar stayed there at the time when her precious jewel, the blue carbuncle, was stolen. *The Adventure of the Blue Carbuncle*, I, 456.

HOTEL DULONG: "I see that it was on the 14th of April that I received a telegram from Lyons, which informed me that Holmes was lying ill in the Hotel Dulong," recalled Watson. *The Reigate Squires*, I, 331.

HOTEL ESCURIAL: In Madrid, it was where the Marquess of Montalva and his secretary, Signor Rulli, were both murdered in their rooms. *The Adventure of Wisteria Lodge*, II, 258.

HOTEL NATIONAL: The vanished Lady Frances Carfax was last heard from by her old governess, Susan Dobney, from the Hôtel National at Lausanne. Watson traveled there to discover the secret of the lady's disappearance. *The Disappearance of Lady Frances Carfax*, II, 657.

HOTSPUR: A brig bound for Australia in 1855, it picked up the survivors of the *Gloria Scott*. *The "Gloria Scott"*, I, 121.

HOUND OF THE BASKERVILLES: The original Hound, which took the life of Hugo Baskerville and was described in 1742 by the second Hugo: "There stood a foul thing, a great, black beast, shaped like a hound, yet larger than any hound that ever mortal eye has rested upon. And even as they looked the thing tore the throat out of Hugo Baskerville, on which, as it turned its blazing eyes and ripping jaws upon them, the three [onlookers] shrieked with fear and rode for dear life, still screaming, across the moor." Watson, years later, described the hell-hound that he, Lestrade, and Holmes faced on the fog-girt moor: "A hound it was, an enormous coal-black hound, but not such a hound as mortal eyes have ever seen. Fire burst from its open mouth, its eyes glowed with a smouldering glare, its muzzle and hackles and dewlap were outlined in flickering flame. Never in the delirious dream of a disordered brain could anything more savage, more appalling, more hellish, be conceived than that dark form and savage face which broke upon us out of the wall of fog." Watson noted of the latter-day Hound, "In mere size and strength it was a terrible creature which was lying stretched before us. It was not pure bloodhound and it was not a pure mastiff; but it appeared to be a combination of the two — gaunt, savage, and as large as a small lioness. ...The huge jaws seemed to be dripping with a bluish flame, and the small, deep-set, cruel eyes were ringed with fire." *The Hound of the Baskervilles*, II, 10, 100–1.

HOWELLS, RACHEL: Second housemaid at Hurlstone, the ancestral home of a branch of the Musgraves, in western Sussex. "Of an excitable Welsh temperament," she was once engaged to the butler, Richard Brunton, but was thrown aside by him. *The Musgrave Ritual*, I, 128–29.

HUDSON: Elias Openshaw's notebook for March, 1869, contained the entry, "4th. Hudson came. Same old platform." *The Five Orange Pips*, I, 397.

HUDSON: A young seaman aboard the barque *Gloria Scott* in 1855, he was the sole survivor of a shipboard explosion which came hard on the heels of a takeover by the barque's cargo of convicts. Some of the convicts had departed the ship in a rowboat just before the explosion, and they pulled the "burned and exhausted" Hudson out of the drink. *The "Gloria Scott"*, I, 121.

HUDSON, MORSE: Proprietor of a shop for the sale of pictures and statues in the Kennington Road. When a plaster bust of Napoleon was smashed in his shop, Hudson attributed it to hooliganism. *The Adventure of the Six Napoleons*, II, 578.

HUDSON, MRS. MARTHA: "The table was all laid, and just as [Watson] was about to ring, Mrs. Hudson entered with the tea and coffee. A few minutes later she brought in the covers, and we all drew up to the table, Holmes ravenous, I curious, and Phelps in the gloomiest state of depression.

"'Mrs. Hudson has risen to the occasion,' said Holmes, uncovering a dish of curried chicken. 'Her cuisine is a little limited, but she has as good an idea of breakfast as a Scotchwoman.'" *The Naval Treaty*, II, 189; see also *The Adventure of the Dancing Men*, II, 534; *The Adventure of Wisteria Lodge*, II, 240.

Mrs. Hudson was thrown into "violent hysterics" when Holmes, supposedly dead above the Fall of Reichenbach in his struggle with Professor Moriarty, returned to his Baker Street rooms. However, she quickly recovered, put the rooms in immediate order, and took a dangerous role in Holmes's plan to foil Sebastian Moran's attempt on his life. *The Adventure of the Empty House*, II, 337.

"Mrs. Hudson, the landlady of Sherlock Holmes, was a long-suffering woman. Not only was her first-floor flat invaded at all hours by throngs of singular and often undesirable characters, but her remarkable lodger showed an eccentricity and irregularity in his life which must have sorely tried her patience. His incredible untidiness, his addiction to music at strange hours, his occasional revolver practice within doors, his weird and often malodorous scientific experiments, and the atmosphere of violence and danger which hung around him made him the very worst tenant in London. On the other hand, his payments were princely. I have no doubt that the house might have been purchased at the price which Holmes paid for his rooms during the years that I was with him.

"The landlady stood in the deepest awe of him, and never dared to interfere with him, however outrageous his proceedings might seem. She was fond of him too, for he had a remarkable way with women. He disliked and distrusted the sex, but he was always a chivalrous opponent. Knowing how genuine was her regard for him, I listened earnestly to her story when she came to my rooms in the second year of my married life and told me of the sad condition to which my poor friend was reduced." *The Adventure of the Dying Detective*, I, 439; see also *The Disappearance of Lady Frances Carfax*, II, 662; *The Adventure of the Mazarin Stone*, II, 747.

HUDSON STREET: "A very quiet thoroughfare" in Aldershot, upon which Mrs. James Barclay, née Nancy Devoy, accompanied by Miss Morrison, met the Crooked Man. *The Crooked Man*, II, 232.

HUGUENOTS, LES: Holmes had a box for *Les Huguenots*, with the De Reszkes performing, to which he invited Watson after his final explanation of the case. *The Hound of the Baskervilles*, II, 112.

HUNGARIAN POLICE: The Hungarian police were of the opinion that the stabbing deaths of Wilson Kemp and Harold Latimer were the result of a quarrel between themselves. Sherlock Holmes was of a different opinion, however. *The Greek Interpreter*, I, 605.

HUNT: A police officer, he was shot because he had ventured to arrest two members of the Scowrers. *The Valley of Fear*, I, 560.

HUNTER, NED: A stable boy who had been on guard the night that the racehorse Silver Blaze disappeared. He had been drugged with opium. *Silver Blaze*, II, 265.

HUNTER, VIOLET: Of Montague Place. "She was plainly but neatly dressed, with a bright, quick face, freckled like a plover's egg, and with the brisk manner of a woman who has had her own way to make in the world." This resourceful governess's acceptance of a peculiar job in Hampshire involved Holmes in mysterious circumstances. *The Adventure of the Copper Beeches*, II, 116.

HURET: In 1894, Sherlock Holmes tracked and arrested "Huret, the Boulevard assassin — an exploit which won for Holmes an autograph letter of thanks from the French President and the Order of the Legion of Honour." *The Adventure of the Golden Pince-Nez*, II, 350.

HURLSTONE: Ancestral home of a cadet branch of the northern Musgraves, in Sussex, it was perhaps the oldest inhabited building in the county. "It is built in the shape of an *L*, the long arm being the more modern portion, and the shorter the ancient nucleus from which the other has developed. Over the low, heavy-lintelled door, in the centre of this old part, is chiselled the date 1607, but experts are agreed that the beams and stonework are really much older than this." *The Musgrave Ritual*, I, 133.

HUXTABLE, DR. THORNEYCROFT: "We have had some dramatic entrances and exits upon our small stage at Baker Street, but I cannot recollect anything more sudden and startling than the first appearance of Dr. Thorneycroft Huxtable, M.A., PH.D., etc." Dr. Huxtable came tumbling into the Baker Street rooms in a state of nervous exhaustion over the disappearance of Lord Saltire, the Duke of Holdernesse's son, from Huxtable's Priory School, near Mackleton. *The Adventure of the Priory School*, II, 607.

HUXTABLE'S SIDELIGHTS ON HORACE: Written by Dr. Thorney-croft Huxtable, founder and principal of the Priory School. *The Adventure of the Priory School*, II, 609.

HYAM, MR.: Jacob Shafter told Jack McMurdo that old Mr. Hyam had been murdered by the Scowrers. *The Valley of Fear*, I, 528.

HYAMS: Jonas Oldacre's tailor. A trouser button marked with the name of "Hyams" was found among the ashes of the burned wood-pile near Oldacre's residence. *The Adventure of the Norwood Builder*, II, 423.

HYDE PARK: Miss Hatty Doran was last seen walking there in the company of Flora Millar, who was later taken into custody. *The Adventure of the Noble Bachelor*, I, 290.

HYNES, MR. HYNES, J.P.: His large house, Purdey Place, lay near Aloysius Garcia's Wisteria Lodge, in Surrey. *The Adventure of Wisteria Lodge*, II, 246.

I

IMPERIAL OPERA OF WARSAW: Irene Adler, famed as *the* woman in Holmes's life, had been prima donna of the Imperial Opera of Warsaw. *A Scandal in Bohemia*, I, 354.

IMPERIAL THEATRE: Violet Smith's father, the late James Smith, had conducted the orchestra at the old Imperial Theatre. *The Adventure of the Solitary Cyclist*, II, 385.

INDIA: When the young Dr. Watson (University of London, 1878) was attached to the Fifth Northumberland Fusiliers as Assistant Surgeon, the regiment was stationed in India. He journeyed thence in time to take part, and be wounded, in the second Afghan War. *A Study in Scarlet*, I, 143; see also *The Sign of the Four*, I, 638; *The Five Orange Pips*, I, 393; *The Naval Treaty*, II, 187; *The Adventure of the Bruce-Partington Plans*, II, 433.

Concerning the "very small, dark fellow, with his hat pushed back and several packages under his arm," whom both Mycroft and Sherlock Holmes viewed from the Strangers' Room of the Diogenes Club, they deduced a great many things, including that he had been a non-commissioned officer of the Royal Artillery who had served in India. *The Greek Interpreter*, I, 594.

INDIAN MUTINY: Colonel James Barclay rose to commissioned rank from full private by the bravery he showed in the Indian Mutiny. The Royal Mallows regiment, which he later commanded, also distinguished itself in action there. *The Crooked Man*, II, 227.

INDIAN PETE: One of the casualties of the expedition across the Great Alkali Plain which only John and Lucy Ferrier survived. *A Study in Scarlet*, I, 198.

INTERLAKEN: Holmes and Watson, in their attempted escape from Professor Moriarty, passed over the Gemmi Pass to Interlaken, and thence to Meiringen. *The Final Problem*, II, 312.

IONIDES OF ALEXANDRIA: An Egyptian cigarette-maker, he "especially prepared...fresh Alexandrian cigarettes" for Professor Coram, who consumed them at a rate of a thousand per fortnight. *The Adventure of the Golden Pince-Nez*, II, 360.

IRIS: The horse run by the Duke of Balmoral for the Wessex Cup. Iris came in a bad third. *Silver Blaze*, II, 278.

ISONOMY: Silver Blaze, the racehorse who disappeared from his stable just before the running of the Wessex Cup, was from Isonomy stock, and held as brilliant a record as his famous ancestor. *Silver Blaze*, II, 264.

ITALY: The naval treaty which strangely disappeared from Percy Phelps's room in the Foreign Office was drawn up between England and Italy, and dealt, in part, with the policy that Britain would pursue "in the event of the French fleet gaining a complete ascendency over that of Italy in the Mediterranean." *The Naval Treaty*, II, 171–72; see also *A Study in Scarlet*, I, 207; *The Adventure of the Red Circle*, II, 698, 703.

IVY PLANT: A pub "round the corner" from the house in which Eduardo Lucas was murdered. It was to the Ivy Plant that Constable MacPherson repaired to procure brandy when the woman he had wrongfully admitted to the murder house "dropped on the floor, and lay as if she were dead." *The Adventure of the Second Stain*, I, 316.

J

JACKSON: Watson had no doubt that Jackson could take over his practice while he accompanied Holmes to Aldershot to investigate the peculiar circumstances surrounding the death of Colonel James Barclay. *The Crooked Man*, II, 226.

JACKSON PRIZE FOR COMPARATIVE PATHOLOGY: Dr. James Mortimer, who sought Holmes's aid in *The Hound of the Baskervilles*, had won the Jackson Prize for Comparative Pathology with his essay entitled "Is Disease a Reversion?" *The Hound of the Baskervilles*, II, 5.

JACOBS: He was butler to the Right Honourable Trelawney Hope and his wife, Lady Hilda Trelawney Hope. *The Adventure of the Second Stain*, I, 320, 321.

JACOBSON: Mordecai Smith's steam launch, *Aurora*, had been removed to Jacobson's shipyard, on the Surrey side of the Thames, ostensibly to receive minor repairs on her rudder. *The Sign of the Four*, I, 662.

JAMES: Son of the postmaster in the hamlet of Grimpen, Devonshire, he delivered a telegram to Baskerville Hall to John Barrymore. *The Hound of the Baskervilles*, II, 44.

JAMES, JACK: An American citizen captured and sentenced to Portland for spying for the Germans before World War I. Von Bork felt that "it was James' own fault. You know that yourself. He was too self-willed for the job." *His Last Bow*, II, 798.

JAMES, LITTLE BILLY: Jacob Shafter told Jack McMurdo that little Billy James had been murdered by the Scowrers. *The Valley of Fear*, I, 528.

JAPAN: One of Holmes's deductions that so impressed Justice of the Peace Trevor was that the latter had visited Japan. *The "Gloria Scott"*, I, 109; see also *The Adventure of the Three Garridebs*, II, 648.

JENKINS: Both he and his younger brother were killed by the Scowrers. *The Valley of Fear*, I, 560.

JEZAIL BULLET: Dr. John H. Watson, newly attached to the Berkshires, participated in "the fatal battle of Maiwand. There I was struck on the shoulder by a Jezail bullet, which shattered the bone and grazed the subclavian artery." *A Study in Scarlet*, I, 143.

Watson sat nursing his wounded leg. "I had had a Jezail bullet through it some time before, and though it did not prevent me from walking, it ached wearily at every change of the weather." *The Sign of the Four*, I, 611.

Watson said, "I had remained indoors all day, for the weather had taken a sudden turn to rain, with high autumnal winds, and the jezail bullet which I brought back in one of my limbs as a relic of my Afghan campaign, throbbed with dull persistency." *The Adventure of the Noble Bachelor*, I, 281.

JOHANNESBURG: The South African city in which, according to Bob Carruthers and Jack Woodley, Violet Smith's Uncle Ralph had died in poverty. Woodley's "name [was] a holy terror from Kimberley to Johannesburg." *The Adventure of the Solitary Cyclist*, II, 385, 395.

JOHN: Irene Adler's coachman, he drove her to her wedding at the Church of St. Monica in the Edgware Road. Later, he kept watch on Holmes, who, disguised as an injured Nonconformist clergyman, had gained access to Adler's sitting-room. *A Scandal in Bohemia*, I, 358, 364.

JOHN: The coachman who picked Holmes and Watson up near the Bar of Gold opium den. *The Man with the Twisted Lip*, I, 373.

JOHN: "A pompous butler" in the employ of Dr. Leslie Armstrong, he "ushered [Holmes and Watson] severely to the door" on the order of his master. *The Adventure of the Missing Three-Quarter*, II, 484.

JOHNSON: One of the two "Oxford fliers" who, in the opinion of Cyril Overton, captain of the Cambridge rugger team, "could romp round" Moorhouse, the slow "first reserve" on Cambridge's squad. *The Adventure of the Missing Three-Quarter*, II, 476.

JOHNSON, "PORKY" SHINWELL: A valuable assistant to Sherlock Holmes in the early years of the twentieth century. "Johnson, I grieve to say, made his name first as a very dangerous villain and served two terms at Parkhurst. Finally, he repented and allied himself to Holmes, acting as his agent in the huge criminal underworld of London, and obtaining information which often proved to be of vital importance." He proved useful in helping Holmes counter the vile schemes of the notorious Baron Adelbert Gruner. Johnson was "a huge, coarse, red-faced, scorbutic man, with a pair of vivid black eyes which were the only external sign of the very cunning mind within." *The Adventure of the Illustrious Client*, II, 675, 677.

JOHNSON, SIDNEY: One of the two men who had a key to the safe from which the Bruce-Partington Plans were stolen, this senior clerk and draftsman was a man of forty, married, with five children who, though "silent [and] morose," had, "on the whole, an excellent record in the public service." *The Adventure of the Bruce-Partington Plans*, II, 437.

JOHNSON, THEOPHILUS: Of Newcastle, he was a coal owner. A very active gentleman, and not much older than Holmes, he and his family were staying at the Northumberland Hotel at the same time as Sir Henry Baskerville. *The Hound of the Baskervilles*, II, 29.

JOHNSTON: One of the four principal Mormon Elders. *A Study in Scarlet*, I, 203.

JONES, ATHELNEY: "A very stout, portly man in a grey suit...red-faced, burly, and plethoric, with a pair of very small, twinkling eyes, which looked keenly out from between swollen and puffy pouches." He carried on the official investigation of the murder of Bartholomew Sholto. *The Sign of the Four*, I, 639–40.

JONES, PETER: The official police agent in the mystery of Jabez Wilson's partial unemployment. Holmes commented, "I thought it as well to have Jones with us also. He is not a bad fellow, though an absolute imbecile in his profession. He has one positive virtue. He is brave as a bulldog, and tenacious as a lobster if he gets his claws upon anyone." *The Red-Headed League*, I, 432, 433.

JOSE: Personal manservant of Mr. Henderson of High Gable, in Surrey, he delivered the note that led to the death of Aloysius Garcia. *The Adventure of Wisteria Lodge*, II, 257.

K

KANSAS: John Garrideb claimed to be a lawyer in Moorville, Kansas. Sherlock Holmes claimed the acquaintance of old Dr. Lysander Starr,

Mayor of Topeka in 1890. And the old land baron, Alexander Hamilton Garrideb, reputedly had made his home in Topeka, where John Garrideb had once practiced law. *The Adventure of the Three Garridebs*, II, 644, 645, 646.

KEMBALL: One of the four principal Mormon Elders. *A Study in Scarlet*, I, 203.

KEMP, WILSON: "A man of the foulest antecedents," he was Harold Latimer's associate in their attempt to gain the property of Sophy and Paul Kratides. *The Greek Interpreter*, I, 597, 599, 605.

KENNINGTON PARK GATE: John Rance, the constable who found the dead body of Enoch J. Drebber in a lonely suburban London apartment just off the Brixton Road, lived at 46 Audley Court, Kennington Park Gate. *A Study in Scarlet*, I, 172.

KENNINGTON ROAD: Morse Hudson had a place for the sale of pictures and statues in the Kennington Road. The first of a series of plaster busts of Napoleon was smashed here. The second bust to be smashed belonged to Dr. Barnicot, who had his residence and principal consulting-room in Kennington Road, within a few yards of Hudson's shop. *The Adventure of the Six Napoleons*, II, 573.

KENSINGTON: At the time of the mystery of Jabez Wilson's partial unemployment, Dr. Watson's house was in Kensington. *The Red-Headed League*, I, 432; see also *The Greek Interpreter*, I, 595; *The Adventure of the Six Napoleons*, II, 575; *The Adventure of Wisteria Lodge*, II, 240; *The Adventure of the Bruce-Partington Plans*, II, 445.

When Holmes investigated the predicament of the unfortunate John Hector McFarlane, Watson had just sold his Kensington practice to a young doctor named Verner, and had moved into Baker Street again with his old companion, Sherlock Holmes. *The Adventure of the Norwood Builder*, II, 414.

KENT: The Cedars, residence of the missing Neville St. Clair, was near Lee, in Kent. *The Man with the Twisted Lip*, I, 372; see also *The Adventure of the Golden Pince-Nez*, II, 352; *The Adventure of the Abbey Grange*, II, 491; *The Adventure of the Lion's Mane*, II, 788.

KENT, MR.: Like Watson, he was an "educated medical man" who shared lodgings (in a "detached house" at Tuxbury Old Park) with a man over whose health he worried. *The Adventure of the Blanched Soldier*, II, 717.

KESWICK: On inquiring for Mrs. Sawyer at 13 Duncan Street, Houndsditch, Holmes "found that the house belonged to a respectable paperhanger, named Keswick, and that no one of the name...of Sawyer... had ever been heard of there." *A Study in Scarlet*, I, 183.

KHALIFA: After his supposed death at the Reichenbach Fall, Sherlock Holmes traveled for two years in Tibet. After leaving Tibet, he had a series of adventures, one of which was "a short but interesting visit to the Khalifa at Khartoum, the results of which [he] communicated to the Foreign Office." *The Adventure of the Empty House*, II, 337.

KHAN, ABDULLAH: A tall and fierce-looking Sikh trooper, he was one of the men bound by the sign of the four. *The Sign of the Four*, I, 676.

KING, MRS.: The cook at Ridling Thorpe Manor, Norfolk, where Mr. Hilton Cubitt was found shot through the heart and his wife with a bullet lodged in her brain. Mrs. King and the housemaid gave the alarm after having been aroused from their sleep by a series of explosions. *The Adventure of the Dancing Men*, II, 536.

KING'S COLLEGE HOSPITAL: After he graduated from London University, Dr. Percy Trevelyan, who came to Holmes with a very curious problem which ended in tragedy, occupied a minor position in King's College Hospital. *The Resident Patient*, I, 269.

KING'S CROSS STATION: Holmes felt that he and Watson ought to journey to Cambridge via King's Cross Station to investigate the sudden disappearance of Godfrey Staunton before the Cambridge-Oxford rugby match. *The Adventure of the Missing Three-Quarter*, II, 482; see also *A Case of Identity*, I, 409.

KING'S PYLAND: The training stables of Colonel Ross, in Dartmoor. It was from here that the horse Silver Blaze disappeared. *Silver Blaze*, II, 271.

KINGSTON: Vernon Lodge, the residence of the notorious Baron Adelbert Gruner, was near Kingston. *The Adventure of the Illustrious Client*, II, 674.

KIRWAN, WILLIAM: Coachman and longtime servant of the Cunninghams at their estate near Reigate, in Surrey. He was killed in a supposed burglary, which Holmes investigated. *The Reigate Squires*, I, 332.

KLEIN: The wealthy German sugar king, he was the first husband of Isadora Klein. *The Adventure of the Three Gables*, II, 731.

KLEIN, ISADORA: Of Grosvenor Square. "*The* celebrated beauty" of her day and the richest widow in the world, her ex-lover had written a romantic novel about their affair, which threatened to ruin her forthcoming marriage to the Duke of Lomond. *The Adventure of the Three Gables*, II, 731, 732.

KLOPMAN: Holmes had, at one time, prevented the murder of Count Von und Zu Grafenstein (uncle of the German spy Von Bork) by the Nihilist Klopman. *His Last Bow*, II, 802.

KNELLER, SIR GODFREY: As he dined with Sir Henry Baskerville, Sherlock Holmes recognized a portrait by Kneller in the family gallery. *The Hound of the Baskervilles*, II, 92.

KNOX, JACK: Of Ironhill. Jack McMurdo thought that the murderers Lawler and Andrews might be after Knox. *The Valley of Fear*, I, 556.

KRATIDES, PAUL: He came to England from Athens to rescue his sister Sophy from an ill-conceived alliance. *The Greek Interpreter*, I, 597.

KRATIDES, SOPHY: She "came of a wealthy Grecian family, and...had been on a visit to some friends in England. While there she had met a young man named Harold Latimer, who had acquired an ascendancy over her, and had eventually persuaded her to fly with him." *The Greek Interpreter*, I, 598, 605.

KU KLUX KLAN: Holmes traced to the Ku Klux Klan the series of mysterious letters that had foreshadowed death for two generations of Openshaws. Holmes referred to his American encyclopedia for specific information about the Klan: "A name derived from a fanciful resemblance to the sound produced by cocking a rifle. This terrible secret society was formed by some ex-Confederate soldiers in the Southern States after the Civil War, and it rapidly formed local branches in different parts of the country, notably Tennessee, Louisiana, the Carolinas, Georgia, and Florida. Its power was used for political purposes, principally for the terrorizing of the negro voters, and the murdering or driving from the country of those who were opposed to its views." *The Five Orange Pips*, I, 400.

L

LA ROTHIERE, LOUIS: The resident of Campden Mansions, Notting Hill, he was one of the three foreign spies in England whom Mycroft Holmes thought capable of handling so big an affair as the theft of the Bruce-Partington submarine plans. *The Adventure of the Bruce-Partington Plans*, II, 445; see also *The Adventure of the Second Stain*, I, 307.

LA SCALA: Irene Adler, famed as *the* woman in Holmes's life, had sung at La Scala. *A Scandal in Bohemia*, I, 354.

LABURNUM LODGE: In Laburnum Vale, Chiswick. Mr. Josiah Brown, whose plaster cast of Devine's bust of Napoleon was smashed, resided there. *The Adventure of the Six Napoleons*, II, 580.

LACHINE: Colonel James Barclay's villa at Aldershot. *The Crooked Man*, II, 227.

LAFTER HALL: On the moor, in Devonshire. Home of Mr. Frankland. *The Hound of the Baskervilles*, II, 12.

LAMBETH: The bird-stuffer, Sherman, and his sleuth-hound, Toby, lived at NO. 3 Pinchin Lane, Lambeth. *The Sign of the Four*, I, 642.

LANCASTER GATE: Aloysius Doran, father of Miss Hatty Doran, had a furnished house there, to which the wedding party returned after her marriage to Lord St. Simon. *The Adventure of the Noble Bachelor*, I, 285.

LANCASTER, JAMES: Captain Basil (Sherlock Holmes in disguise) did not want him as a harpooner for his exploring expedition. *The Adventure of Black Peter*, II, 409.

LANDER: A Scowrer, both he and one Egan claimed the head-money for the shooting of old man Crabbe at Stylestown. *The Valley of Fear*, I, 564.

LANGHAM HOTEL: Captain Morstan's address when he returned to England in 1878 to visit his daughter, Mary, was the Langham Hotel. *The Sign of the Four*, I, 616; see also *A Scandal in Bohemia*, I, 355; *The Disappearance of Lady Frances Carfax*, II, 662.

LANGMERE: Donnithorpe, the site of Holmes's first criminal investigation, was a little hamlet just to the north of Langmere, in the country of the Broads. *The "Gloria Scott"*, I, 108.

LANNER, INSPECTOR: He was in charge of the investigation of Mr. Blessington's death. At first, he differed with Holmes's statement that the death was not suicide, but murder. Later, however, he acknowledged the cogent facts that the Master Detective mustered in favor of his hypothesis. *The Resident Patient*, I, 276.

LARBEY: He was almost beaten to death upon the orders of Boss McGinty of the Scowrers. His wife was cruelly shot, while nursing him. *The Valley of Fear*, I, 560.

LASCAR: "The rascally Lascar" who ran the Bar of Gold opium den had sworn vengeance upon Sherlock Holmes. *The Man with the Twisted Lip*, I, 372.

LASSUS, ROLAND DE: Sherlock Holmes wrote a "monograph upon the the Polyphonic Motets of Lassus, which [was] printed for private circulation, and is said by experts to be the last word upon the subject." *The Adventure of the Bruce-Partington Plans*, II, 449.

LATIMER, HAROLD: This "fashionably dressed young man" was "a powerful, broad-shouldered young fellow" who had gained control over Greek beauty Sophy Kratides. When Sophy's brother came from Athens to rescue her, Latimer and an associate enslaved him, and procured the services of Mr. Melas to act as interpreter. *The Greek Interpreter*, I, 595ff.

LATIMER'S: Watson had purchased his boots from Latimer's, in Oxford Street. Holmes, however, wasn't interested in the boots — only the manner in which their laces were tied. *The Disappearance of Lady Frances Carfax*, II, 656.

LAUDER: Holmes was convinced that Colonel Sebastian Moran was at the bottom of the death of Mrs. Stewart of Lauder, in 1887. Nothing could be proved at the time, however. *The Adventure of the Empty House*, II, 347.

LAURISTON GARDENS: The body of Enoch J. Drebber had been found in an empty house at NO. 3 Lauriston Gardens. Inspector Tobias Gregson sought Holmes's aid in untangling the case. *A Study in Scarlet*, I, 166.

LAUSANNE: Watson, acting as Holmes's agent, traveled to Lausanne to search for the missing Lady Frances Carfax. She had last been heard of from the Hôtel National at Lausanne. *The Disappearance of Lady Frances Carfax*, II, 657.

LAW: In Watson's famous catalogue of "Sherlock Holmes — his limits," he noted that the Great Detective had "a good practical knowledge of British law." *A Study in Scarlet*, I, 156; see also *The Five Orange Pips*, I, 399.

LAWLER: He was sent by the Scowrers' county delegate, Evans Pott, to murder the manager of the Crow Hill mine. He lodged with Jack Mc-Murdo. *The Valley of Fear*, I, 555.

LE BRUN: Baron Adelbert Gruner warned Holmes that his fate might be the same as that of Le Brun, the French agent, who was beaten by some Apaches in the Montmartre district and crippled for life, after making inquiries into the Baron's affairs only a week before. *The Adventure of the Illustrious Client*, II, 677.

LE VILLARD, FRANCOIS: "Who, as you probably know, has come rather to the front lately in the French detective service. He has all the Celtic power of quick intuition, but he is deficient in the wide range of exact knowledge which is essential to the higher development of his art." Le Villard had consulted Holmes in a case concerning a will, which "possessed some features of interest," and he was also translating Holmes's works into French. *The Sign of the Four*, I, 612.

LEADENHALL STREET: Hosmer Angel, who suddenly disappeared on the day of his wedding to Mary Sutherland, supposedly worked as a cashier in a Leadenhall Street office. He said that he lived on the premises there, and that he received all of his mail from Mary at the Leadenhall Street Post Office. *A Case of Identity*, I, 408, 409.

LECOQ: Watson queried his new companion whether he had read Gaboriau's works. "Does Lecoq come up to your idea of a detective?"

Sherlock Holmes sniffed sardonically. "Lecoq was a miserable bungler. He had only one thing to recommend him, and that was his energy. That book made me positively ill. The question was how to identify an unknown prisoner. I could have done it in twenty-four hours. Lecoq took six months or so. It might be made a text-book for detectives to teach them what to avoid." *A Study in Scarlet*, I, 162.

LEE: He sold his Vermissa Valley mine to the State and Merton County Railroad Company. *The Valley of Fear*, I, 542.

LEE: Neville St. Clair's residence, the Cedars, was near Lee, in Kent. *The Man with the Twisted Lip*, I, 372; see also *The Adventure of Wisteria Lodge*, II, 241.

LEFEVRE: Holmes was jubilant over his discovery of "an infallible test for blood stains." He felt it would have been decisive in the cases of the "notorious Muller, and Lefevre of Montpellier," among others. *A Study in Scarlet*, I, 150, 151.

LEGION OF HONOUR, ORDER OF THE: For tracking and arresting Huret, the Boulevard assassin, Sherlock Holmes was awarded the French Order of the Legion of Honour. *The Adventure of the Golden Pince-Nez*, II, 350.

LEONARDO: "The strong man" in "Ronder's wild beast show," he had also been Mrs. Ronder's lover and her husband's murderer. *The Adventure of the Veiled Lodger*, II, 456ff.

LESTRADE, INSPECTOR: Inspector Lestrade was Tobias Gregson's co-worker in the investigation of the mysterious death of Enoch J. Drebber in an empty house just off the Brixton Road. Gregson had called in Holmes to assist in the unraveling of the mystery. The Great Detective remarked, "Gregson is the smartest of the Scotland Yarders; he and Lestrade are the pick of a bad lot. They are both quick and energetic, but conventional—shockingly so. They have their knives into one another, too. They are as jealous as a pair of professional beauties." Later, Watson gave us his conventional description of Lestrade as "lean and ferret-like as ever." *A Study in Scarlet*, I, 165, 168.

Holmes said, "I am the last and highest court of appeal in detection. When Gregson, or Lestrade, or Athelney Jones are out of their depths —which, by the way, is their normal state—the matter is laid before me." *The Sign of the Four*, I, 611.

Inspector Lestrade had been retained by Miss Turner to prove the innocence of James McCarthy, who was accused of the murder of his father. "Lestrade, being rather puzzled, has referred the case to me, and hence it is that two middle-aged gentlemen are flying westward at fifty miles an hour, instead of quietly digesting their breakfasts at home. ...We may chance to hit upon some other obvious facts which may have been by no means obvious to Mr. Lestrade. You know me too well to think that I am boasting when I say that I shall either confirm or destroy his theory by means which he is quite incapable of employing, or even of understanding." Later, Watson described Lestrade as "a lean, ferret-like man, furtive and sly-looking." *The Boscombe Valley Mystery*, II, 136, 137, 140.

Inspector Lestrade was already investigating the Adventure of the Noble Bachelor when it was brought to Holmes's attention. "Mr. Lestrade, of Scotland Yard, is acting already in the matter, but he assures me that he sees no objection to your co-operation, and that he even thinks that it might be of some assistance." *The Adventure of the Noble Bachelor*, I, 282.

Lestrade also assisted Holmes in *The Hound of the Baskervilles*. He arrived in Devonshire aboard the five-forty. "The London express came roaring into the station, and a small, wiry bulldog of a man had sprung from a first-class carriage. We all three shook hands, and I saw at once from the reverential way in which Lestrade gazed at my companion that he had learned a good deal since the days when they had first worked together. I could well remember the scorn which the theories of the reasoner used then to excite in the practical man." Holmes thought that Lestrade was "the best of the professionals." *The Hound of the Baskervilles*, II, 94, 96.

Lestrade had taken on the case of Holmes's assassination himself. He felt that it was "good to see [Holmes] back in London," after the latter had been supposed dead at the Reichenbach Fall. *The Adventure of the Empty House*, II, 342.

In the eyes of the press, Inspector Lestrade possessed both "energy and sagacity." He proved that he had at least a modicum of the latter quality by acknowledging that Sherlock Holmes had "been of use to the [Police] Force once or twice in the past." With tongue firmly in cheek, Holmes lamented the fact that Lestrade did not, however, "add imagination to [his] other great qualities." This lacking of the Inspector's resulted in his taking the "too obvious" course of arresting one John Hector McFarlane for the murder of the Norwood builder, Jonas Oldacre — an action which nearly resulted in the loss of both an innocent man's life and Lestrade's reputation in the Force. Lestrade testified that "I am a practical man, Mr. Holmes, and when I have got my evidence I come to my conclusions." Fortunately, for McFarlane, his evidence proved to be false. *The Adventure of the Norwood Builder*, II, 426, 429.

In the Adventure of Charles Augustus Milverton, Watson referred to Lestrade as "very solemn and impressive." *The Adventure of Charles Augustus Milverton*, II, 570

Watson relates: "It was no unusual thing for Mr. Lestrade, of Scotland

Yard, to look in upon us of an evening, and his visits were welcome to Sherlock Holmes, for they enabled him to keep in touch with all that was going on at police headquarters. In return for the news which Lestrade would bring, Holmes was always ready to listen with attention to the details of any case upon which the detective was engaged, and was able occasionally, without any active interference, to give some hint or suggestion drawn from his own vast knowledge and experience." Lestrade congratulated Holmes on his successful conclusion to the Adventure of the Six Napoleons: "I've seen you handle a good many cases, Mr. Holmes, but I don't know that I ever knew a more workmanlike one than that. We're not jealous of you at Scotland Yard. No, sir, we are very proud of you, and if you come down to-morrow there's not a man, from the oldest inspector to the youngest constable, who wouldn't be glad to shake you by the hand." *The Adventure of the Six Napoleons*, II, 572, 587.

In *The Adventure of the Second Stain*, Lestrade is described as having "bulldog features." *The Adventure of the Second Stain*, I, 313.

Lestrade sought Holmes's advice in *The Cardboard Box*. A newspaper report at the time called the Scotland Yard inspector "one of the smartest of our detective officers...." Lestrade joined Holmes at Croydon, where Watson described him "as dapper, and as ferret-like as ever. ..." Holmes felt that Lestrade would secure the criminal, for "although he is absolutely devoid of reason, he is as tenacious as a bulldog when he once understands what he has to do, and indeed, it is just this tenacity which has brought him to the top at Scotland Yard." *The Cardboard Box*, II, 195, 196, 201.

"Thin and austere," Lestrade was dubbed "our old friend" by Watson. *The Adventure of the Bruce-Partington Plans*, II, 435.

Lestrade finally came up with a warrant for the arrest of the abductors of the Lady Frances Carfax, but Holmes feared that they had flown the coop: "If our ex-missionary friends escape the clutches of Lestrade, I shall expect to hear of some brilliant incidents in their future career." *The Disappearance of Lady Frances Carfax*, II, 669, 670.

Holmes sought out Inspector Lestrade when he wished to find the true identity of John Garrideb. "There may be an occasional want of imaginative intuition down there [at Scotland Yard], but they lead the world for thoroughness and method." *The Adventure of the Three Garridebs*, II, 651.

LESURIER, MADAME: Milliner, of Bond Street. There was a milliner's account for thirty-seven pounds fifteen made out by Madame Lesurier, of Bond Street, to William Darbyshire, in the pocket of John Straker, who was found dead on the moor. *Silver Blaze*, II, 272.

LETURIER: Holmes, in analyzing his successful investigation of the mysterious death of Enoch J. Drebber, said, "The forcible administration of poison is by no means a new thing in criminal annals. The cases of Dolsky in Odessa, and of Leturier in Montpellier, will occur at once to any toxicologist." *A Study in Scarlet*, I, 232.

LEVERSTOKE, LORD: He had entrusted his son to Dr. Thorneycroft Huxtable's care at the Priory School in Hallamshire. *The Adventure of the Priory School*, II, 609.

LEVERTON: A detective employed by Pinkerton's American Agency. In London, "on the trail of [his] life," Leverton was disguised as a cabman when he was introduced to Sherlock Holmes by Gregson, the Scotland Yard detective. Like any other young detective, Leverton was greatly flattered when he received words of commendation from Holmes: the latter declared himself quite pleased to meet the hero of the Long Island Cave mystery. *The Adventure of the Red Circle*, II, 698, 699.

LEWIS, SIR GEORGE: Sir James Damery had managed the delicate negotiations with Sir George Lewis over the Hammerford Will case. *The Adventure of the Illustrious Client*, II, 671.

LEWISHAM: In 1896, Josiah Amberley retired from business and bought a house at Lewisham. *The Adventure of the Retired Colourman*, II, 546; see also *The Adventure of the Abbey Grange*, II, 492.

LEXINGTON, MRS.: Housekeeper to Jonas Oldacre. By her account, she had let John Hector McFarlane, Oldacre's supposed killer, into her master's house; and then she had gone to bed, hearing nothing of what transpired between the two. Holmes felt that she was concealing some vital information, however, for "there was a sort of sulky defiance in her eyes which only goes with guilty knowledge." *The Adventure of the Norwood Builder*, II, 423ff.

LHASSA: After his supposed death at the Reichenbach Fall, Sherlock Holmes "travelled for two years in Tibet" and amused himself "by visiting Lhassa and spending some days with the head Llama [*sic*]." *The Adventure of the Empty House*, II, 337.

LIEGE: As Holmes sat down to await the expected arrival of the murderer of Enoch J. Drebber, he took up "a queer old book I picked up at a stall yesterday — *De Jure inter Gentes* — published in Latin at Liege in the Lowlands, in 1642." *A Study in Scarlet*, I, 180.

LINDER, MAX, AND CO.: Paid five hundred dollars to the Scowrers to be left alone. *The Valley of Fear*, I, 542.

LITERATURE: In Watson's famous catalogue of "Sherlock Holmes — his limits," he rated the Great Detective's knowledge of literature as "Nil." *A Study in Scarlet*, I, 156.

LITERATURE, SENSATIONAL: In Watson's famous catalogue of "Sherlock Holmes — his limits," he rated the Great Detective's knowledge of "Sensational Literature" as "Immense. He appears to know every detail of every horror perpetrated in this century." *A Study in Scarlet*, I, 156; see also *The Five Orange Pips*, I, 399.

LITTLE GEORGE STREET: Joseph Stangerson was found stabbed to death in his room in Halliday's Private Hotel, in Little George Street. *A Study in Scarlet*, I, 191.

LITTLE PURLINGTON: In Essex, not far from Frinton. J. C. Elman was vicar of Mossmoor-cum-Little Purlington. Watson felt that it was "the most primitive village in England." *The Adventure of the Retired Colourman*, II, 551, 552.

LITTLE RYDER STREET, W.: The London street in which Nathan Garrideb made his residence, it was "one of the smaller offshoots from the Edgware Road, within a stone-cast of old Tyburn Tree of evil memory." *The Adventure of the Three Garridebs*, II, 647.

LIVERPOOL: The two letters found in the pockets of the dead Enoch J. Drebber were both from the Guion Steamship Company, referring to the sailing of Drebber's and Joseph Stangerson's boats from Liverpool. *A Study in Scarlet*, I, 169; see also *The Adventure of the Priory School*, II, 610; *The Cardboard Box*, II, 199; *The Adventure of the Illustrious Client*, II, 684; *The Adventure of the Mazarin Stone*, II, 744.

LIVERPOOL, DUBLIN, AND LONDON STEAM PACKET COMPANY: Jim Browner was a steward aboard one of their vessels, the s.s. *May Day*. *The Cardboard Box*, II, 204.

LLAMA [SIC], HEAD: After his supposed death at the Reichenbach Fall,

Sherlock Holmes "travelled for two years in Tibet" and amused himself "by visiting Lhassa and spending some days with the head Llama." These remarkable adventures were reported as being those of a Norwegian named Sigerson. *The Adventure of the Empty House*, II, 337.

LLOYD'S: Holmes spent one whole day poring over Lloyd's registers and files of old papers in order to find the source of the problem that had led two generations of Openshaws to their deaths. *The Five Orange Pips*, I, 403.

LOMAX: Watson's friend, sub-librarian at the London Library in St. James's Square. He directed the Doctor to a "goodly volume" on Chinese pottery in which Watson, at Holmes's request, could pursue his researches. *The Adventure of the Illustrious Client*, II, 684.

LOMOND, DUKE OF: Isadora Klein was to marry the young Duke of Lomond, and wished to prevent the scandal that was sure to arise if her previous lover's unpublished novel saw the light of day. *The Adventure of the Three Gables*, II, 732.

LONDON: Recently invalided home from the second Afghan War, Dr. John H. Watson "naturally gravitated to London, that great cesspool into which all the loungers and idlers of the Empire are irresistibly drained.... The sight of a friendly face in the great wilderness of London is a pleasant thing indeed to a lonely man," he later observed, after running into his former dresser, young Stamford, in the Criterion Bar one day. *A Study in Scarlet*, I, 145.

"It is a hobby of mine to have an exact knowledge of London," said Holmes, as he strolled around the corner from Jabez Wilson's Coburg Square pawnshop. *The Red-Headed League*, I, 431.

Holmes lamented that "London has become a singularly uninteresting city since the death of the late lamented Professor Moriarty." Before Moriarty's death, "To the scientific student of the higher criminal world no capital in Europe offered the advantages which London then possessed." At about this time, the unhappy John Hector McFarlane came to Holmes with a most gratifying problem. McFarlane felt that at the moment he was the most unfortunate man in London. *The Adventure of the Norwood Builder*, II, 414, 415.

On their way to investigate the source of the smashed plaster casts of

Napoleon's head, Holmes and Watson "passed through the fringe of fashionable London, hotel London, theatrical London, literary London, commercial London, and, finally, maritime London, till we came to a river-side city of a hundred thousand souls, where the tenement houses swelter and reek with the outcasts of Europe." *The Adventure of the Six Napoleons*, II, 579.

LONDON BRIDGE: The Bar of Gold opium den lay in Upper Swandam Lane, "a vile alley lurking behind the high wharves which line the north side of the river to the east of London Bridge." *The Man with the Twisted Lip*, I, 369; see also *The Adventure of the Retired Colourman*, II, 549.

LONDON BRIDGE STATION: John Hector McFarlane came to seek Sherlock Holmes's aid in proving his innocence in the murder of Jonas Oldacre. He knew the police were already on his trail. He told Holmes, "I have been followed from London Bridge Station, and I am sure that they are only waiting for the warrant to arrest me." *The Adventure of the Norwood Builder*, II, 416; see also *The Adventure of the Bruce-Partington Plans*, II, 437.

LONDON LIBRARY: At Holmes's behest, Watson studied Chinese pottery intensively, in a goodly volume he obtained from his friend Lomax, the sub-librarian at the London Library in St. James's Square. *The Adventure of the Illustrious Client*, II, 684.

LONDON, UNIVERSITY OF: Dr. Watson took his degree of Doctor of Medicine at the University of London in the year 1878, as he tells us at the beginning of his narrative of his first meeting with Sherlock Holmes. *A Study in Scarlet*, I, 143.

Dr. Percy Trevelyan, who came to Holmes with a curious problem which ended in tragedy, had graduated from the University of London where his "student career was considered by [his] professors to be a very promising one." *The Resident Patient*, I, 268, 269.

LONE STAR: The barque *Lone Star*, out of Savannah, Georgia, was commanded by James Calhoun. It had touched at Pondicherry, Dundee, and London just prior to the deaths of two generations of Openshaws. It was presumed lost in the Atlantic, for "a shattered sternpost of a boat was seen swinging in the trough of a wave, with the letters 'L.S.' carved upon it." *The Five Orange Pips*, I, 402, 403.

LONG ISLAND CAVE MYSTERY: The case from which Mr. Leverton,

of Pinkerton's American Agency, emerged as the hero. Leverton had distinguished himself to such a degree that, when Holmes met him during the Adventure of the Red Circle, he bestowed words of commendation upon the American. *The Adventure of the Red Circle*, ii, 699.

LOPEZ: Secretary to Don Juan Murillo, the Tiger of San Pedro. Lopez escaped with Murillo from San Pedro during the popular revolt against Murillo's tyranny. He traveled with Murillo throughout Europe. *The Adventure of Wisteria Lodge*, ii, 257.

LOWENSTEIN, H.: The notorious Lowenstein of Prague was "an obscure scientist who was striving in some unknown way for the secret of rejuvenescence and the elixir of life." His "wondrous strength-giving serum" had been "tabooed by the [medical] profession because he refused to reveal its source." *The Adventure of the Creeping Man*, ii, 765.

LOWER BRIXTON ROAD: Dr. Barnicot, a well-known London medical practitioner, had his branch surgery and dispensary there. *The Adventure of the Six Napoleons*, ii, 573.

LOWER BURKE STREET: Mr. Culverton Smith, the planter and prominent resident of Sumatra, had his house at 13 Lower Burke Street. *The Adventure of the Dying Detective*, i, 443, 444.

LOWER GILL MOOR: A great rolling moor, extending for ten miles, that lay between the Priory School, Holdernesse Hall, and the Chesterfield high road. *The Adventure of the Priory School*, ii, 616.

LOWER NORWOOD: The London suburb of which Jonas Oldacre had been a well-known resident, as a result of his having carried on his business as a builder for many years there. *The Adventure of the Norwood Builder*, ii, 416.

LOWTHER ARCADE: It was to the Strand end of the Lowther Arcade that Watson directed his cab in his mad dash to join Holmes aboard the Continental Express at Victoria Station. *The Final Problem*, ii, 307.

LUCAS, EDUARDO: "Well known in society circles both on account of his charming personality and because he [had] the well-deserved reputation of being one of the best amateur tenors in [Britain]," this "unmarried man, thirty-four years of age" was also the international spy responsible for engineering the theft of a valuable State document from the bedroom of Britain's Secretary for European Affairs, the Right

Honourable Trelawney Hope. *The Adventure of the Second Stain*, i, 307ff.

LUCAS, MR.: Secretary to Mr. Henderson of High Gable, near Oxshott, in Surrey. *The Adventure of Wisteria Lodge*, ii, 253.

LUCCA, EMILIA: Born in Posilippo, near Naples, she was the daughter of Augusto Barelli, the chief lawyer and once the deputy of that part of Italy. She had become attracted to Gennaro Lucca, one of her father's employees, and even though Lucca had neither money nor position, his positive personal attributes won her heart to such a degree that she consented to flee with him, first to Bari (where they were married), and then to New York (where they settled, in Brooklyn). *The Adventure of the Red Circle*, ii, *passim*.

LUCCA, GENNARO: In his wild and fiery days in Italy, he had joined the Neapolitan terrorist society, the Red Circle, an impetuous act he was later to rue for "once within its rule no escape was possible." Gennaro thought that he had cast it all off forever when he and his wife Emilia moved to New York because her father forbade their marrying; then, one sad day, he was met by Giuseppe Gorgiano, the very man who had initiated him in Naples. Gorgiano had organized a scion society of the Red Circle in New York, and he ordered Gennaro to attend one of their forthcoming meetings. A few days prior to the meeting, however, Gorgiano made lewd advances toward Emilia; Gennaro then attacked him, and the vindictive Gorgiano rigged the meeting in such a way that Gennaro must either kill his best friend, or expose himself and Emilia to vengeance. *The Adventure of the Red Circle*, ii, *passim*.

LUCERNE: The luggage of the dead Douglas Maberley was labeled "Milano" and "Lucerne." *The Adventure of the Three Gables*, ii, 728; see also *The Final Problem*, ii, 314.

LUXEMBOURG: On their Continental journey, Holmes and Watson made their way, at their leisure, into Switzerland, via Luxembourg and Basel. *The Final Problem*, ii, 310.

LYCEUM THEATRE: Mary Morstan received a mysterious note asking her to "Be at the third pillar from the left outside the Lyceum Theatre tonight at seven o'clock. If you are distrustful bring two friends. You are a wronged woman, and shall have justice. Do not bring the police. If you do, all will be in vain. Your unknown friend." The two friends that she brought with her were Sherlock Holmes and Dr. Watson. *The Sign of the Four*, I, 618.

LYNCH, VICTOR: Sherlock Holmes's "good old index" contained "the record of old cases, mixed with the accumulated information of a lifetime." The volume devoted to the letter *V* was especially interesting: one of its items concerned "Victor Lynch, the forger." *The Adventure of the Sussex Vampire*, II, 463.

LYON PLACE: Mary Sutherland, who resided at 31 Lyon Place, Camberwell, came to Holmes after her fiancé disappeared on the way to their wedding. *A Case of Identity*, I, 410.

LYONS: An artist who married Laura Frankland, of Coombe Tracey, in Devonshire, and then deserted her. *The Hound of the Baskervilles*, II, 71.

LYONS, FRANCE: Watson writes, "I see it was on the 14th of April that I received a telegram from Lyons, which informed me that Holmes was lying ill in the Hotel Dulong." *The Reigate Squires*, I, 331.

LYONS, LAURA: Mr. Frankland's daughter, of Coombe Tracey. She had had a mysterious assignation with Sir Charles Baskerville on the night that he died. "She married an artist named Lyons, who came sketching on the moor. He proved to be a blackguard and deserted her. The fault, from what I hear, may not have been entirely on one side. Her father refused to have anything to do with her, because she had married without his consent, and perhaps for one or two other reasons as well. So, between the old sinner and the young one the girl has had a pretty bad time." She had been forced to take in typewriting. *The Hound of the Baskervilles*, II, 71-72, 74.

M

MABERLEY, DOUGLAS: Son of Mary and Mortimer Maberley. Holmes remembered him as a "magnificent creature," but Douglas's mother saw him turn into a "moody, morose, brooding creature" in the time before he left for Rome to become Britain's Attaché there. *The Adventure of the Three Gables*, II, 724, 725.

MABERLEY, MORTIMER: He had once consulted Holmes in "some trifling matter," and his widow sought Holmes's aid once again. *The Adventure of the Three Gables*, II, 724.

MABERLEY, MRS. MARY: "A most engaging elderly person, who bore every mark of refinement and culture," she sought Holmes's aid in solving the strange events surrounding the attempted purchase of her house, The Three Gables. *The Adventure of the Three Gables*, II, 724.

MCCARTHY, CHARLES: Ex-Australian acquaintance of John Turner, he was once a wagon-driver in the gold fields there. He later lived on one of Turner's farms, Hatherley. He was found brutally murdered, apparently by his own son, on the Turner estate. His son said of him, "he was not a popular man, being somewhat cold and forbidding in his manners," and John Turner felt that McCarthy "was a devil incarnate." *The Boscombe Valley Mystery*, II, 135, 138, 149.

MCCARTHY, JAMES: He was seen on his father's trail shortly before the latter was murdered. Although the evidence pointed strongly to the young man's guilt, Holmes felt that he might be innocent. *The Boscombe Valley Mystery*, II, 135.

MCCAULEY: Elias Openshaw's notebook for March, 1869, contained the entries: "7th. Set the pips on McCauley, Paramore, and Swain of St. Augustine. 8th. McCauley cleared." *The Five Orange Pips*, I, 397.

MACDONALD, INSPECTOR ALEC: Watson writes, "He was a young but trusted member of the detective force, who had distinguished himself in several cases which had been entrusted to him. His tall, bony figure gave promise of exceptional physical strength, while his great cranium and deep-set, lustrous eyes spoke no less clearly of the keen intelligence which twinkled out from behind his bushy eyebrows. He was a silent, precise man, with a dour nature and a hard Aberdonian accent. Twice already in his career had Holmes helped him to attain success, his own sole reward being the intellectual joy of the problem." "Mr. Mac" assisted Holmes in investigating the tragedy of Birlstone. *The Valley of Fear*, I, 476.

MCFARLANE, JOHN HECTOR: Obviously "a bachelor, a solicitor, a

Freemason, and an asthmatic," he stormed into the quarters Holmes shared with Watson, hoping that the detective could prove him innocent of "the charge of murdering Mr. Jonas Oldacre." In the opinion of the police, McFarlane's tale was weak, for he claimed that Oldacre, an old suitor of his mother's, had, under bizarre circumstances, decided to leave almost all his property to young McFarlane. One of the conditions was that McFarlane visit Oldacre's home to inspect a number of documents—he did so, but he swore that, all evidence to the contrary, he had left his host healthy and whole, not as "charred remains." *The Adventure of the Norwood Builder*, II, 415ff.

MCFARLANE, MRS.: Mother of the unfortunate John Hector McFarlane. Her hand had once been sought by Jonas Oldacre, whom she described as a "cunning ape" and whom she rejected for a better, but poorer, man. Much later, her son was the recipient of a generous bequest from Oldacre. *The Adventure of the Norwood Builder*, II, 422.

MCFARLANE'S: McFarlane's carriage-building depot lay just around the corner from Jabez Wilson's Coburg Square pawnshop. *The Red-Headed League*, I, 431.

MCGINTY, BOSS JOHN ("BLACK JACK"): Bodymaster of Lodge 341, Vermissa Valley, of the Ancient Order of Freemen. He was leader of the Scowrers within the same valley, and, also, owner of the Union House hotel and saloon in Vermissa. "Besides those secret powers which it was universally believed that he exercised in so pitiless a fashion, he was a high public official, a municipal councillor, and a commissioner for roads, elected to the office through the votes of the ruffians who in turn expected to receive favours at his hands." *The Valley of Fear*, I, 523, 532.

MCGREGOR, MRS.: One of the casualties of the expedition across the Great Alkali Plain which only John and Lucy Ferrier survived. *A Study in Scarlet*, I, 198.

MACKINNON, INSPECTOR: The "smart young police inspector" who was in charge of the investigation of the disappearance of Josiah Amberley's wife and fortune. Holmes felt that he was "a good fellow." *The Adventure of the Retired Colourman*, II, 553, 554, 557.

MACKLETON: Dr. Thorneycroft Huxtable's Priory School, from which the young Lord Saltire disappeared, was near Mackleton, in the north of England. *The Adventure of the Priory School*, II, 607.

MCLAREN, MILES: A scholar at the College of St. Luke's. He was a candidate for the Fortescue Scholarship. "He is a brilliant fellow when he chooses to work—one of the brightest intellects of the University; but he is wayward, dissipated, and unprincipled." *The Adventure of the Three Students*, II, 374.

MCMURDO: An ex-prizefighter, employed as porter at Pondicherry Lodge, Upper Norwood. He recognized Sherlock Holmes as the amateur who had fought three rounds with him at Alison's rooms on the night of his benefit. He told Holmes, "If instead o' standin' there so quiet you had just stepped up and given me that cross-hit of yours under the jaw, I'd ha' known you without a question." *The Sign of the Four*, I, 631, 632.

MCMURDO, JACK: "He is a fresh-complexioned, middle-sized young man, not far, one would guess, from his thirtieth year. He has large, shrewd, humorous grey eyes which twinkle inquiringly from time to time as he looks round through his spectacles at the people about him. It is easy to see that he is of a sociable and possibly simple disposition, anxious to be friendly to all men.... And yet the man who studied him more closely might discern a certain firmness of jaw and grim tightness about the lips which would warn him that there were depths beyond and that this pleasant, brown-haired young Irishman might conceivably leave his mark for good or evil upon any society to which he was introduced." *The Valley of Fear*, I, 521–22.

MACNAMARA, WIDOW: Mike Scanlan and Jack McMurdo boarded at her lodgings in Vermissa, after Jacob Shafter kicked McMurdo out of his boardinghouse because of the latter's affiliation with the Scowrers. *The Valley of Fear*, I, 536.

MACPHAIL: An able-bodied man, he served Professor Presbury as coachman. The uproar caused by Presbury's faithful wolfhound's attack on his own master "brought the sleepy and astonished coachman from his room above the stables." *The Adventure of the Creeping Man*, II, 762.

MACPHERSON: A "big constable," he had been in charge of guarding 16 Godolphin Street after the murder of that house's master, international spy Eduardo Lucas. Thus, it was understandable that MacPherson seemed "very hot and penitent" after Lestrade, acting on instructions from Sherlock Holmes, called him on the carpet for allowing a certain lady into the murder room. MacPherson's heat was turned into amazement when Holmes showed him a cardboard portrait of the lady, whose identity was thought to be unknown. *The Adventure of the Second Stain*, I, 315, 318.

MCPHERSON, FITZROY: "Fitzroy McPherson was the science master [at The Gables], a fine upstanding young fellow whose life had been crippled by heart trouble following rheumatic fever." He was engaged to Maud Bellamy at the time of his brutal murder, and she was certain that, because of McPherson's bravery and strength, "no single person could ever have inflicted such an outrage upon him." *The Adventure of the Lion's Mane*, II, 777.

MCQUIRE'S CAMP: Aloysius Doran worked a mining claim near the Rockies. It was the place where Francis Hay Moulton and Hatty Doran met and were engaged. *The Adventure of the Noble Bachelor*, I, 296.

MADRID: Don Juan Murillo, the Tiger of San Pedro, escaped to Madrid after a revolution in his country. He finally met his death there some time later, when he and his secretary were murdered in their rooms at the Hotel Escurial. *The Adventure of Wisteria Lodge*, II, 256, 258; see also *The Adventure of the Second Stain*, I, 321.

MAFIA: The secret political society, which enforced "its decrees by murder." Pietro Venucci was a member. *The Adventure of the Six Napoleons*, II, 581.

MAIWAND: Dr. Watson admitted to Holmes that the murder of Enoch J. Drebber had indeed upset him. "I ought to be more case-hardened after my Afghan experiences. I saw my own comrades hacked to pieces at Maiwand without losing my nerve." Watson himself had received a serious wound at Maiwand. *A Study in Scarlet*, I, 143, 179.

MALINGERING: Holmes said, "The best way of successfully acting a part is to be it. I give you my word that for three days I have tasted neither food nor drink until you were good enough to pour me out that glass of water.... Three days of absolute fast does not improve one's beauty.... For the rest, there is nothing which a sponge may not cure. With vaseline upon one's forehead, crusts of beeswax around one's lips, a very satisfying effect can be produced. Malingering is a subject upon which I have sometimes thought of writing a monograph." *The Adventure of the Dying Detective*, I, 449, 450; see also *The Reigate Squires*, I, 337.

MANAOS: Maria Pinto Gibson, the ill-fated wife of Neil Gibson, the Gold King, was the daughter of a Government official in Manaos, Brazil. *The Problem of Thor Bridge*, II, 594.

MANDERS: A Scowrer, he was a reckless youngster who accompanied Jack McMurdo in an unsuccessful attempt on the life of Chester Wilcox. *The Valley of Fear*, I, 558.

MANOR HOUSE CASE: Mycroft Holmes had expected his brother Sherlock to consult him over the Manor House case. Both Sherlock and Mycroft had come to the same conclusion that the guilty party was Adams. *The Greek Interpreter*, I, 594.

MANSEL: A Scowrer, he participated in the assault on James Stanger, editor of the Vermissa *Herald*. *The Valley of Fear*, I, 545.

MANSON: He sold his Vermissa Valley ironworks to the West Wilmerton General Mining Company. *The Valley of Fear*, I, 543.

MARCINI'S: Holmes invited Watson to stop for a little dinner there on their way to see the De Reszkes in *Les Huguenots*. *The Hound of the Baskervilles*, II, 112.

MARGATE: Municipal borough on the Isle of Thanet in Kent. It was at Margate that Sherlock Holmes suspected a woman because she had "manoeuvered to have the light at her back." Holmes had believed that the woman did so in order to mask her facial expression, but was proved quite wrong: in truth, she had done so because she wished to conceal the fact that she had "no powder on her nose." Holmes believed this a perfect example of the inscrutability of women's motives. *The Adventure of the Second Stain*, I, 311; see also *The Adventure of the Veiled Lodger*, II, 460.

MARKER, MRS.: An elderly housekeeper, she was employed by Professor Coram of Yoxley Old Place. Of excellent character, she was understandably sad-faced when Sherlock Holmes questioned her after the murder of Coram's secretary. *The Adventure of the Golden Pince-Nez*, II, 352, 359.

MARSEILLES: At the time Holmes took up the case of Miss Mary Sutherland, he had a number of other cases on hand, but "save for one rather intricate matter which has been referred to me from Marseilles, there is nothing which presents any features of interest." *A Case of Identity*, I, 405.

MARTHA: Housekeeper for the German spy, Von Bork, just before the outbreak of World War I. It was said she might almost personify Britannia. *His Last Bow*, II, 796.

MARTIN, INSPECTOR: Of the Norfolk Constabulary. He was investigating the tragic death of Hilton Cubitt of Ridling Thorpe Manor and welcomed Holmes's interest in the case. *The Adventure of the Dancing Men*, II, 535.

MARTIN, LIEUTENANT: He remained loyal to his captain during the convict uprising on board the barque *Gloria Scott* in 1855. He was killed trying to put down the rebellion. *The "Gloria Scott"*, I, 119.

MARTYRDOM OF MAN: Written by Winwood Reade. Holmes considered it "one of the most remarkable [books] ever penned." *The Sign of the Four*, I, 619.

MARVIN, CAPTAIN TEDDY: Of the Coal and Iron Police, in the Vermissa Valley. He professed to know Jack McMurdo from the latter's gangster days in Chicago, and was instrumental in the extirpation of the Scowrers from the Valley. *The Valley of Fear*, I, 537.

MARX & CO.: Of High Holborn. A good deal of clothing bearing their stamp had been left behind in the house of Aloysius Garcia, who was found brutally murdered. They said they knew nothing of their customer, save that he was a good payer. *The Adventure of Wisteria Lodge*, II, 248.

MARY: She prepared the fire in Elias Openshaw's room, in which he burned most of the evidence of his days in Florida. *The Five Orange Pips*, I, 393.

MARY: The "little maid-servant" to Mrs. Mary Maberley of The Three Gables, Harrow Weald. Her screams scared away some robbers and brought police to Mrs. Maberley's aid. *The Adventure of the Three Gables*, II, 729, 730.

MARY JANE: The Watsons' incorrigible servant girl, who had scarred the Doctor's shoes in removing the mud from their soles. Mrs. Watson was forced to give her notice. *A Scandal in Bohemia*, I, 348.

MARYLEBONE LANE: The van that narrowly missed Holmes at the corner of Bentinck Street and Welbeck Street rushed round from Marylebone Lane and was gone in an instant. *The Final Problem*, II, 306.

MASON: Holmes was jubilant over his discovery of an "infallible test for blood stains." He felt it would have been decisive in the case of Mason of Bradford. *A Study in Scarlet*, I, 150, 151.

MASON: "A platelayer," he had discovered the dead body of Arthur Cadogan West lying "just outside Aldgate Station on the Underground system in London" at six o'clock one Tuesday morning. *The Adventure of the Bruce-Partington Plans*, II, 434.

MASON, JOHN: The head trainer at Sir Robert Norberton's Shoscombe Park Stables. He had come to Holmes because of the exceedingly strange behavior of his master prior to the running of the Derby. *The Adventure of Shoscombe Old Place*, II, 631.

MASON, MRS.: "A tall, gaunt woman...who seemed to be a sour, silent kind of creature," she was the nurse to Robert Ferguson's younger son, whom she tenderly loved. Her devotion to the child compelled her, first, to inform her master that his wife had been seen sucking "at a small wound in the [child's] neck," and then to guard the infant day and night. *The Adventure of the Sussex Vampire*, II, 466, 471.

MASON, WHITE: The local officer in charge of the investigation surrounding the horrible death of John Douglas, of Birlstone Manor, in Sussex. He called in Inspector Alec MacDonald of the Metropolitan Police who, in turn, called in his friend Sherlock Holmes. Mason described the case as "a real downright snorter." *The Valley of Fear*, I, 488.

MATHEWS: Holmes felt that his index of biographies was especially illustrious in the section devoted to those persons whose names began with the letter *M*. One of those persons was "Mathews, who knocked out [Sherlock Holmes's] left canine in the waiting-room at Charing Cross." *The Adventure of the Empty House*, II, 346.

MATILDA BRIGGS: Sherlock Holmes had had successful action in the case of Matilda Briggs, but Matilda Briggs was not the name of a young woman. Rather, "it was a ship which [was] associated with the giant rat of Sumatra, a story for which the world [was] not yet prepared." *The Adventure of the Sussex Vampire*, II, 462.

MAUDSLEY: A friend of James Ryder's. "I had a friend once called

Maudsley, who went to the bad, and has just been serving his time in Pentonville. One day he had met me, and fell into talk about the ways of thieves and how they could get rid of what they stole. I knew that he would be true to me, for I knew one or two things about him, so I made up my mind to go right on to Kilburn, where he lived, and rake him into my confidence." *The Adventure of the Blue Carbuncle*, 1, 465.

MAUPERTUIS, BARON: Watson wrote, "The whole question of the Netherland-Sumatra Company and of the colossal schemes of Baron Maupertuis is too recent in the minds of the public, and too intimately concerned with politics and finance, to be a fitting subject for this series of sketches." *The Reigate Squires*, 1, 331.

MAURITIUS, ISLAND OF: After his marriage to Alice Rucastle, Mr. Fowler took a Government appointment on the Island of Mauritius. *The Adventure of the Copper Beeches*, 11, 132.

MAWSON & WILLIAMS': A giant stockbroking firm in Lombard Street. Hall Pycroft, who had lost his job at Coxon & Woodhouse owing to the failure of the Venezuelan loan, managed to obtain a job at Mawson & Williams', when they had an opening. He was persuaded, however, not to show up for his first day's work, and the strange circumstances surrounding this event prompted him to consult Sherlock Holmes. *The Stockbroker's Clerk*, 11, 155.

MAY DAY: It was aboard the Liverpool, Dublin, and London Steam Packet Company vessel s.s. *May Day* that Jim Browner was employed as a steward. *The Cardboard Box*, 11, 204.

MAYNOOTH, EARL OF: In the spring of 1894, he was "Governor of one of the Australian colonies." As his wife required an operation for a cataract, the Earl had sent her back to England, along with their son, Ronald, and daughter, Hilda. *The Adventure of the Empty House*, 11, 330.

MAYNOOTH, LADY: Wife of the "Governor of one of the Australian colonies," she had returned to England to undergo an eye operation. Her son, Ronald, and daughter, Hilda, had accompanied her, and the three made their residence together at 427 Park Lane. One night in the spring of 1894, after spending the evening with a relation, Lady Maynooth returned to their residence, attempted to enter her son's room to say good night, found the door locked on the inside, and finally — after getting no answer — had the door forced open. Her son was, in fact, inside, "his head...horribly mutilated by an expanded revolver bullet." *The Adventure of the Empty House*, ii, 330.

MECCA: After his supposed death at the Reichenbach Fall, Sherlock Holmes "travelled for two years in Tibet." Shortly after leaving Tibet, he "looked in at Mecca." *The Adventure of the Empty House*, ii, 337.

MEEK, SIR JASPER: According to Watson, he was one of the best medical practitioners in London. Thus, Watson proposed to consult Meek for Holmes in view of Holmes's strange malady. *The Adventure of the Dying Detective*, i, 441.

MEIRINGEN: In their attempted escape from Professor Moriarty, Holmes and Watson paused at Meiringen, and spent the night at the Englischer Hof there. *The Final Problem*, ii, 312.

MELAS, MR.: Mycroft Holmes said, "Mr. Melas is a Greek by extraction...and he is a remarkable linguist. He earns his living partly as interpreter in the law courts, partly by acting as guide to any wealthy Orientals who may visit the Northumberland Avenue hotels." *The Greek Interpreter*, i, 595.

MELVILLE: A retired brewer who lived at Albemarle Mansion, Kensington. John Scott Eccles was a guest at his table when he met the ingenious Aloysius Garcia, who later visited him at his own home and then invited Eccles out to visit him at Wisteria Lodge. *The Adventure of Wisteria Lodge*, ii, 240.

MENDELSSOHN, FELIX: Watson knew that Holmes could play pieces, and difficult ones at that, on the violin, because, at Watson's request, Holmes had played some of Mendelssohn's Lieder, which were a favorite of the good Doctor's. *A Study in Scarlet*, i, 158.

MENZIES: The engineer of the Crow Hill mine, he was murdered by the Scowrers. *The Valley of Fear*, i, 557.

MERCER: Second mate of the barque *Gloria Scott*, he was in league with Jack Prendergast in the convict rebellion aboard that ship. *The "Gloria Scott"*, i, 118.

MERCER: Holmes's "general utility man who [looked] up routine business," he was said to have come into the Great Detective's employ since Watson's time. Mercer's telegram regarding one Dorak helped Holmes clear up the case. *The Adventure of the Creeping Man*, ii, 760.

MEREDITH, GEORGE: Holmes had already decided upon the major

points in the death of Charles McCarthy. Thus, he wished to "talk about George Meredith, if you please, and we shall leave minor points until tomorrow." *The Boscombe Valley Mystery*, II, 144.

MERIVALE: Of Scotland Yard. He asked Holmes to look into the St. Pancras murder case, in which Holmes, through the use of his microscope, positively connected a suspect with a cap found at the scene of the crime. *The Adventure of Shoscombe Old Place*, II, 630.

MERRIDEW: Holmes felt that his "index of biographies" was especially "illustrious" in the section devoted to those persons whose names began with the letter *M*. One of those persons was "Merridew of abominable memory." *The Adventure of the Empty House*, II, 346.

MERRILOW, MRS.: "An elderly, motherly woman of the buxom landlady type," she came to Sherlock Holmes on behalf of her "terribly mutilated" lodger, Mrs. Eugenia Ronder. The lodger's nighttime cries had so alarmed Mrs. Merrilow that she suggested consulting either the clergy or the police. Then, when Mrs. Ronder rejected both of those options, Mrs. Merrilow suggested Holmes, and the lodger "fair jumped" at the idea. *The Adventure of the Veiled Lodger*, II, 453–55.

MERRIPIT HOUSE: Home of the Stapletons, on the Devonshire moor. *The Hound of the Baskervilles*, II, 49.

MERROW, LORD: The Right Honourable Trelawney Hope had had a valuable State document taken from among the papers he kept in a locked dispatch-box in his bedroom. Another of those papers was a letter from Lord Merrow. *The Adventure of the Second Stain*, I, 321.

MERRYWEATHER, MR.: Chairman of directors of the City and Suburban Bank. He accompanied Holmes, Watson, and Peter Jones into the cellar of the Coburg branch of his bank in order to thwart a crime. *The Red-Headed League*, I, 432–34.

MERTON COUNTY: Purely agricultural county on the railroad line which ran through the coal-and-iron-producing Gilmerton Mountains and Vermissa Valley, site of the American action in *The Valley of Fear*. *The Valley of Fear*, I, 521.

MERTON, SAM: A boxer, he was Count Negretto Sylvius's companion in the filching of the Mazarin stone. Holmes said, "Not a bad fellow, Sam, but the Count has used him. Sam's not a shark. He is a great big silly bull-headed gudgeon. But he is flopping about in my net all the same." *The Adventure of the Mazarin Stone*, II, 737, 742.

MEUNIER, MONSIEUR OSCAR: An artist of Grenoble, who spent some days in doing the molding of a bust of Sherlock Holmes in wax. The bust was such a perfect reproduction of Holmes that, on first seeing it, Watson "threw out [his] hand to make sure that the man himself was standing beside [him]." *The Adventure of the Empty House*, II, 339-40.

MEXBOROUGH PRIVATE HOTEL: In Craven Street. Jack and Beryl Stapleton lodged there while he, disguised in a beard, followed Dr. Mortimer to Baker Street, and afterwards to the station and to the Northumberland Hotel. *The Hound of the Baskervilles*, II, 108-9.

MEYER, ADOLPH: He resided at 13 Great George Street, Westminster, and was one of the three foreign spies in England whom Mycroft Holmes thought capable of handling so big an affair as the theft of the Bruce-Partington submarine plans. *The Adventure of the Bruce-Partington Plans*, II, 445.

MICHAEL: A stable-hand in the employment of Robert Ferguson, he slept in his master's house. *The Adventure of the Sussex Vampire*, II, 466.

MIDDLESEX: Mrs. Effie Hebron had a maiden aunt at Pinner, in Middlesex, with whom she stayed after she returned to England following the death of her husband in America. *The Yellow Face*, I, 579; see also *The Man with the Twisted Lip*, I, 378.

MIDIANITES: Dr. Shlessinger, while recuperating, at the Englischer Hof in Baden, from a disease contracted while carrying out his missionary duties in South America, "was preparing a map of the Holy Land, with special reference to the Kingdom of the Midianites, upon which he was writing a monograph." *The Disappearance of Lady Frances Carfax*, II, 659.

MIDLAND ELECTRIC COMPANY: At the time of *The Adventure of the Solitary Cyclist*, Violet Smith's fiancé, Cyril Morton, was employed by the Midland Electric Company at Coventry. *The Adventure of the Solitary Cyclist*, II, 387.

MILES, THE HONOURABLE MISS: A victim of Charles Augustus Milverton's machinations, she saw her wedding to Colonel Dorking called off only two days before it was to take place. *The Adventure of Charles Augustus Milverton*, II, 561.

MILLAR, FLORA: Former *danseuse* at the Allegro, she was once an intimate companion of Lord St. Simon, who eventually married Hatty Doran. Millar "endeavoured to force her way into the house after the bridal party, alleging that she had some claim upon Lord St. Simon. It was only after a painful and prolonged scene that she was ejected by the butler and the footman." Later, she was arrested because she was the last person seen in the company of the bride, who had mysteriously disappeared. *The Adventure of the Noble Bachelor*, i, 286.

MILLER HILL: Ill-kept public park in the very center of Vermissa, where Jack McMurdo and Brother Morris met. *The Valley of Fear*, i, 547.

MILMAN: Apparently murdered by the Scowrers in the Vermissa Valley. *The Valley of Fear*, i, 528.

MILNER, GODFREY: With Lord Balmoral, he had lost as much as £420 in a sitting of cards to Ronald Adair and Colonel Sebastian Moran, some weeks before Adair's murder. *The Adventure of the Empty House*, ii, 330.

MILVERTON, CHARLES AUGUSTUS: "The king of all the blackmailers," Milverton was considered "the worst man in London" by Sherlock Holmes. "A genius in his way," Milverton had "something of Mr. Pickwick's benevolence in his appearance," an appearance marred only by a perpetually frozen smile and deadly eyes. He was in the process of blackmailing Holmes's client, Lady Eva Brackwell, when Holmes took on the case. *The Adventure of Charles Augustus Milverton*, ii, 558, 560.

MING DYNASTY: Watson, in the guise of Dr. Hill Barton, used a delicate little saucer of the most beautiful deep-blue color to distract Baron Adelbert Gruner. The saucer was real egg-shell pottery of the Ming dynasty. *The Adventure of the Illustrious Client*, ii, 685.

MITTON, JOHN: Valet to the international spy Eduardo Lucas, he had been out for the evening, visiting a friend at Hammersmith the night his master was "stabbed to the heart." Though the authorities arrested Mitton "as an alternative to absolute inaction," no case could be sustained against him because his alibi was complete. *The Adventure of the Second Stain*, i, 308, 311.

MOFFAT: A member of the Worthingdon bank gang. They pulled their heist in 1875, but were caught, and Moffat was sentenced to fifteen years. The gang swore, and achieved, revenge on their erstwhile partner, Sutton, who had testified against them. *The Resident Patient*, i, 279, 280.

MOLESEY MYSTERY: A case successfully handled by Inspector Lestrade. Holmes acknowledged Lestrade's success by saying that the Inspector had "handled the Molesey Mystery with less than [his] usual—that's to say, [he] handled it fairly well." *The Adventure of the Empty House*, ii, 342.

MONGOOSE: Henry Wood carried a pet mongoose named Teddy with him to entertain soldiers in their canteens. *The Crooked Man*, II, 237.

MONTAGUE PLACE: Miss Violet Hunter had her lodgings in Montague Place, and it was from there that she wrote Holmes the note which involved him in the strange affair. *The Adventure of the Copper Beeches*, II, 115.

MONTAGUE STREET: Holmes said, "When I first came up to London I had rooms in Montague Street, just round the corner from the British Museum, and there I waited, filling in my too abundant leisure time by studying all those branches of science which might make me more efficient." *The Musgrave Ritual*, I, 125–26.

MONTALVA, MARQUESS OF: He and Signor Rulli, his secretary, were both murdered in their rooms at the Hotel Escurial at Madrid. "The crime was ascribed to Nihilism, and the murderers were never arrested." *The Adventure of Wisteria Lodge*, II, 258.

MONTANA: Francis Hay Moulton traveled there after his marriage to Hatty Doran. *The Adventure of the Noble Bachelor*, I, 296.

MONTGOMERY, INSPECTOR: Jim Browner made his statement before Inspector Montgomery at the Shadwell Police Station. *The Cardboard Box*, II, 204.

MONTPELLIER: Holmes was jubilant over his discovery of "an infallible test for blood stains." He felt it would have been decisive in the case of the notorious Muller, and Lefevre of Montpellier, among others. Later, he said, "The forcible administration of a poison is by no means a new thing in criminal annals. The cases of Dolsky in Odessa, and of Leturier in Montpellier, will occur at once to any toxicologist." *A Study in Scarlet*, I, 150, 151, 232.

In a laboratory in Montpellier, in the south of France, Sherlock Holmes "spent some months in a research into the coal-tar derivatives." *The Adventure of the Empty House*, II, 337; see also *The Disappearance of Lady Frances Carfax*, II, 658.

MONTPENSIER, MME: The full explanation of the adventure of *The Hound of the Baskervilles* had to wait until Holmes had concluded two cases of "the utmost importance.... in the second he had defended the unfortunate Mme Montpensier from the charge of murder which hung over her in connection with the death of her step-daughter, Mlle Carère, the young lady who, as it will be remembered, was found six months later alive and married in New York." *The Hound of the Baskervilles*, 11, 105.

MOORHOUSE: "First reserve" on the rugger team of Cambridge Varsity, it was he who was the logical choice to replace Godfrey Staunton, the crack three-quarter who had vanished just before Cambridge's big match with Oxford. The captain of the Cambridge squad, Cyril Overton, questioned Moorhouse's abilities, however, saying that "he [Moorhouse] is trained as a half, and he always edges right in on to the scrum instead of keeping out on the touch-line. He's a fine place-kick, it's true, but, then, he has no judgment, and he can't sprint for nuts." *The Adventure of the Missing Three-Quarter*, 11, 476.

MORAN: The lodgekeeper at the Boscombe Valley Estate. Holmes had a word with him at the conclusion of his field investigation of the brutal slaying of Charles McCarthy. *The Boscombe Valley Mystery*, 11, 146.

MORAN, COLONEL SEBASTIAN: "The second most dangerous man in London," after Professor Moriarty, he had been educated at the best schools, had written two books, and — for a time, at least — lived the life of "an honourable soldier." Then, for whatever reason, he began to go wrong, and was sought out by Professor Moriarty, whom he served for a time as chief of staff. "With the brow of a philosopher above and the jaw of a sensualist below, the man must have started with great capacities for good or for evil. But one could not look upon his cruel blue eyes, with their drooping, cynical lids, or upon the fierce, aggressive nose and the threatening, deep-lined brow, without reading Nature's plainest danger-signals." Sherlock Holmes had had even more tangible proofs of Moran's evil nature, however, for it had been the Colonel who had hurled boulders down at Holmes when the latter lay on a ledge above the pathway from which Professor Moriarty had plummeted to his death. Thus, when the detective heard of the murder of Ronald Adair, a crime which bore Moran's stamp, he hastened back to London in such obvious fashion that he brought the old "shikari" (hunter) out into the open. *The Adventure of the Empty House*, 11, *passim*.

Holmes said, "I happen to know who is the first link in [Moriarty's] chain — a chain with this Napoleon-gone-wrong at one end and a hundred broken fighting men, pickpockets, blackmailers, and cardsharpers at the other, with every sort of crime in between. His chief of staff is

Colonel Sebastian Moran, as aloof and guarded and inaccessible to the law as himself. What do you think he pays him?"

"I'd like to hear," said Inspector Alec MacDonald.

"Six thousand a year. That's paying for brains, you see — the American business principle." *The Valley of Fear*, I, 480.

Sir James Damery described Baron Adelbert Gruner as "the most dangerous man in Europe," and Holmes replied that if he was "more dangerous than the late Professor Moriarty, or than the living Colonel Sebastian Moran, then he is indeed worth meeting." *The Adventure of the Illustrious Client*, II, 672; see also *His Last Bow*, II, 801.

MORAN, PATIENCE: Fourteen-year-old daughter of the lodgekeeper of John Turner's Boscombe Valley Estate. She was picking flowers in the woods when she chanced upon Charles McCarthy and his son, James, having a violent quarrel. Soon afterwards, the elder man was found murdered on the same spot. *The Boscombe Valley Mystery*, II, 136.

MORAN, SIR AUGUSTUS, C.B.: Former British Minister to Persia, Sir Augustus was the father of Colonel Sebastian Moran. *The Adventure of the Empty House*, II, 346.

MORCAR, COUNTESS OF: Owner of the stolen blue carbuncle. *The Adventure of the Blue Carbuncle*, I, 455.

MORECROFT: The criminal who called himself John Garrideb was a man of many names; he was also known as "James Winter, *alias* Morecroft, *alias* Killer Evans." *The Adventure of the Three Garridebs*, II, 651.

MORGAN: Holmes felt that his index of biographies was especially illustrious in the section devoted to those persons whose names began with the letter *M*. One of those persons was Morgan, the poisoner. *The Adventure of the Empty House*, II, 346.

MORIARTY, COLONEL JAMES: His letters defending the memory of his brother, Professor Moriarty, who had apparently plunged to his death over the Fall of Reichenbach, forced Watson "to lay the facts before the public exactly as they occurred." *The Final Problem*, II, 301.

MORIARTY, PROFESSOR JAMES: Holmes said: "His career has been an extraordinary one. He is a man of good birth and excellent education, endowed by Nature with a phenomenal mathematical faculty. At the age of twenty-one he wrote a treatise upon the Binomial Theorem, which had a European vogue. On the strength of it, he won the Mathematical Chair at one of our smaller Universities, and had, to all appearance, a most brilliant career before him. But the man had hereditary tendencies of the most diabolical kind. A criminal strain ran in his blood, which, instead of being modified, was increased and rendered infinitely more dangerous by his extraordinary mental powers. Dark rumours gathered round him in the University town, and eventually he was compelled to resign his Chair and to come down to London, where he set up as an Army coach.... For years past I have continually been conscious of some power behind the malefactor, some deep organizing power which for ever stands in the way of the law, and throws its shield over the wrongdoer. Again and again in cases of the most varying sorts—forgery cases, robberies, murders—I have felt the presence of this force, and I have deduced its action in many of those undiscovered crimes in which I have endeavoured to break through the veil which shrouded it, and at last the time came when I seized the thread and followed it until it led me, after a thousand cunning windings, to ex-Professor Moriarty of mathematical celebrity. He is the Napoleon of crime, Watson. He is the organizer of half that is evil and of nearly all that is undetected in this great city. He is a genius, a philosopher, an abstract thinker. He has a brain of the first order. He sits motionless, like a spider in the centre of its web, but that web has a thousand radiations, and he knows well every quiver of each of them. He does little himself. He only plans. But his agents are numerous and splendidly organized.... This was the organization I deduced, Watson, and which I devoted my whole energy to exposing and breaking up." Holmes described Moriarty's personal appearance, "He is extremely tall and thin, his forehead domes out in a white curve, and his two eyes are deeply sunken in his head. He is clean-shaven, pale, and ascetic-looking, retaining something of the professor in his features. His shoulders are rounded from much study, and his face protrudes forward, and is for ever slowly oscillating from side to side in a curiously reptilian fashion." *The Final Problem*, ii, 303, 304.

According to Holmes, Moriarty "had one of the great brains of the [19th] century." *The Adventure of the Empty House*, ii, 346.

"From the point of view of [a] criminal expert," like Sherlock Holmes, "London [had] become a singularly uninteresting city since the death of the late lamented Professor Moriarty," for "with that man in the field one's morning paper presented infinite possibilities. Often it was only the smallest trace...and yet it was enough to tell [Holmes] that the great malignant brain was there, as the gentlest tremors of the edges of the web remind one of the foul spider which lurks in the centre." Holmes concluded this unusual eulogy to the man who had been his archenemy by saying that "to the scientific student of the higher criminal world no capital in Europe offered the advantages which London then possessed." *The Adventure of the Norwood Builder*, II, 414.

Holmes felt that Dr. Leslie Armstrong was a man, "who if he turned his talents that way, was more calculated to fill the gap left by the illustrious Moriarty." *The Adventure of the Missing Three-Quarter*, II, 484.

Said Holmes to Watson: "In calling Moriarty a criminal you are uttering libel in the eyes of the law, and there lies the glory and the wonder of it. The greatest schemer of all time, the organizer of every devilry, the controlling brain of the underworld.... That's the man." *The Valley of Fear*, I, 472.

Von Bork said to Holmes, "I shall get level with you, Altamont, if it takes me all my life I shall get level with you!"

"The old sweet song," said Holmes. "How often have I heard it in days gone by. It was the favourite ditty of the late lamented Professor Moriarty. Colonel Sebastian Moran has also been known to warble it. And yet I live and keep bees upon the South Downs." *His Last Bow*, II, 801.

Sir James Damery felt that there was "no more dangerous man in Europe" than Baron Adelbert Gruner. Holmes responded that if he was "more dangerous than the late Professor Moriarty, or than the living Colonel Sebastian Moran, then he is indeed worth meeting." *The Adventure of the Illustrious Client*, II, 672.

MORMONS: It was the migrating Mormon band of nearly ten thousand souls which rescued John and Lucy Ferrier upon the Great Alkali Plain. They joined the group and became successful farmers in Utah. *A Study in Scarlet*, I, 202, 207.

MORPHY, ALICE: "A very perfect girl both in mind and body," she was the daughter of Professor Morphy, holder of the Chair of Comparative Anatomy at Camford University. Moreover, she became engaged to one of her father's colleagues, Professor Presbury, who had won her hand (over several younger candidates) with his frenziedly youthful courtship. *The Adventure of the Creeping Man*, II, 753.

MORPHY, PROFESSOR: Professor Presbury's colleague in the Chair of Comparative Anatomy at Camford University, Morphy was also the father of the woman to whom Presbury had become engaged. *The Adventure of the Creeping Man*, II, 753.

MORRIS: "An elderly, clean-shaven man, with a kindly face and a good brow," he talked in favor of some moderation and conciliation on the part of the Scowrers. *The Valley of Fear*, I, 542.

MORRIS, WILLIAM: The red-headed gentleman who temporarily occupied rooms at Pope's Court, Fleet Street, cultivated at least two separate identities. To Jabez Wilson, he was known as Duncan Ross, manager of the offices of the Red-Headed League. To the landlord at Pope's Court, however, he was known as William Morris, "a solicitor [who] was using my room as a temporary convenience until his new premises were ready." *The Red-Headed League*, I, 427.

MORRISON, ANNIE: She had some relationship with the murdered William Kirwan. *The Reigate Squires*, I, 345.

MORRISON, MISS: The next-door neighbor to the Barclays, at Aldershot, she accompanied Mrs. Barclay to a meeting of the Guild of St. George, and was witness to Mrs. Barclay's confrontation with the Crooked Man on their way home. *The Crooked Man*, II, 228, 232.

MORRISON, MORRISON, AND DODD: Robert Ferguson's lawyers, they specialized "entirely upon the assessment of machinery." Thus, when Ferguson sent them "a communication...concerning vampires," they recommended that their client take the matter to Sherlock Holmes. It was not by chance that they recommended Holmes for such a bizarre case: they had not forgotten his successful action in the case of the *Matilda Briggs*, a ship which was associated with the giant rat of Sumatra. *The Adventure of the Sussex Vampire*, II, 462.

MORSTAN, CAPTAIN ARTHUR: Upon returning to England from his Indian regiment in 1878 to visit his daughter, Mary, he mysteriously disappeared. He had been a close friend of Major John Sholto, with whom he had served at the Blair Island penal colony in the Andaman Islands. *The Sign of the Four*, I, 616, 682.

MORSTAN, MISS MARY: Daughter of Captain Morstan, she sought Holmes's aid in solving the strange events surrounding the disappearance of her father. Later, she married Dr. Watson, who said of her, "She was a blonde young lady, small, dainty, well gloved, and dressed in the most perfect taste. There was, however, a plainness and simplicity about her costume which bore with it a suggestion of limited means.... Her face had neither regularity of feature nor beauty of complexion, but her expression was sweet and amiable, and her large blue eyes were singularly spiritual and sympathetic. In an experience of women which extends over many nations and three separate continents, I have never looked upon a face which gave a clearer promise of a refined and sensitive nature." After the course of the adventure, Watson related to Holmes that Mary had done him the honor of accepting him as "a husband in prospective." *The Sign of the Four*, 1, 615, 616.

MORTIMER: The gardener at Yoxley Old Place, he was "an Army pensioner—an old Crimean man of excellent character." He did not live in the main house, but in a three-roomed cottage at the other end of the garden. Aside from his obvious horticultural chores, Mortimer's duties included pushing his crippled employer "around the grounds...in a bath-chair." *The Adventure of the Golden Pince-Nez*, 11, 352, 353.

MORTIMER, JAMES: "M.R.C.S., 1882, Grimpen, Dartmoor, Devon. House-surgeon, from 1882 to 1884, at Charing Cross Hospital. Winner of the Jackson Prize for Comparative Pathology, with an essay entitled 'Is Disease a Reversion?' Corresponding member of the Swedish Pathological Society. Author of 'Some Freaks of Atavism' (*Lancet*, 1882), 'Do We Progress?' (*Journal of Psychology*, March, 1883). Medical Officer for the parishes of Grimpen, Thorsley, and High Barrow." Close friend of Sir Charles Baskerville and administrator of his estate, he brought Holmes the problems of Sir Charles's mysterious death, and of the fateful decision facing Sir Henry Baskerville, his heir. He described himself as "a dabbler in science...a picker-up of shells on the shores of the great unknown ocean." *The Hound of the Baskervilles*, 11, 5, 6, 7.

MORTIMER STREET: After discussing with Watson their plans to escape Professor Moriarty by a mad dash to the Continental express, and thence, through Europe, Holmes clambered over the garden wall of Watson's house into Mortimer Street. *The Final Problem*, 11, 307.

MORTON: One of the two "Oxford fliers" who, in the opinion of Cyril Overton, captain of the Cambridge varsity rugger team, "could romp round" Moorhouse, the slow first reserve on Cambridge's squad. *The Adventure of the Missing Three-Quarter*, ii, 476.

MORTON, CYRIL: An electrical engineer employed by the Midland Electric Company, at Coventry, he was engaged to marry Miss Violet Smith, "the solitary cyclist of Charlington." *The Adventure of the Solitary Cyclist*, ii, 385, 397.

MORTON, INSPECTOR: An old acquaintance of Holmes's, from the Yard, he participated in *The Adventure of the Dying Detective*, "dressed in unofficial tweeds." *The Adventure of the Dying Detective*, i, 444.

MORTON & WAYLIGHT'S: The firm in Tottenham Court Road at which Mr. Warren was employed as a timekeeper. Mrs. Warren had come to Sherlock Holmes, saying that her husband was as nervous over the actions of one of their lodgers as she was. *The Adventure of the Red Circle*, ii, 691, 695.

MOSER, M.: Watson was searching for some clues as to the whereabouts of the vanished Lady Frances Carfax. "Two days later found me at the National Hotel at Lausanne, where I received every courtesy at the hands of M. Moser, the well-known manager." *The Disappearance of Lady Frances Carfax*, ii, 658.

MOULTON, FRANCIS HAY: He made the acquaintance of Hatty Doran in 1881. They were engaged, and he eventually married her secretly in San Francisco. He was presumed dead when a miners' camp in New Mexico, where he was prospecting, was attacked by Apache Indians. *The Adventure of the Noble Bachelor*, i, 296, 297.

MOUNT-JAMES, LORD: Uncle to Godfrey Staunton, he was thought to be Staunton's nearest living relative. He was also one of the richest men in England and "an absolute miser." *The Adventure of the Missing Three-Quarter*, ii, 480ff.

MOUNTS BAY: From the windows of their little whitewashed vacation cottage in Cornwall, Holmes and Watson "looked down upon the whole sinister semicircle of Mounts Bay, that old death trap of sailing vessels, with its fringe of black cliffs and surge-swept reefs on which innumerable seaman [had] met their end." *The Adventure of the Devil's Foot*, ii, 509.

MULLER: Holmes was jubilant over his discovery of "an infallible test for blood stains." He felt it would have been decisive in the cases of the "notorious Muller, and Lefevre of Montpellier," among others. *A Study in Scarlet*, I, 150, 151.

MUNICH: Holmes noted that there was a case similar to *The Adventure of the Noble Bachelor* in Munich, the year after the Franco-Prussian War. *The Adventure of the Noble Bachelor*, I, 291.

MUNRO, COLONEL SPENCE: Miss Violet Hunter, whose acceptance of a peculiar position in Hampshire involved Holmes in *The Adventure of the Copper Beeches*, had been a governess in the family of Colonel Spence Munro for five years, until he accepted a post in Halifax, Nova Scotia. *The Adventure of the Copper Beeches*, II, 116.

MUNRO, EFFIE: Wife of Grant Munro. She originally married John Hebron, of Atlanta, Georgia. She was widowed when he died of the yellow fever, and she returned to England, met, and then married Munro. *The Yellow Face*, I, 579.

MUNRO, GRANT ("JACK"): He came to Holmes because of his worry over his wife's strange behavior. *The Yellow Face*, I, 577.

MURCHER, HARRY: On the night that Constable John Rance discovered the dead body of Enoch J. Drebber in an empty house just off the Brixton Road, he had met with Harry Murcher, who had the Holland Grove beat, at the corner of Henrietta Street. Murcher later came to his aid when the body was discovered. *A Study in Scarlet*, I, 176.

MURDOCH, IAN: Mathematical coach at The Gables, "a tall, dark, thin man, so taciturn and aloof" that, initially, Holmes thought him quite friendless. "He seemed to live in some high, abstract region of surds and conic sections with little to connect him with ordinary life." A man of "ferocious" temper, Murdoch had once hurled Fitzroy McPherson's dog through a plate-glass window. *The Adventure of the Lion's Mane*, II, 778.

MURDOCH, JAMES: Mutilated by the Scowrers. *The Valley of Fear*, I, 560.

MURGER, HENRI: As Holmes went out to pursue the elusive Mrs. Sawyer, Watson passed the time "skipping over the pages of Henri Murger's *Vie de Bohème*. *A Study in Scarlet*, I, 182.

MURILLO, DON JUAN: The Tiger of San Pedro. "The whole history of the man came back to me in a flash. He had made his name as the most lewd and bloodthirsty tyrant that had ever governed any country with a pretence to civilization. Strong, fearless, and energetic, he had sufficient virtue to enable him to impose his odious vices upon a cowering people for ten or twelve years. His name was a terror through all of Central America. At the end of that time there was a universal rising against him. But he was as cunning as he was cruel, and at the first whisper of coming trouble he had secretly conveyed his treasures aboard a ship which was manned by devoted adherents. It was an empty palace which was stormed by the insurgents next day. The Dictator, his two children, his secretary, and his wealth had all escaped them. From that moment he had vanished from the world, and his identity had been a frequent subject for comment in the European press. *The Adventure of Wisteria Lodge*, ii, 255–56.

MURILLO, EX-PRESIDENT: Sherlock Holmes felt that his first few months back in London following the death of Professor Moriarty were uneventful. Watson, who had resumed his partnership with Holmes during that period, disagreed, citing, among others, "the case of the papers of ex-President Murillo." *The Adventure of the Norwood Builder*, ii, 414.

MURPHY: A gypsy horse-dealer, who had been on the moor at the time of the death of Sir Charles Baskerville. Although he had been under the influence of drink, he declared that he had heard cries, but he was unable to state from which direction they had come. *The Hound of the Baskervilles*, ii, 12.

MURPHY: Jack McMurdo told Jacob Shafter that in Chicago, a man of the name of Murphy had given him the address of Shafter's Vermissa boarding-house. *The Valley of Fear*, i, 526.

MURPHY, MAJOR: Of the Royal Mallows regiment, he was stationed at Aldershot. He was Holmes's primary informant concerning Colonel James Barclay and his wife (who was born Nancy Devoy). *The Crooked Man*, ii, 227.

MURRAY: Dr. John H. Watson, newly attached to the Berkshires during the second Afghan War, was seriously wounded in the battle of Maiwand. He would "have fallen into the hands of the murderous Ghazis had it not been for the devotion and courage shown by Murray, my orderly, who threw me across a packhorse, and succeeded in bringing me safely to the British lines." *A Study in Scarlet*, 1, 143.

MURRAY, MR.: In the afternoon of March 30, 1894, he had, along with two others, played whist with Ronald Adair. *The Adventure of the Empty House*, 11, 330.

MUSGRAVE, SIR RALPH: A prominent Cavalier, and the right-hand man of Charles 11 in his wanderings. *The Musgrave Ritual*, 1, 138.

MUSGRAVE, REGINALD: Holmes said: "In appearance he was a man of an exceedingly aristocratic type, thin, high-nosed, and large-eyed, with languid and yet courtly manners. He was indeed a scion of one of the very oldest families in the kingdom, though his branch was a cadet one which had separated from the Northern Musgraves some time in the sixteenth century, and had established itself in Western Sussex, where the manor house of Hurlstone is perhaps the oldest inhabited building in the county." He was an old college acquaintance of Holmes's, who brought him an intriguing adventure. *The Musgrave Ritual*, 1, 126.

MUSIC: Holmes and Watson were going to the St. James's Hall to hear Sarasate on the violin. Holmes observed that "there is a good deal of German music on the programme, which is rather more to my taste than Italian or French. It is introspective, and I want to introspect. Come along!" *The Red-Headed League*, 1, 428; see also *The Adventure of the Bruce-Partington Plans*, 11, 432; *The Adventure of the Retired Colourman*, 11, 550.

MUTTRA: Site of Abel White's indigo plantation, where Jonathan Small was employed as an overseer. *The Sign of the Four*, 1, 674.

MYRTLES, THE: At the time of Mr. Melas's strange, late-night employment, Sophy Kratides was staying at Mr. Harold Latimer's residence, The Myrtles, in Beckenham. *The Greek Interpreter*, 1, 602, 603.

N

NAPLES: Pietro Venucci, "one of the greatest cut-throats in London," was from Naples. *The Adventure of the Six Napoleons*, 11, 581; see also *The Adventure of the Red Circle*, 11, 702, 703.

NAPOLEON I: Plaster casts of the famous head of Napoleon by the French sculptor Devine were being systematically smashed. Lestrade came to Holmes thinking that there was some "queer madness" behind the whole affair. *The Adventure of the Six Napoleons*, II, 573.

NARBONNE: Watson received a note from Holmes, dated from Narbonne, when the Great Detective was engaged by the French Government in a matter of supreme importance. *The Final Problem*, II, 301.

NEALE, OUTFITTER, VERMISSA, U.S.A.: A tailor's tab found on the neck of an overcoat that Holmes fished out of the shallow moat which surrounded the Manor House of Birlstone, in Sussex, where John Douglas had supposedly been murdered. *The Valley of Fear*, I, 516.

NED, UNCLE: Of Auckland, New Zealand, he left his niece, Mary Sutherland, some New Zealand Stock valued at two thousand five hundred pounds, and paying 4½ percent. *A Case of Identity*, I, 407.

NEGRO, THE: A horse run by Mr. Heath Newton for the Wessex Cup against Silver Blaze. *Silver Blaze*, II, 278.

NELIGAN, JOHN HOPLEY: Son of the Neligan of Dawson & Neligan who disappeared after the failure of that West Country banking firm. John Hopley Neligan had traced the securities that his father had supposedly stolen back to Captain Peter Carey, who was subsequently found murdered. Neligan naturally came under suspicion for the murder. Holmes was called into the case by Inspector Stanley Hopkins. *The Adventure of Black Peter*, II, 406.

NETHERLAND-SUMATRA COMPANY: Watson wrote, "The whole question of the Netherland-Sumatra Company and of the colossal schemes of Baron Maupertuis is too recent in the minds of the public, and too intimately concerned with politics and finances, to be a fitting subject for this series of sketches." *The Reigate Squires*, I, 331.

NETLEY: After receiving his Doctor of Medicine degree from the University of London in 1878, John H. Watson "proceeded to Netley to go through the course prescribed for surgeons in the army." *A Study in Scarlet*, I, 143.

NEW BRIGHTON: Mary Browner and her friend took tickets for New Brighton when they thought her husband was at sea. *The Cardboard Box*, II, 207.

NEW FOREST: On that blazing hot day in August that saw Holmes and Watson begin the investigation of the grisly events surrounding *The Cardboard Box*, Watson "yearned for the glades of the New Forest or the shingle of Southsea. A depleted bank account had caused me to postpone my holiday...." *The Cardboard Box*, II, 193.

NEW JERSEY: Irene Adler, famed as *the* woman in Holmes's life, was born in New Jersey in 1858. *A Scandal in Bohemia*, I, 354.

NEW MEXICO: Francis Hay Moulton was reported killed in an Apache attack on a miners' camp in New Mexico. *The Adventure of the Noble Bachelor*, I, 296.

NEW YORK: The two letters found in the pockets of the dead Enoch J. Drebber were both from the Guion Steamship Company and referred to the sailing of Drebber's and Joseph Stangerson's ships from Liverpool. Holmes concluded, "It is clear that this unfortunate man was about to return to New York." *A Study in Scarlet*, I, 169; see also *The Hound of the Baskervilles*, II, 105; *The Adventure of the Abbey Grange*, II, 504; *The Adventure of the Red Circle*, II, 702; *His Last Bow*, II, 799.

NEW YORK POLICE BUREAU: Holmes cabled his friend Wilson Hargreave, of the New York Police Bureau, "who has more than once made use of my knowledge of London crime." *The Adventure of the Dancing Men*, II, 542.

NEW ZEALAND: One of Holmes's deductions that so impressed Justice of the Peace Trevor was that the latter had been to New Zealand. *The "Gloria Scott"*, I, 109; see also *A Case of Identity*, I, 407; *The Stockbroker's Clerk*, II, 157.

NEWHAVEN: Leaving the Continental Express at Canterbury, Holmes and Watson traveled overland to Newhaven, and from there to Dieppe. *The Final Problem*, II, 309.

NEWTON, MR. HEATH: Ran The Negro for the Wessex Cup against Silver Blaze. *Silver Blaze*, II, 278.

NICHOLSON FAMILY: Jacob Shafter told Jack McMurdo that they had been murdered by the Scowrers. *The Valley of Fear*, I, 528.

NIHILISM: Mr. Morse Hudson, shopkeeper, felt that the epidemic of smashing plaster casts of Napoleonic busts was a Nihilist plot. *The Ad-*

venture of the Six Napoleons, II, 578; see also *The Adventure of the Golden Pince-Nez*, II, 365; *The Adventure of Wisteria Lodge*, II, 258; *His Last Bow*, II, 802.

NIMES: Dr. Watson received a note from Holmes, dated from Nîmes, in 1891. The Great Detective was engaged in a matter of supreme importance at the request of the French Government. *The Final Problem*, II, 301.

NONPAREIL CLUB: The full explanation of the adventure of *The Hound of the Baskervilles* had to wait until Holmes had concluded two cases of "the utmost importance." In the first, "he had exposed the atrocious conduct of Colonel Upwood in connection with the famous card scandal of the Nonpareil Club." *The Hound of the Baskervilles*, II, 105.

NORAH CREINA: A steamer lost with all hands on the Portuguese coast, some leagues north of Oporto. The remaining members of the Worthingdon bank gang were surmised by Scotland Yard to have been aboard the ill-fated ship. *The Resident Patient*, I, 280.

NORBERTON, SIR ROBERT: He resided at Shoscombe Old Place with his sister, Lady Beatrice Falder. "He has the name of a dangerous man. He is about the most daredevil rider in England — second in the Grand National a few years back. He is one of those men who have overshot their true generation. He should have been a buck in the days of the Regency — a boxer, an athlete, a plunger on the Turf, a lover of fair ladies, and, by all account, so far down Queer Street that he may never find his way back again." He had his whole fortune riding on Shoscombe Prince in the Derby, but his trainer went to Holmes claiming that Norberton had gone mad. *The Adventure of Shoscombe Old Place*, II, 631, 633, 639.

NORBURY: Grant Munro had an eighty-pound-a-year villa there. It was the site of the adventure of *The Yellow Face*, a case which Holmes found so instructive that he said, "Watson, if it should ever strike you that I am getting a little over-confident in my powers, or giving less pains to a case than it deserves, kindly whisper 'Norbury' in my ear, and I shall be infinitely obliged to you." *The Yellow Face*, I, 579, 589.

NORFOLK: The father of Victor Trevor, Holmes's only friend at college, had a place at Donnithorpe, in Norfolk. *The "Gloria Scott"*, I, 108; see also *The Adventure of the Dancing Men*, II, 535.

NORLETT, MR.: "A small, rat-faced man with a disagreeably furtive manner," he was employed by Sir Robert Norberton for an unusual assignment. *The Adventure of Shoscombe Old Place*, II, 640.

NORLETT, MRS. CARRIE: Her maiden name was Carrie Evans, under which she served as Lady Beatrice Falder's confidential maid. *The Adventure of Shoscombe Old Place*, II, 640.

NORMAN-NERUDA (WILMA; VIOLINIST): Holmes wanted to speed up his investigation of the lonely death of Enoch J. Drebber in an empty London suburban apartment, for "I want to go to Hallé's concert to hear Norman Neruda this afternoon.... Her attack and her bowing are splendid. What's that little thing of Chopin's she plays so magnificently: Tra-la-la-lira-lira-lay." *A Study in Scarlet*, I, 174, 178.

NORTH CAROLINA: The Anderson murders, which were similar to the case that Holmes investigated in *The Hound of the Baskervilles*, took place in North Carolina. *The Hound of the Baskervilles*, II, 96.

NORTHUMBERLAND AVENUE: It is in the Northumberland Avenue Turkish Bath that we find Holmes and Watson at the beginning of the adventure. *The Adventure of the Illustrious Client*, II, 671; see also *The Adventure of the Noble Bachelor*, I, 299; *The Greek Interpreter*, I, 595.

NORTHUMBERLAND FUSILIERS, FIFTH: After completing his surgical training at Netley, the young Dr. Watson "was attached to the Fifth Northumberland Fusiliers as Assistant Surgeon." The regiment, at that time, was stationed in India. *A Study in Scarlet*, I, 143.

NORTHUMBERLAND HOTEL: Sir Henry Baskerville, on his arrival in London from Canada to claim his inheritance of the Baskerville estate, stayed at the Northumberland Hotel. *The Hound of the Baskervilles*, II, 21.

NORTON, GODFREY: Close friend of Irene Adler, whom he finally married. A lawyer of the Inner Temple, "he was a remarkably handsome man, dark, aquiline, and moustached...." He asked Holmes, disguised as an unemployed groom, to witness the marriage at the Church of St. Monica. *A Scandal in Bohemia*, I, 358.

NORWAY: After his supposed death at the Fall of Reichenbach, Sherlock Holmes traveled for two years in Tibet. His explorations were so remarkable that news of them reached London, but—as Holmes had been posing as a Norwegian named Sigerson—Watson never knew that he was receiving news of the friend he thought dead. *The Adventure of the Empty House*, II, 337.

Neligan, of the ruined banking firm, Dawson & Neligan, had set off for Norway in his private yacht, hoping to invest the securities he took with him and make good the investment of those whom the failure of his firm had hurt. He was thought lost at sea. Later, after the investigation of the true circumstances of Neligan's death, Watson and Holmes traveled to Norway. *The Adventure of Black Peter*, II, 407, 413.

NORWOOD DISAPPEARANCE CASE: Holmes correctly entitled the supposed murder of Jonas Oldacre by the unfortunate John Hector McFarlane "the Norwood Disappearance Case." *The Adventure of the Norwood Builder*, II, 424.

NOTTING HILL: Louis La Rothiere, of Campden Mansions, Notting Hill, was one of three foreign agents in England capable of handling as large an affair as the stealing of the Bruce-Partington submarine plans. *The Adventure of the Bruce-Partington Plans*, II, 445; see also *The Adventure of the Red Circle*, II, 701.

O

OAKSHOTT, MRS. MAGGIE: Of 117 Brixton Road, she was an egg and poultry supplier and sold the goose that figured in *The Adventure of the Blue Carbuncle* to Mr. Breckinridge of Covent Garden Market. *The Adventure of the Blue Carbuncle*, I, 461.

OAKSHOTT, SIR LESLIE: The famous surgeon who treated Holmes after the murderous attack made upon him outside the Café Royal at the direction of the notorious Baron Adelbert Gruner. *The Adventure of the Illustrious Client*, II, 683.

OBERSTEIN, HUGO: Oberstein was one of the three "foreign spies" in England whom Mycroft Holmes thought capable of handling so big an affair as the theft of the Bruce-Partington Plans. After perusing a large-scale map of London, Sherlock Holmes was quick to see the significance of the fact that Oberstein's residence, at 13 Caulfield Gardens, Kensington, abutted on the Underground. Shortly thereafter, Oberstein found that even the most intricate plans could not purchase a pardon from fifteen years in a British prison. *The Adventure of the Bruce-Partington Plans*, II, *passim*; see also *The Adventure of the Second Stain*, I, 307.

ODESSA: Holmes, in analyzing his successful investigation of the mysterious death of Enoch J. Drebber, said, "The forcible administration of poison is by no means a new thing in criminal annals. The cases of Dolsky in Odessa, and of Leturier in Montpellier, will occur at once to any toxicologist." *A Study in Scarlet*, I, 232.

At the time of *A Scandal in Bohemia*, Watson had, from time to time, heard some vague account of Holmes's doings, such as his summons to Odessa in the case of the Trepoff murder. *A Scandal in Bohemia*, I, 347.

OLD DEER PARK: Watson had played rugby for Blackheath when Big Bob Ferguson was three-quarter for Richmond. In one of their athletic confrontations, Ferguson "threw [Watson] over the ropes into the crowd at the Old Deer Park." *The Adventure of the Sussex Vampire*, II, 465.

OLD JEWRY: The London street in which Robert Ferguson's lawyers, Morrison, Morrison, and Dodd, had their offices. *The Adventure of the Sussex Vampire*, II, 462.

OLD RUSSIAN WOMAN, THE ADVENTURE OF: One of Holmes's untold tales. *The Musgrave Ritual*, I, 124.

OLDACRE, JONAS: A well-known resident of Lower Norwood, where he carried on his business as a builder for many years, Oldacre was a bachelor, fifty-two years of age, who, it appeared, had been brutally murdered by John Hector McFarlane. Under bizarre circumstances, Oldacre had, "with some reservations...left all his property" to McFarlane, the son of a woman to whom he had once been engaged. The police felt that the bequest had been so tempting to McFarlane that he hastened his benefactor's demise. *The Adventure of the Norwood Builder*, II, *passim*.

OLDMORE, MRS.: Of High Lodge, Alton, her husband was once Mayor of Gloucester. She and her maid always stayed at the Northumberland Hotel while in London, and were staying there at the same time as Sir Henry Baskerville. *The Hound of the Baskervilles*, II, 29.

OPENSHAW, ELIAS: Uncle of John Openshaw, Elias "had emigrated to America when he was a young man, and became a planter in Florida, where he was reported to have done well. At the time of the [American Civil] war he fought in Jackson's army, and afterwards under Hood, where he rose to be a colonel. When Lee laid down his arms my uncle returned to his plantation, where he remained for three or four years. About 1869 or 1870 he came back to Europe, and took a small estate in Sussex, near Horsham. He had made a very considerable fortune in the States, and his reason for leaving them was his aversion to the negroes, and his dislike of the Republican policy in extending the franchise to them. He was a singular man, fierce and quick tempered, very foul-mouthed when he was angry, and of a most retiring disposition." His nephew John came to live with him, and was shocked at his uncle's fearful reaction to a mysterious letter from India, which contained five dried orange seeds and the letters "K.K.K." Elias met his death in a shallow pool of water shortly thereafter. *The Five Orange Pips*, I, 392, 393, 394.

OPENSHAW, JOHN: He had inherited his uncle's fortune and estate from his father, but along with this legacy, he had inherited a strange dread of dried orange seeds. *The Five Orange Pips*, I, 390.

OPENSHAW, JOSEPH: Father of John Openshaw, Joseph "had a small factory at Coventry, which he enlarged at the time of the invention of bicycling. He was the patentee of the Openshaw unbreakable tire, and his business met with such success that he was able to sell it, and to retire upon a handsome competence." He inherited his brother's estate, but later met his death in a chalk-pit, after having received a letter from Scotland containing five dried orange seeds and the message, "Put the papers on the sundial." *The Five Orange Pips*, I, 392, 395.

OPIUM: Watson wrote that Isa Whitney "was much addicted to opium. The habit grew upon him, as I understand, from some foolish freak when he was at college, for having read De Quincey's description of his dreams and sensations, he had drenched his tobacco in laudanum in an attempt to produce the same effects. He found, as so many more have done, that the practice is easier to attain than to get rid of, and for many years he continued to be a slave to the drug, an object of mingled horror and pity to his friends and relatives." Also, Holmes's search for the missing Neville St. Clair centered around the Bar of Gold, the Upper Swandam Lane opium den Isa frequented. When Watson found Holmes there, Holmes greeted him with, "I suppose...that you imagine that I have added opium-smoking to cocaine injections and all the other little weaknesses on which you have favoured me with your medical views." In truth, Holmes had not succumbed to the drug which had Isa Whitney in its grip. *The Man with the Twisted Lip*, I, 368, 371; see also *Silver Blaze*, II, 268.

ORDER, THE: One of the two names used by the Russian Nihilistic group of which the man "who gave the name of Professor Coram," his estranged wife Anna, and "the friend of [her] heart," Alexis, had been members. *The Adventure of the Golden Pince-Nez*, II, 365.

ORIGIN OF TREE WORSHIP, THE: One of the several books which Watson knocked out of the arms of an "elderly deformed...bibliophile" when both of them were gazing up at the house in which the Honourable Ronald Adair had been murdered. *The Adventure of the Empty House*, II, 331.

ORONTES: Dr. John H. Watson, after being seriously wounded at the battle of Maïwand during the second Afghan War, and recovering from a severe bout of enteric fever contracted at the base hospital at Peshawar, was invalided home aboard the troopship *Orontes*, which duly landed at Portsmouth jetty one month later. *A Study in Scarlet*, I, 143.

OVERTON, CYRIL: Skipper of the Cambridge varsity rugger team. An excellent player himself—he had been first reserve for England against Wales—Overton conceded that one Godfrey Staunton was the best man on his squad. Thus, he was understandably upset when Staunton disappeared just prior to Cambridge's important match against Oxford. Overton had been referred to Sherlock Holmes by Inspector Stanley Hopkins, and hoped that the detective could find Staunton before the match. *The Adventure of the Missing Three-Quarter*, II, 475ff.

OXFORD: "John Clay, the murderer, thief, smasher, and forger," had "royal blood in [his] veins" and had attended Eton and Oxford. *The Red-Headed League*, I, 433, 436.

Colonel Sebastian Moran, Moriarty's right-hand man, was educated at Eton and Oxford. *The Adventure of the Empty House*, II, 346.

Godfrey Staunton, the crack three-quarter of the Cambridge rugby team, disappeared just before their match with the Oxford team. Oxford won by a goal and two tries. *The Adventure of the Missing Three-Quarter*, ii, 487.

OXFORD STREET: Holmes went out about midday to conduct some business in Oxford Street, when Professor Moriarty's hired agents made the first of a series of promised attacks on Holmes's life. *The Final Problem*, ii, 306; see also *The Red-Headed League*, i, 432; *The Resident Patient*, i, 274; *The Greek Interpreter*, i, 596; *The Adventure of Charles Augustus Milverton*, ii, 564, 571; *The Adventure of the Golden Pince-Nez*, ii, 351; *The Disappearance of Lady Frances Carfax*, ii, 656.

OXSHOTT COMMON: The brutally beaten body of Mr. Aloysius Garcia was found on Oxshott Common, about a mile from Garcia's home, Wisteria Lodge. *The Adventure of Wisteria Lodge*, ii, 243.

OXSHOTT TOWERS: Sir George Folliott's large house, Oxshott Towers, lay near Aloysius Garcia's Wisteria Lodge, in Surrey. *The Adventure of Wisteria Lodge*, ii, 246.

OYSTERS: Holmes said to Athelney Jones, "I insist upon your dining with us. It will be ready in half an hour. I have oysters and a brace of grouse, with something a little choice in white wines." *The Sign of the Four*, i, 661.

Holmes: "Indeed, I cannot think why the whole bed of the ocean is not one solid mass of oysters, so prolific the creatures seem. No doubt there are natural enemies which limit the increases of the creatures. You and I, Watson, we have done our part. Shall the world, then, be overrun by oysters? No, no; horrible!" The Master Detective's simulated delirium was only part of a trap set to catch a suspected murderer with designs on Holmes's own life. *The Adventure of the Dying Detective*, i, 444.

P

PADDINGTON STATION: Sherlock Holmes was pacing up and down the platform at Paddington Station, "his tall, gaunt figure made even gaunter and taller by his long grey travelling-cloak and close-fitting cloth cap." He was waiting for Watson to join him in traveling to Hereford-shire to investigate the murder of Charles McCarthy. *The Boscombe Valley Mystery*, ii, 134; see also *The Adventure of the Engineer's Thumb*, ii, 209; *Silver Blaze*, ii, 261; *The Stockbroker's Clerk*, ii, 153.

PAGANINI, NICCOLO: After telling Watson how he had purchased his Stradivarius at a ridiculously low price, Holmes went on to discuss Paganini. "We sat for an hour over a bottle of claret while he told me anecdote after anecdote of that extraordinary man." *The Cardboard Box*, ii, 200.

PALL MALL: Mycroft Holmes's rooms were in Pall Mall, just across the street from the Diogenes Club. *The Greek Interpreter*, i, 592; see also *The Adventure of the Solitary Cyclist*, ii, 388, 389; *The Adventure of the Abbey Grange,* ii, 502; *The Adventure of the Bruce-Partington Plans*, ii, 433.

PALMER: Holmes said, "When a doctor does go wrong he is the first of criminals. He has nerve and he has knowledge. Palmer and Pritchard were among the heads of their profession." *The Adventure of the Speckled Band*, i, 257.

PALMYRA: The Douglases sailed aboard the *Palmyra* for South Africa, at the conclusion of Holmes's investigation. *The Valley of Fear*, i, 573.

PARADOL CHAMBER, THE ADVENTURE OF THE: "The year '87 furnished us with a long series of cases of greater or less interest, of which I retain the records. Among my headings under this one twelve months, I find an account of the adventure of the Paradol Chamber...." *The Five Orange Pips*, i, 389.

PARAMORE: Elias Openshaw's notebook for March, 1869, contained the entries, "7th. Set the pips on McCauley, Paramore, and Swain of St. Augustine....12th. Visited Paramore. All well." *The Five Orange Pips*, i, 397.

PARIS: Enoch Drebber and Joseph Stangerson fled the pursuing Jefferson Hope from St. Petersburg to Paris. When Hope arrived in Paris, they had just departed for Copenhagen. *A Study in Scarlet*, i, 222; see also *The Stockbroker's Clerk*, ii, 159; *The Adventure of the Second Stain*, i, 312; *The Adventure of the Bruce-Partington Plans*, ii, 452.

PARK LANE: Lady Maynooth lived at 427 Park Lane with her second son, Ronald Adair, and her daughter, Hilda Adair. *The Adventure of the Empty House*, ii, 330, 331.

PARK LANE MYSTERY: The popular name given to the mystery which Sherlock Holmes solved in *The Adventure of the Empty House*. *The Adventure of the Empty House*, II, 331.

PARKER: Arthur Pinner claimed that a certain Parker, who used to be Coxon's manager, raved about Hall Pycroft's financial ability. *The Stockbroker's Clerk*, II, 156.

PARKER: A "sentinel" for the Moriarty gang, he was deemed "a harmless enough fellow" by Sherlock Holmes. He was "a remarkable performer upon the jews' harp" and "a garrotter by trade." *The Adventure of the Empty House*, II, 340.

PARKER: The vicar of Hilton Cubitt's parish in Norfolk, he was staying at a boarding house in Russell Square, in London. When Cubitt came up to London for the Jubilee, he stayed at the same boarding house. There, he met his wife-to-be, Elsie Patrick. *The Adventure of the Dancing Men*, II, 529.

PARKHURST: Shinwell Johnson, Holmes's valuable assistant in the London underworld, had previously served two terms at Parkhurst. *The Adventure of the Illustrious Client*, II, 675.

PARR, LUCY: Second waiting-maid at Fairbank, residence of Alexander Holder, the great financier. One of the most precious treasures of the Empire had been stolen from his residence, and she was somewhat under suspicion, having been employed for only a few months. *The Adventure of the Beryl Coronet*, II, 286.

PATRICK, ELSIE: She married Hilton Cubitt after meeting him at a Russell Square boarding house. She was very much in love with him, but made him promise not to inquire into her previous life in America. Cubitt kept his promise, even in the affair of the grotesque writings that were found all around his house. *The Adventure of the Dancing Men*, II, 529.

PATRICK, OLD: Father of Elsie Patrick and boss of the Joint in Chicago. He invented the writing that would pass as a child's scrawl, which Holmes encountered in *The Adventure of the Dancing Men*. *The Adventure of the Dancing Men*, II, 544.

PATTERSON, INSPECTOR: In charge of the investigation that was supposed to net Professor Moriarty and his gang. In a final note to Watson, left under a silver cigarette-case above the Fall of Reichenbach, Holmes said, "Tell Inspector Patterson that the papers which he needs to convict the gang are in pigeon-hole M., done up in a blue envelope and inscribed 'Moriarty.'" *The Final Problem*, II, 317.

PATTINS, HUGH: Captain Basil (Sherlock Holmes in disguise) did not want him as harpooner for his exploring expedition. *The Adventure of Black Peter*, II, 409.

PAUL, JEAN: Pseudonym of J. P. F. Richter. Holmes said, "He makes one curious but profound remark. It is that the chief proof of man's real greatness lies in his perception of his own smallness. It argues, you see, a power of comparison and of appreeiation which is in itself a proof of nobility." *The Sign of the Four*, I, 648.

PEACE, CHARLIE: "A complex mind," said Holmes of Baron Adelbert Gruner. "All great criminals have that. My old friend Charlie Peace was a violin virtuoso." *The Adventure of the Illustrious Client*, II, 675.

PENNSYLVANIA: Ezekiah Hopkins, supposed founder of the Red-Headed League, was reportedly from Lebanon, Pennsylvania. *The Red-Headed League*, I, 421.

PENNSYLVANIA SMALL ARM COMPANY: Its initials, "PEN," were on the fluting between the barrels of the sawed-off shotgun that presumably killed John Douglas of Birlstone Manor, in Sussex. *The Valley of Fear*, I, 489.

PENTONVILLE: Maudsley, a friend of James Ryder, had just been released from Pentonville. *The Adventure of the Blue Carbuncle*, I, 465.

PERKINS: The groom at Baskerville Hall, in Devonshire, he had been sent to fetch Dr. James Mortimer, on the discovery of the dead body of Sir Charles Baskerville. *The Hound of the Baskervilles*, II, 13, 38.

PERKINS: Holmes confronted the fighter, Steve Dixie, with the killing of young Perkins outside the Holborn Bar. *The Adventure of the Three Gables*, II, 723.

PERNAMBUCO, BRAZIL: Isadora Klein's people had been leaders in Pernambuco for generations. *The Adventure of the Three Gables*, II, 731.

PERSANO, ISADORA: One of Holmes's unfinished tales, mentioned by Watson, involved "Isadora Persano, the well-known journalist and duellist, who was found stark staring mad with a match-box in front of him which contained a remarkable worm, said to be unknown to science." *The Problem of Thor Bridge*, 11, 588.

PERSIA: Holmes "passed through Persia" during his wanderings after his supposed death above the Fall of Reichenbach. Also, Sir Augustus Moran, father of the notorious Colonel Sebastian Moran, was once British Minister to Persia. *The Adventure of the Empty House*, 11, 337, 346.

PERU: Bob Ferguson's devoted wife was a Peruvian lady. *The Adventure of the Sussex Vampire*, 11, 464.

PESHAWAR: Dr. John H. Watson, seriously wounded at the battle of Maiwand, during the second Afghan War, was removed to the base hospital at Peshawar. *A Study in Scarlet*, 1, 143.

PETER: A groom in the employ of Bob Carruthers, he was driving Miss Violet Smith to Farnham Station in a dog-cart when they were attacked. "The beasts [pulled Peter] off and clubbed him." Then, they dragged Violet off. *The Adventure of the Solitary Cyclist*, 11, 393.

PETERS, HENRY ("HOLY"): "One of the most unscrupulous rascals that Australia has ever evolved," he posed as the good Dr. Shlessinger, and won the Lady Frances Carfax's confidence. *The Disappearance of Lady Frances Carfax*, 11, 662, 666.

PETERSFIELD: Lord Backwater had a residence near here, where Lord and Lady St. Simon were to have spent their honeymoon. *The Adventure of the Noble Bachelor*, 1, 285.

PETERSON: Peterson, the commissionaire, brought the mysterious goose and battered billycock to Holmes that led to an interesting investigation. *The Adventure of the Blue Carbuncle*, 1, 452.

PETRARCH: After discussing some of the facts of the murder of Charles McCarthy with Watson, Holmes read his pocket Petrarch until they arrived at the scene of the crime. *The Boscombe Valley Mystery*, 11, 140.

PHELPS, PERCY ("TADPOLE"): An old school friend of Watson's, "he was a very brilliant boy, and carried away every prize which the school had to offer, finishing his exploits by winning a scholarship, which sent him on to continue his triumphant career at Cambridge." Phelps's family had good connections, and this combined with his great skill to land him a good position at the Foreign Office. This was the last Watson heard of Phelps until he received a letter imploring help in the "horrible misfortune" which had come to "blast his career." A top-secret naval treaty had disappeared, under strange circumstances, from Phelps's office. *The Naval Treaty*, II, 167, 170.

PHILADELPHIA: Jephro Rucastle claimed that his daughter, Alice, had left England on a trip to Philadelphia. *The Adventure of the Copper Beeches*, II, 119.

PHILLIMORE, JAMES: One of Holmes's unfinished tales, mentioned by Watson: "Mr. James Phillimore, who, stepping back into his own house to get an umbrella, was never more seen in this world." *The Problem of Thor Bridge*, II, 588.

"PIERROT": A pseudonym used in *The Daily Telegraph*'s "agony column" by a person who was definitely *not* clownish. Holmes was able to adopt the pseudonym long enough to ensnare "Pierrot's" partner in crime. *The Adventure of the Bruce-Partington Plans*, II, 449.

PIKE, LANGDALE: Holmes's "human book of reference upon all matters of social scandal. This strange, languid creature spent his waking hours in the bow window of a St. James' Street club, and was the receiving-station, as well as the transmitter, for all the gossip of the Metropolis. He made, it was said, a four-figure income by the paragraphs which he contributed every week to the garbage papers which cater for an inquisitive public. If ever, far down in the turbid depths of London life, there was some strange swirl or eddy, it was marked with automatic exactness by this human dial upon the surface. Holmes discreetly helped Langdale to knowledge, and on occasion was helped in turn." *The Adventure of the Three Gables*, II, 728–29.

PINCHIN LANE: The bird-stuffer, Sherman, and his sleuth-hound, Toby, lived at NO. 3 Pinchin Lane, Lambeth. *The Sign of the Four*, I, 642.

PINKERTON'S: The private detective agency employed by large railroad and steel companies to break the hold of the Scowrers on the coal mining districts of the Gilmerton Mountains. Birdy Edwards was their primary operative in this effort. *The Valley of Fear*, I, 561, 570.

Mr. Leverton, of Pinkerton's American Agency, had "tracked [a vicious killer] over from New York, and [had] been close to him for a week in London, waiting some excuse to get [a] hand on his collar." *The Adventure of the Red Circle*, II, 699.

PINNER: In Middlesex. Mrs. Effie Hebron had a maiden aunt there, with whom she had stayed after she returned to England following the death of her husband in America. *The Yellow Face*, I, 579.

PINNER, ARTHUR: Supposedly a financial agent, he said that his brother, Harry Pinner, was promoter and managing director of the Franco-Midland Hardware Company, Limited, and was looking for "a young, pushing man" to add to the organization. Harry had asked Arthur to find someone who could fit the job, and Arthur set upon Hall Pycroft and offered him a good position. Arthur Pinner also went under the name Beddington. *The Stockbroker's Clerk*, II, 160.

PINNER, HARRY: Supposedly promoter for, and managing director of, the Franco-Midland Hardware Company, Limited. He sought "a young, pushing man," and his brother, Arthur, suggested Hall Pycroft. He very closely resembled his brother, except that he was clean shaven and his hair was lighter. Pycroft noticed that each brother had a second tooth on the left-hand side which had been very poorly filled with gold. *The Stockbroker's Clerk*, II, 157.

PINTO, JONAS: He was shot to death in the Lake Saloon, Market Street, Chicago, in the New Year week of 1874. Jack McMurdo said, "I was helping Uncle Sam to make dollars. Maybe mine were not as good gold as his, but they looked as well and were cheaper to make. This man Pinto helped me to shove the queer...to pass the dollars out into circulation. Then he said he would split. Maybe he did split. I didn't wait to see. I just killed him and lighted out for the coal country." *The Valley of Fear*, I, 534.

PINTO, MARIA: The maiden name of the ill-used and tragic Brazilian wife of Neil Gibson, the Gold King. She was the daughter of a Government official in Manáos. Her jealousy of her husband's attentions toward their children's governess drove her to mad deeds. *The Problem of Thor Bridge*, II, 591, 594.

PITT: Sir William Baskerville had been "Chairman of Committees of the House of Commons under Pitt." *The Hound of the Baskervilles*, II, 92.

PITT STREET: "...a quiet little backwater just beside one of the briskest currents of London life." A man was found brutally slain on the steps of NO. 131 Pitt Street, the residence of Horace Harker. Harker had been the possessor of one of the plaster casts of Devine's bust of Napoleon. *The Adventure of the Six Napoleons*, II, 575.

PLYMOUTH: Holmes claimed that he had seen Mrs. John Straker in Plymouth, at a garden-party, in an expensive costume of dove-colored silk with ostrich-feather trimming. She replied that he was mistaken. *Silver Blaze*, II, 272; see also *The Hound of the Baskervilles*, II, 57; *The Adventure of the Devil's Foot*, II, 516.

POE, EDGAR ALLAN: Watson told the Great Detective that he reminded him of Edgar Allan Poe's Dupin. Holmes replied, "Now, in my opinion, Dupin was a very inferior fellow. That trick of his of breaking in on his friends' thoughts with an apropos remark after a quarter of an hour's silence is really very showy and superficial. He had some analytical genius, no doubt; but he was by no means such a phenomenon as Poe appeared to imagine." *A Study in Scarlet*, I, 162; see also *The Cardboard Box*, II, 194.

POLDHU BAY: In the early spring of 1897, Sherlock Holmes, following doctor's orders to relax, adjourned with Watson to "a small cottage near Poldhu Bay, at the further extremity of the Cornish peninsula." *The Adventure of the Devil's Foot*, II, 508, 509.

THE POLITICIAN, THE LIGHTHOUSE, AND THE TRAINED CORMORANT: Even though Watson assured his readers that "no confidence [would] be abused" in the memoirs which Sherlock Holmes allowed to be published, at least one reader made efforts to get at and destroy those papers. Thus, Watson was compelled to state that the source of the outrages was known, and if they were repeated he had Holmes's "authority for saying that the whole story concerning the politician, the lighthouse, and the trained cormorant [would] be given to the public." *The Adventure of the Veiled Lodger*, II, 453.

POLLACK, CONSTABLE: Together with Sergeant Tuson, he succeeded, after a desperate struggle, in arresting the famous forger Beddington, following the latter's attempted robbery of Mawson & Williams, the famous financial house. *The Stockbroker's Clerk*, II, 165, 166.

POMPEY: In Sherlock Holmes's opinion, Pompey was "a detective who was a very eminent specialist in [the art of tracking]." Physically, he was "a squat, lop-eared, white-and-tan dog, something between a beagle and a foxhound." "The pride of the [Cambridge] draghounds," Pompey was "no great flier, as his build [showed], but a staunch hound on a scent." With the assistance of his canine "detective," Holmes was finally able to discover the whereabouts of Godfrey Staunton, the missing star of Cambridge University's rugger team. *The Adventure of the Missing Three-Quarter*, 11, 488.

PONCHO: It was the stampeding of her horse, Poncho, in a herd of cattle that first introduced Lucy Ferrier to Jefferson Hope. *A Study in Scarlet*, I, 205.

PONDICHERRY: One day in 1883, Elias Openshaw received a letter from India bearing a Pondicherry postmark. "Opening it hurriedly, out there jumped five little dried orange pips, which pattered down upon his plate." These signaled the poor man's coming death in a "little green-scummed pool." Significantly, the barque *Lone Star* had touched at Pondicherry in January and February of 1883. *The Five Orange Pips*, I, 393, 394, 403.

PONDICHERRY LODGE: Home of Major John Sholto, and later, of his son Bartholomew. *The Sign of the Four*, I, 631, 633.

POPE, HIS HOLINESS THE: In his anxiety to oblige the Pope in the little affair of the Vatican cameos, Holmes had overlooked the newspaper reports of the mysterious death of Sir Charles Baskerville. *The Hound of the Baskervilles*, 11, 12.

One of Holmes's cases of the year 1895 most memorable to Watson was his "investigation of the sudden death of Cardinal Tosca—an inquiry which was carried out by him at the express desire of his Holiness the Pope...." *The Adventure of Black Peter*, 11, 398.

POPE'S COURT: The offices of the Red-Headed League were at 7 Pope's Court, Fleet Street. *The Red-Headed League*, I, 421, 423.

PORLOCK, FRED: Holmes said, "Porlock, Watson, is a *nom de plume*, a mere identification, but behind it lies a shifty and evasive personality. In a former letter he frankly informed me that the name was not his own, and defied me ever to trace him among the teeming millions of this great city. Porlock is important, not for himself, but for the great man with whom he is in touch.... Led on by some rudimentary aspirations towards right, and encouraged by the judicious stimulation of an occasional ten-pound note sent to him by devious methods, he has once or twice given me advance information which has been of value—the highest value which anticipates and prevents rather than avenges crime."

A cipher letter from Porlock first drew Holmes into the strange events surrounding the case *The Valley of Fear*. *The Valley of Fear*, I, 471, 472.

PORTER, MRS.: The elderly Cornish housekeeper who, with the aid of a young girl, looked after the wants of the Tregennis family. An "evidently harmless" person, she had been understandably distressed by the great harm which had befallen her employers. *The Adventure of the Devil's Foot*, II, 513, 515,

PORTLAND: Jack James, an American citizen, was sentenced to Portland for spying for the Germans before the First World War. *His Last Bow*, II, 798.

PORTSDOWN HILL: Major Freebody was in command of one of the forts on Portsdown Hill. His friend, Joseph Openshaw, went to visit him, and met death at the bottom of a deep chalk-pit. *The Five Orange Pips*, I, 395.

PORTSMOUTH: Dr. John H. Watson, after being seriously wounded at the battle of Maiwand during the second Afghan War, and recovering from a severe bout of enteric fever contracted at the base hospital at Peshawar, was invalided home aboard the troopship *Orontes*, which duly landed at Portsmouth jetty one month later. *A Study in Scarlet*, I, 143; see also *The Naval Treaty*, II, 179; *His Last Bow*, II, 795, 796.

POSILIPPO: A town near Naples, it produced two vastly dissimilar persons, Emilia Barelli Lucca and Giuseppe Gorgiano. *The Adventure of the Red Circle*, II, 702.

POTT, EVANS: County delegate of the Ancient Order of Freemen, he lived at Hobson's Patch. *The Valley of Fear*, I, 555.

POTTER'S TERRACE: Hall Pycroft, whose strange new job prompted him to consult with Sherlock Holmes, had his rooms "out Hampstead way—17 Potter's Terrace." *The Stockbroker's Clerk*, II, 156.

POULTNEY SQUARE: Annie Fraser and Henry Peters's residence was NO. 36 Poultney Square, Brixton. *The Disappearance of Lady Frances Carfax*, II, 664.

PRACTICAL HANDBOOK OF BEE CULTURE, WITH SOME OBSERVATIONS UPON THE SEGREGATION OF THE QUEEN: Holmes passed the small blue book over to Von Bork, who thought it contained the British naval signals. Later, Holmes described it to Watson: "Here is the fruit of my leisured ease, the *magnum opus* of my latter years!... Alone I did it. Behold the fruit of pensive nights and laborious days, when I watched the little working gangs as once I watched the criminal world of London." *His Last Bow*, II, 800–1.

PRAGUE: Wilhelm Gottsreich Sigismond von Ormstein had come incognito from Prague in order to consult Holmes in a "matter... so delicate that I could not confide it to an agent without putting myself in his power." *A Scandal in Bohemia*, I, 353.

Concerning Baron Adelbert Gruner and the death of his wife in the Splügen Pass, Holmes felt, "Who could possibly have read what happened at Prague and have any doubts as to the man's guilt! It was a purely technical legal point and the suspicious death of a witness that saved him!" *The Adventure of the Illustrious Client*, II, 672.

Professor Presbury of Camford University broke his lifelong habits and went away on a journey without notifying anyone where he was going. Later, Holmes's client, Mr. Bennett, received a letter from a fellow student saying that he was glad to have seen the Professor in Prague, but he had not been able to talk with him. Later, it was learned that Presbury had visited the infamous H. Lowenstein of that city. *The Adventure of the Creeping Man*, II, 754, 764.

PRENDERGAST, JACK: "He was a man of good family and of great ability, but of incurably vicious habits, who had, by an ingenious system of fraud, obtained huge sums of money from the leading London merchants." Eventually, in 1855, he was caught and sentenced to transportation to the Australian colonies aboard the barque *Gloria Scott*. He bribed the crew, and led a successful convict uprising with the help of fellow convicts Armitage and Evans. He was killed in an explosion which destroyed the ship shortly after the uprising. *The "Gloria Scott"*, I, 117.

PRENDERGAST, MAJOR: John Openshaw had heard of Holmes from Major Prendergast, whom Holmes had saved in the Tankerville Club Scandal.

"Ah, of course. He was wrongfully accused of cheating at cards," said Holmes.

"He said that you could solve anything."

"He said too much."

"That you are never beaten."

"I have been beaten four times — three times by men and once by a woman." *The Five Orange Pips*, I, 392.

PRESBURY, EDITH: The only daughter of the famous Camford physiologist, she was engaged to her father's professional assistant, Trevor Bennett. She was deeply concerned about her father's bizarre behavior. *The Adventure of the Creeping Man*, II, 756.

PRESBURY, PROFESSOR: "The famous Camford physiologist" whose bizarre behavior was brought to Holmes's attention in *The Adventure of the Creeping Man*. A sixty-one-year-old widower, Presbury was a man of European reputation, who, in a "passionate frenzy of youth," had become engaged to Alice Morphy, daughter of one of his colleagues and a woman about the same age as that of Presbury's own daughter, Edith. It was not the difference in age between Presbury and Alice that led Edith's fiancé to seek Holmes's advice, it was the "violent and unnatural" manner in which he had conducted his courtship, for though the Professor was naturally "combative," he had turned quite savage — so savage, in fact, that his faithful wolfhound, Roy, had tried to bite him. *The Adventure of the Creeping Man*, II, 758, *passim*.

PRESCOTT, RODGER: Once famous as a forger and coiner in Chicago, he was shot by Killer Evans in the Waterloo Road [in London] in January, 1895. He "died, but [as Prescott] was shown to have been the aggressor in the row," Killer Evans got off with a relatively light sentence. Prescott was known as the greatest counterfeiter London had ever seen. *The Adventure of the Three Garridebs*, II, 652ff.

PRICE, MR.: Watson posed as a clerk, Mr. Price, of Birmingham, in his and Holmes's interview with Harry Pinner. *The Stockbroker's Clerk*, II, 162.

PRINCETOWN: The prison in Dartmoor from which Selden, the murderer, had escaped. *The Hound of the Baskervilles*, II, 38.

PRINGLE, MRS.: An elderly housekeeper, she was employed at 16 Godolphin Street by Eduardo Lucas, an international spy. *The Adventure of the Second Stain*, I, 308.

PRIORY SCHOOL, THE: Preparatory school near Mackleton, in Hallamshire, it was founded by Dr. Thorneycroft Huxtable. It was one of the most select schools in England, boasting some of the best names in the realm among its students. The Duke of Holdernesse's son, Lord Saltire, was entrusted to Dr. Huxtable's care, but he mysteriously disappeared, and Holmes was called in to investigate. *The Adventure of the Priory School*, II, 609.

PRITCHARD: "When a doctor does go wrong he is the first of criminals. He has nerve and he has knowledge. Palmer and Pritchard were among the heads of their profession." *The Adventure of the Speckled Band*, I, 257.

PROSPER, FRANCIS: Greengrocer for Alexander Holder's household in Streatham, he was a beau of the second waiting-maid at Fairbank. He had a wooden leg. *The Adventure of the Beryl Coronet*, II, 293.

PUGILIST: Horse run by Colonel Wardlaw against Silver Blaze for the Wessex Cup. *Silver Blaze*, II, 278.

PUNJAB: After traveling through Nepal and Afghanistan, Henry Wood went back to the Punjab, where he "lived mostly among the natives, and picked up a living by the conjuring tricks [he] had learned." *The Crooked Man*, II, 236.

PURDEY PLACE: Purdey Place, the large house of Mr. Hynes Hynes, J.P., lay near Aloysius Garcia's Wisteria Lodge, in Surrey. *The Adventure of Wisteria Lodge*, II, 246.

PYCROFT, HALL: An unemployed clerk, he accepted a seemingly good berth with the Franco-Midland Hardware Company, but was puzzled over some of the terms of his employment, and came to Holmes for a solution. *The Stockbroker's Clerk*, II, 155.

Q

QUEEN ANNE STREET: At the time of *The Adventure of the Illustrious Client*, Dr. Watson was living in his own rooms in Queen Anne Street. *The Adventure of the Illustrious Client*, II, 672.

R

RAE, ANDREW: Of Rae and Sturmash, coal-owners, Merton County. The Merton County Lodge of the Ancient Order of Freemen petitioned for his murder by the Vermissa Lodge. *The Valley of Fear*, I, 541.

RAGGED SHAW: Grove of trees between the Priory School and Lower Gill Moor, in Hallamshire. Lord Saltire disappeared through the Ragged Shaw. *The Adventure of the Priory School*, II, 615.

RAILWAY ARMS: Country inn in Little Purlington, "the most primitive village in England," where Watson and Josiah Amberley were forced to spend the night. *The Adventure of the Retired Colourman*, II, 552.

RALPH: Butler for the Emsworth family, Ralph "seemed about the same age as [Tuxbury Old Hall]," and his wife seemed even older. *The Adventure of the Blanched Soldier*, II, 709.

RALPH, MRS.: She had been Godfrey Emsworth's nurse at Tuxbury Old Hall, near Bedford. He had spoken of her "as second only to his mother in his affections." *The Adventure of the Blanched Soldier*, II, 709.

RANCE, JOHN: The constable who found the dead body of Enoch J. Drebber in a lonely suburban apartment just off the Brixton Road. Rance lived at 46 Audley Court, Kennington Park Gate. He narrowly missed capturing the true murderer. *A Study in Scarlet*, I, 172.

RANDALL: Surname of a Lewisham gang of burglars — a father and his two sons. The Randalls had committed a burglary at Sydenham a fortnight before the murder of Sir Eustace Brackenstall at the Abbey Grange, and they were suspected of the latter crime as well — that is, until they were arrested in New York the morning following the murder. *The Adventure of the Abbey Grange*, II, 492, 504.

RAO, LAL: Indian butler of Bartholomew Sholto, of Pondicherry Lodge, Upper Norwood. *The Sign of the Four*, I, 647, 653, 688.

RAS, DAULAT: Indian student at the College of St. Luke's, in one of England's great university towns. He lived on the same stair as Hilton Soames, a tutor, and was a candidate for the Fortescue Scholarship. *The Adventure of the Three Students*, II, 374, 376.

RASPER: Horse run by Lord Singleford against Silver Blaze for the Wessex Cup. *Silver Blaze*, II, 278.

RATCLIFF HIGHWAY: Sumner, the shipping agent whom Captain Basil (Sherlock Holmes in disguise) solicited for three harpooners, was located there. *The Adventure of Black Peter*, II, 408.

RATCLIFF HIGHWAY MURDERS: In attributing the death of Enoch J.

Drebber to political refugees and revolutionists, the *Daily Telegraph* made mention of the Ratcliff Highway murders. *A Study in Scarlet*, 1, 184.

READE, WINWOOD: Holmes recommended that Watson read Reade's *Martyrdom of Man*, while Holmes was out investigating the facts surrounding the sign of the four. Later, when Watson suggested that someone had called man "a soul concealed in an animal," Holmes replied, "Winwood Reade is good upon the subject. He remarks that, while the individual man is an insoluble puzzle, in the aggregate he becomes a mathematical certainty." *The Sign of the Four*, 1, 619, 666.

READING: Mr. Sandeford, whose plaster cast of Devine's bust of Napoleon was the last to be smashed, resided in Lower Grove Road, Reading. *The Adventure of the Six Napoleons*, 11, 580; see also *The Boscombe Valley Mystery*, 11, 134; *The Adventure of the Speckled Band*, 1, 249; *The Adventure of the Engineer's Thumb*, 11, 213; *Silver Blaze*, 11, 262.

RED BULL, THE: Inn on the High Road, near Mackleton. Its landlady was sick one night and had sent to Mackleton for a doctor. Thus, the patrons of the inn were up all night awaiting the doctor and could swear that no one, including the missing Lord Saltire and the Priory School's German master, Heidegger, had passed in the night. *The Adventure of the Priory School*, 11, 615.

RED CIRCLE, THE: A Neapolitan terrorist society which was allied to the old Carbonari, its oaths and secrets were "frightful; but once within its rule no escape was possible." Gennaro Lucca, who had joined the Red Circle "in his wild and fiery days," found out as much when, years after his initiation, he met one "Black Gorgiano" in the streets of New York. *The Adventure of the Red Circle*, 11, 700, 703.

RED-HEADED LEAGUE, THE: Vincent Spaulding outlined the history of the League to Jabez Wilson: "As far as I can make out, the League was founded by an American millionaire, Ezekiah Hopkins, who was very peculiar in his ways. He himself was red-headed, and he had a great sympathy for all red-headed men; so, when he died, it was found that he had left his enormous fortune in the hands of trustees, with instructions to apply the interest to the providing of easy berths to men whose hair is of that colour. From all I hear it is splendid pay, and very little to do." Holmes said of the case itself, "In the present instance I am forced to admit that the facts are, to the best of my belief, unique." *The Red-Headed League*, i, 419, 423.

RED INDIAN: Watson wrote of Sherlock Holmes, "For an instant the veil had lifted upon his keen, intense nature, but for an instant only. When I glanced again his face had resumed that Red Indian composure which had made so many regard him as a machine rather than a man." *The Crooked Man*, ii, 226; see also *The Naval Treaty*, ii, 183.

RED LEECH, THE: One of the many cases Sherlock Holmes handled in 1894 was "the repulsive story of the red leech and the terrible death of Crosby the banker." *The Adventure of the Golden Pince-Nez*, ii, 350.

REGENT CIRCUS: When Sherlock Holmes and Watson strolled out into the London evening to take in two of the city's great curiosities, Mycroft Holmes and the Diogenes Club, they found themselves walking toward Regent Circus. *The Greek Interpreter*, i, 591; see also *The Adventure of Charles Augustus Milverton*, ii, 571.

REGENT STREET: Holmes spotted a man with a bushy black beard and a pair of piercing eyes trailing Dr. Mortimer and Sir Henry Baskerville in a cab as they strolled down Regent Street. *The Hound of the Baskervilles*, ii, 26; see also *A Scandal in Bohemia*, i, 358; *The Boscombe Valley Mystery*, ii, 150; *The Adventure of the Illustrious Client*, ii, 682.

REICHENBACH FALL: Watson said: "It is, indeed, a fearful place. The torrent, swollen by the melting snow, plunges into a tremendous abyss, from which the spray rolls up like the smoke from a burning house. The shaft into which the river hurls itself is an immense chasm, lined by glistening, coal-black rock, and narrowing into a creaming, boiling pit of incalculable depth, which brims over and shoots the stream onward over its jagged lip. The long sweep of green water roaring for ever down, and the thick flickering curtain of spray hissing for ever upwards, turn a man giddy with their constant whirl and clamour." Holmes and Watson visited there on their Continental trek through Switzerland, and it was against this wild backdrop that the fateful struggle between the Great Detective and the Evil Genius, Professor Moriarty, took place. *The Final Problem*, ii, 314.

REIGATE: In Surrey. Watson's friend and onetime patient, Colonel Hayter, invited Holmes and Watson to his home there. While on vacation, they became involved in the adventure of *The Reigate Squires*. *The Reigate Squires*, I, 331.

REILLY: A reckless youngster, he accompanied Jack McMurdo in an unsuccessful attempt on the life of Chester Wilcox. *The Valley of Fear*, I, 558.

REILLY: Lawyer for the Scowrers, he succeeded in freeing the men jailed for the assault upon James Stanger, editor of the Vermissa *Herald*. *The Valley of Fear*, I, 551.

RELIGION: "'There is nothing in which deduction is so necessary as in religion,' said [Holmes], leaning with his back against the shutters. 'It can be built up as an exact science by the reasoner. Our highest assurance of the goodness of Providence seems to me to rest in the flowers. All other things, our powers, our desires, our food, are really necessary for our existence in the first instance. But this rose is an extra. Its smell and its colour are an embellishment of life, not a condition of it. It is only goodness which gives extras, and so I say again that we have much to hope from the flowers.'" *The Naval Treaty*, II, 178.

REYNOLDS, SIR JOSHUA: As he dined with Sir Henry Baskerville, Sherlock Holmes thought he recognized a portrait by Reynolds in the family gallery. It was the one of a "stout gentleman with the wig." *The Hound of the Baskervilles*, II, 92.

RHODESIAN POLICE: After his disgrace concerning the Fortescue Scholarship, the guilty party accepted the offer of a commission in the Rhodesian Police and left for South Africa at once. *The Adventure of the Three Students*, II, 381.

RHONE, VALLEY OF THE: Holmes and Watson spent a charming week wandering up the valley of the Rhône in their attempted escape from Professor Moriarty. *The Final Problem*, II, 312.

RICHARDS, DR.: He had been sent for on an urgent call to Tredannick Wartha, the house of the Tregennis family, in Cornwall. The three persons for whom the doctor had been summoned were so far beyond any assistance he could offer, however, that he turned "white as a sheet" and "fell into a chair in a sort of faint." *The Adventure of the Devil's Foot*, II, 510, 513.

RICHTER: The real name of "Jean Paul." Holmes felt that "there is much food for thought in Richter." *The Sign of the Four*, I, 648.

RICOLETTI OF THE CLUB FOOT AND HIS ABOMINABLE WIFE, THE CASE OF: One of Holmes's untold tales. *The Musgrave Ritual*, I, 124.

RIDLING THORPE MANOR: In Norfolk, home of the Hilton Cubitts and scene of the curious incident of the childish stick figures. *The Adventure of the Dancing Men*, II, 535.

RIGA: François le Villard consulted Holmes about a case which "was concerned with a will, and possessed some features of interest." Holmes "was able to refer him to two parallel cases," one of which occurred "at Riga in 1857." *The Sign of the Four*, I, 612.

RIPLEY: A "pretty little village" in Surrey, near Woking. While investigating the disappearance of the top-secret naval treaty from Percy Phelps's office, Holmes stopped for tea in Ripley and "took the precaution of filling [his] flask and of putting a paper of sandwiches in [his] pocket." *The Naval Treaty*, II, 189.

RIVIERA: Holmes had all the facts in a squat notebook concerning the robbery in the train-de-luxe to the Riviera on February 13, 1892, which apparently implicated Count Negretto Sylvius. *The Adventure of the Mazarin Stone*, II, 741; see also *The Adventure of the Three Gables*, II, 731.

ROBERT STREET: Holmes, Watson, and Mary Morstan passed by Robert Street on their journey to Thaddeus Sholto's house. *The Sign of the Four*, I, 623.

ROBERTS, LORD: A military man as esteemed in his field as was Sir James Saunders in medical circles. Holmes believed that, were a "raw subaltern" to have been granted an interview with Lord Roberts, the subaltern's "wonder and pleasure" could not have exceeded that expressed by Mr. Kent, when that country surgeon met Sir James. *The Adventure of the Blanched Soldier*, II, 719.

ROBINSON, JOHN: Alias of James Ryder. *The Adventure of the Blue Carbuncle*, I, 463.

ROCHESTER ROW: Holmes, Watson, and Mary Morstan passed by Rochester Row on their journey to Thaddeus Sholto's house. *The Sign of the Four*, I, 623.

ROCK OF GIBRALTAR: The "largest and best boat" of the Adelaide-Southampton line. On board the *Rock of Gibraltar*, sailing out of Adelaide, Mary Fraser and Jack Croker began the friendship which, over eighteen months later, would figure prominently in one of Holmes's cases. *The Adventure of the Abbey Grange*, II, 502.

ROME: Douglas Maberley had been Attaché at Rome before he died there of pneumonia. *The Adventure of the Three Gables*, II, 724.

RONDER: "One of the greatest showmen of his day" before he took to drink. "Ruffian, bully, beast—it was all written on [his] heavy-jowled face." Ronder's actions were every bit as ugly as his face: he deserted his wife for others, and he tied her down and lashed her with his riding whip when she complained. *The Adventure of the Veiled Lodger*, II, 458ff.

RONDER, MRS. EUGENIA: Once "a very magnificent woman," she had been terribly mutilated by "a very fine North African lion" which was one of the primary exhibits in the wild beast show she ran with her husband. Her face had been transformed into a "grisly ruin," but her spirit had been even more disfigured by the awful incident. She felt that "it would ease [her] mind if someone knew the truth [about the incident] before [she] died," and she chose Sherlock Holmes as her confessor. *The Adventure of the Veiled Lodger*, II, *passim*.

ROSA, SALVATOR: A connoisseur might have thrown a doubt on the Salvator Rosa that hung in Thaddeus Sholto's small house, "an oasis of art in the howling desert of South London." *The Sign of the Four*, I, 626.

ROSENLAUI: On that fateful May 4, 1891, Holmes and Watson set off from Meiringen with the intention of crossing the hills and spending the night in the Hamlet of Rosenlaui. On the way, they paused to view the Fall of Reichenbach. *The Final Problem*, II, 312.

ROSS, COLONEL: Owner of Silver Blaze and the King's Pyland stables in Dartmoor from which the horse disappeared. He invited Holmes to look into the case in conjunction with Inspector Gregory. *Silver Blaze*, II, 269.

ROSS, DUNCAN: Manager of the offices of the Red-Headed League in London, he claimed to be a member himself. He set Jabez Wilson on the arduous task of copying the *Encyclopaedia Britannica*. Also known as William Morris. *The Red-Headed League*, I, 424.

ROSS AND MANGLES: Animal dealers, in Fulham Road, they sold the "strongest and most savage" dog in their possession to Sir Henry Baskerville's neighbor. *The Hound of the Baskervilles*, II, 107.

ROTHERHITHE: Mrs. Hudson reported that Holmes had been working at a case down at Rotherhithe, in an alley near the river, and had brought the illness with which he had supposedly been stricken in *The Adventure of the Dying Detective* back with him to Baker Street. The case had involved some Chinese sailors down on the docks. *The Adventure of the Dying Detective*, I, 439, 446.

ROTTERDAM: Sherlock Holmes, in the guise of Altamont, the Irish-American spy, said that he was hoping to catch a boat from Rotterdam to New York. *His Last Bow*, II, 799; see also *The Boscombe Valley Mystery*, II, 148.

ROUNDHAY, MR.: "The vicar of the parish" centered in the Cornish hamlet of Tredannick Wollas, Mr. Roundhay "was something of an archaeologist, and as such Holmes had made his acquaintance." *The Adventure of the Devil's Foot*, II, 509.

ROY: Professor Presbury's faithful wolfhound, he had, seemingly without reason, twice attempted to bite his master. *The Adventure of the Creeping Man*, II, 752.

ROYAL ARTILLERY: Concerning the "very small, dark fellow, with his hat pushed back and several packages under his arm" that both Mycroft and Sherlock Holmes viewed from the window of the Strangers' Room of the Diogenes Club, they deduced a great many things, including that he had been a non-commissioned officer of the Royal Artillery who had served in India. *The Greek Interpreter*, I, 594.

ROYAL MALLOWS: The "old 117th," was "one of the most famous Irish regiments in the British Army. It did wonders both in the Crimea and the Mutiny, and has since that time distinguished itself upon every possible occasion." Its commanding officer was Colonel James Barclay, "a gallant veteran, who started as a full private, was raised to commissioned rank for his bravery at the time of the Mutiny, and so lived to command the regiment in which he had once carried a musket." He was found mysteriously dead in his locked morning-room. *The Crooked Man*, II, 227.

ROYAL MARINE LIGHT INFANTRY: Holmes deduced that the commissionaire who delivered Inspector Gregson's summons was a retired sergeant of Marines. Shortly thereafter, the man identified himself to an astonished Watson as "A [former] sergeant, sir. Royal Marine Light Infantry, sir." *A Study in Scarlet*, I, 163.

ROYLOTT, DR. GRIMESBY: Stepfather of Helen and Julia Stoner; last of the Roylott family of Stoke Moran, in Surrey. His "family was at one time among the richest in England, and the estate extended over the borders into Berkshire in the north, and Hampshire in the west. In the last century, however, four successive heirs were of a dissolute and wasteful disposition, and the family ruin was eventually completed by a gambler, in the days of the Regency. Nothing was left save a few acres of ground and the two-hundred-year-old house, which is itself crushed under a heavy mortgage. The last squire dragged out his existence there, living the horrible life of an aristocratic pauper; but his only son, [Grimesby Roylott], seeing that he must adapt himself to the new conditions, obtained an advance from a relative, which enabled him to take a medical degree, and went to Calcutta, where, by his professional skill and his force of character, he established a large practice. In a fit of anger, however, caused by some robberies which had been perpetrated in the house, he beat his native butler to death, and narrowly escaped a capital sentence. As it was, he suffered a long term of imprisonment, and afterwards returned to England a morose and disappointed man." While in India, Roylott married Mrs. Stoner. *The Adventure of the Speckled Band*, I, 245, 251.

RUCASTLE, ALICE: Daughter of Jephro Rucastle. She was apparently away in Philadelphia at the time Jephro hired Miss Violet Hunter — who bore a remarkable resemblance to his daughter — as governess, at quite a generous salary. Miss Rucastle's fiancé was nevertheless of the opinion that she had remained at home. *The Adventure of the Copper Beeches*, II, 119.

RUCASTLE, EDWARD: Son of Jephro Rucastle, who said of his son, "One child — one dear little romper just six years old. Oh, if you could see him killing cockroaches with a slipper! Smack! smack! smack! Three gone before you could wink!" But his governess, Miss Violet Hunter, who called Holmes into *The Adventure of the Copper Beeches*, noted, "I have never met so utterly spoilt and so ill-natured a little creature. He is small for his age, with a head which is quite disproportionately large. His whole life appears to be spent in an alternation between savage fits of passion and gloomy intervals of sulking. Giving pain to any creature weaker than himself seems to be his one idea of amusement, and he shows quite remarkable talent in planning the capture of mice, little birds, and insects." And Holmes told Watson pointedly: "My dear Watson, you as a medical man are continually gaining light as to the tendencies of a child by the study of the parents. Don't you see that the converse is equally valid. I have frequently gained my first real insight into the character of parents by studying their children. This child's disposition is abnormally cruel, merely for cruelty's sake, and whether he derives this from his smiling father, as I should suspect, or from his mother, it bodes evil for the poor girl [Miss Violet Hunter] who is in their power." *The Adventure of the Copper Beeches*, II, 117, 123, 129.

RUCASTLE, JEPHRO: He sought out Miss Violet Hunter as a governess for his young son, Edward. However, his and his wife's peculiar whims and fancies as to Miss Hunter's dress, appearance, and activities soon involved Holmes. *The Adventure of the Copper Beeches*, II, 116.

RUCASTLE, MRS. JEPHRO: Violet Hunter described her as "a silent, pale-faced woman, much younger than her husband, not more than thirty," who seemed to be "colourless in mind as well as in feature. She impressed me neither favourably nor the reverse. She was a nonentity. It was easy to see that she was passionately devoted to her husband and to her little son." *The Adventure of the Copper Beeches*, II, 123.

RUFTON, EARL OF: The Lady Frances Carfax, whom Holmes rescued, was the sole survivor of the direct family of the late Earl of Rufton. *The Disappearance of Lady Frances Carfax*, II, 657.

RUGBY: Watson had played rugby for Blackheath when Big Bob Ferguson was three-quarter for Richmond. *The Adventure of the Sussex Vampire*, II, 465.

RULLI, SIGNOR: Secretary to the Marquess of Montalva. Both were murdered in their rooms at the Hotel Escurial at Madrid. The crime was ascribed to Nihilism, and the murderers were never arrested. Signor Rulli was also known as Lucas and Lopez. *The Adventure of Wisteria Lodge*, II, 258.

RUSSELL, CLARK: "It was in the latter days of September, and the equinoctial gales had set in with exceptional violence....Sherlock Holmes sat moodily at one side of the fireplace cross-indexing his records of crime, whilst I at the other was deep in one of Clark Russell's fine sea stories, until the howl of the gale from without seemed to blend with the text, and the splash of the rain to lengthen out into the long swash of the sea waves." *The Five Orange Pips*, I, 389–90.

RUSSELL SQUARE: Hilton Cubitt, having come up to London for the Queen's Jubilee, stopped at a boarding-house in Russell Square because Parker, the vicar of his parish, had been staying there. There he met Elsie Patrick, the woman who was to become his wife. *The Adventure of the Dancing Men*, II, 529.

RUSSIA: Holmes's investigation of the tragedy of Yoxley Old Place revealed the multilevel intrigues of the Russian Nihilists of the Order and Brotherhood. *The Adventure of the Golden Pince-Nez*, II, 364ff; see also *The Naval Treaty*, II, 171; *The Adventure of the Second Stain*, I, 321.

RUTLAND ISLAND: In the Andaman Islands. In return for a share of the great Agra treasure, Major John Sholto was to leave there a small yacht provisioned for a sea voyage, for the men bound by the sign of the four. *The Sign of the Four*, I, 684.

RYDER, JAMES ("JEM"): Upper attendant at the Cosmopolitan Hotel, from which the Countess of Morcar's fabulous jewel, the blue carbuncle, was stolen. His goose figured prominently in *The Adventure of the Blue Carbuncle*. *The Adventure of the Blue Carbuncle*, I, 456.

S

SAHARA KING: Ronder's wild beast show had among its exhibits a very fine North African lion named Sahara King. *The Adventure of the Veiled Lodger*, II, 455, 459.

ST. CLAIR, NEVILLE: He disappeared into the wretched beggar Hugh Boone's room at the Bar of Gold opium den. All that was found of him there were his clothes. Holmes then entered the case. St. Clair "had no occupation, but was interested in several companies, and went into town as a rule in the morning, returning by the 5.14 from Cannon Street every night. Mr. St. Clair is now 37 years of age, is a man of temperate habits, a good husband, a very affectionate father, and a man who is popular with all who know him." *The Man with the Twisted Lip*, I, 373, 384.

ST. CLAIR, MRS. NEVILLE: On her return from the Aberdeen Shipping Company, Mrs. St. Clair spied her husband in a second-floor window of the Bar of Gold opium den. When she reached the room, however, he had mysteriously disappeared. *The Man with the Twisted Lip*, I, 374, 378.

ST. GEORGE'S: Church in Hanover Square where Lord St. Simon and Miss Hatty Doran were married. *The Adventure of the Noble Bachelor*, I, 285.

ST. GEORGE'S, THEOLOGICAL COLLEGE OF: Elias Whitney, whose brother Isa was "much addicted to opium," was the principal of the Theological College of St. George's. *The Man with the Twisted Lip*, I, 368.

ST. JAMES'S HALL: Sarasate was playing the violin at St. James's Hall, and Holmes invited Watson to accompany him to the performance. They were "off to violin land, where all is sweetness, and delicacy, and harmony, and there are no red-headed clients to vex us with their conundrums." *The Red-Headed League*, I, 428, 431.

ST. JAMES'S SQUARE: At Holmes's behest, Watson intensively studied Chinese pottery. He obtained a goodly volume upon the subject from the London Library in St. James's Square. *The Adventure of the Illustrious Client*, II, 684.

ST. JAMES'S STREET: In the bow window of a St. James's Street club, Langdale Pike spent his waking hours as "the receiving station, as well as the transmitter, for all the gossip of the Metropolis." *The Adventure of the Three Gables*, II, 728.

ST. JOHN'S WOOD: Irene Adler's residence was Briony Lodge, Serpentine Avenue, St. John's Wood. *A Scandal in Bohemia*, I, 355.

ST. LOUIS: Jefferson Hope, Senior, and John Ferrier had been good friends in St. Louis. *A Study in Scarlet*, I, 205; see also *The Sign of the Four*, I, 612.

ST. LUKE'S, COLLEGE OF: Hilton Soames, who came to Holmes over a very painful problem surrounding the Fortescue Scholarship examination, was a tutor and lecturer at the College of St. Luke's, in one of England's great university towns. *The Adventure of the Three Students*, II, 368.

ST. MONICA, CHURCH OF: It was here, in the Edgware Road, that Godfrey Norton and Irene Adler were married. *A Scandal in Bohemia*, I, 358.

ST. OLIVER'S PRIVATE SCHOOL: In York, it was run for a time by Mr. and Mrs. Vandeleur. *The Hound of the Baskervilles*, II, 95.

ST. PANCRAS CASE: Holmes said: "In the St. Pancras case you may remember that a cap was found beside the dead policeman. The accused man denies that it is his. But he is a picture-frame maker who habitually handles glue." Holmes had positively identified the glue under his microscope. The case was brought to him by Merivale of the Yard. *The Adventure of Shoscombe Old Place*, II, 630.

ST. PANCRAS HOTEL: Hosmer Angel and Mary Sutherland were to be married at St. Saviour's Church, near King's Cross, and later to have their wedding breakfast at the St. Pancras Hotel; but when their cabs pulled up in front of the church, Angel had disappeared. *A Case of Identity*, I, 409.

ST. PETERSBURG, RUSSIA: Enoch Drebber and Joseph Stangerson fled from Jefferson Hope to St. Petersburg. *A Study in Scarlet*, I, 222.

ST. SAVIOUR'S: Hosmer Angel and Mary Sutherland were to be married at St. Saviour's, near King's Cross. *A Case of Identity*, I, 409.

ST. SIMON, LADY CLARA: Sister of Lord Robert St. Simon, whose bride mysteriously disappeared. *The Adventure of the Noble Bachelor*, I, 285.

ST. SIMON, LORD EUSTACE: Younger brother of Lord Robert St. Simon, whose bride mysteriously disappeared. *The Adventure of the Noble Bachelor*, I, 285.

ST. SIMON, LORD ROBERT: Robert Walsingham de Vere St. Simon, second son of the Duke of Balmoral. Born in 1846. Under-Secretary for the Colonies in a late Administration. He sought Holmes's aid to find his bride. *The Adventure of the Noble Bachelor*, I, 287.

ST. VITUS'S DANCE: Old Mr. Farquhar, from whom Watson purchased a medical practice in the Paddington district, had seen the practice decline because of his age and "an affliction of the nature of St. Vitus' dance from which he suffered." *The Stockbroker's Clerk*, II, 153; see also *The Greek Interpreter*, I, 599.

SALTIRE, LORD: Only legitimate son of, and heir to, the Duke of Holdernesse, he disappeared mysteriously from Dr. Huxtable's Priory School. *The Adventure of the Priory School*, II, 608.

SALT LAKE CITY: John Ferrier prospered so much that there were not half a dozen men in the whole of Salt Lake City who could compare with him. *A Study in Scarlet*, I, 204.

SAMSON: Holmes was jubilant over his discovery of "an infallible test for blood stains." He felt it would have been decisive in the case of Samson of New Orleans. *A Study in Scarlet*, I, 151.

SAN FRANCISCO: Aloysius Doran took his daughter there so that she would not marry against his wishes. *The Adventure of the Noble Bachelor*, I, 296.

SAN PAULO: One of the headings in a notebook, containing Stock Exchange securities, found on the floor of Captain Peter Carey's cabin after his bloody death. *The Adventure of Black Peter*, II, 402.

SAN PEDRO: Country in Central America whose colors were green and white. It was ruled by the vicious dictator, Don Juan Murillo, the Tiger of San Pedro, for ten or twelve years. He was deposed in a revolution, but escaped. *The Adventure of Wisteria Lodge*, II, 255.

SAND, GEORGE: Holmes, drifting into ennui after unraveling the mystery surrounding Jabez Wilson's partial unemployment, found solace in Gustave Flaubert's comment to George Sand, *"L'homme c'est rien — l'oeuvre c'est tout* [The man is nothing, the work is everything]." *The Red-Headed League*, I, 438.

SANDEFORD, MR.: He possessed the sixth significant plaster cast of Devine's bust of Napoleon, which Holmes purchased and smashed. *The Adventure of the Six Napoleons*, II, 584.

SANDERS, IKEY: He refused to cut up the stolen Crown diamond for Count Negretto Sylvius. Holmes had his testimony against the Count. *The Adventure of the Mazarin Stone*, II, 741.

SANGER: "One of the greatest showmen of his day," he was the rival of Wombwell and of Ronder. *The Adventure of the Veiled Lodger*, II, 455.

SARASATE, PABLO DE: Sarasate was playing the violin at St. James's Hall, and Holmes invited Watson to accompany him to the performance. *The Red-Headed League*, I, 428, 431.

SAUNDERS: Housemaid at Ridling Thorpe Manor, Norfolk, where Hilton Cubitt was found fatally shot through the heart, and his wife barely alive with a bullet lodged in her brain. The housemaid gave the alarm, after having been aroused from her sleep by the explosion. *The Adventure of the Dancing Men*, II, 536.

SAUNDERS, MRS.: Caretaker of the house in which Nathan Garrideb had his curious apartment, she remained on the premises each day up to four o'clock. *The Adventure of the Three Garridebs*, II, 650, 652.

SAUNDERS, SIR JAMES: A great dermatologist for whom Holmes had once done a professional service. *The Adventure of the Blanched Soldier*, II, 715, 719, 721.

SAVAGE, VICTOR: "A strong, hearty fellow" who surprisingly contracted an out-of-the-way Asiatic disease in the heart of London and died a horrible death. *The Adventure of the Dying Detective*, I, 447.

SAVANNAH: The barque *Lone Star*, commanded by James Calhoun, was out of Savannah, Georgia. *The Five Orange Pips*, I, 402, 403.

SAWYER, MRS.: A person using this name picked up the wedding ring which Holmes had advertised as found in the roadway between the White Hart Tavern and Holland Grove on the night that Enoch J. Drebber was murdered. She appeared to be "a very old and wrinkled woman." *A Study in Scarlet*, I, 181, 183.

SCANDINAVIA, KING OF: The hereditary King of Bohemia's marriage to Clotilde Lothman von Saxe-Meningen, second daughter of the King of Scandinavia, was threatened by a compromising photograph in Irene Adler's possession. *A Scandal in Bohemia*, I, 354; see also *The Adventure of the Noble Bachelor*, I, 287.

SCANDINAVIA, ROYAL FAMILY OF: By the time of *The Final Problem*, Holmes had been of assistance to the Royal Family of Scandinavia, and he hinted to Watson that this had garnered him great financial remuneration. *The Final Problem*, II, 303.

SCANLAN, MIKE: He met Jack McMurdo and later became his roommate. *The Valley of Fear*, I, 527.

SCOTLAND YARD: Holmes sent Watson to Lausanne to see what he could find out concerning the whereabouts of the vanished Lady Frances Carfax. He felt that he could not leave London because "on general principles it is best that I should not leave the country. Scotland Yard feels lonely without me, and it causes an unhealthy excitement among the criminal classes." *The Disappearance of Lady Frances Carfax*, II, 658; see also *The Adventure of the Norwood Builder*, II, 418; *The Adventure of the Lion's Mane*, II, 789; *The Adventure of the Empty House*, II, 349.

SCOTT, J. H.: Bodymaster of Lodge 29, Chicago, of the Ancient Order of Freemen. Jack McMurdo claimed to be a member of that Lodge. *The Valley of Fear*, I, 523.

SCOWRERS: The secret society that terrorized the Vermissa Valley through murder and other harsh methods in an attempt to organize the mineworkers. It exacted a harsh penalty from anyone who violated its oath of secrecy. Jack McMurdo became a member. *The Valley of Fear*, I, *passim*.

SEA UNICORN: The steam sealer commanded by Captain Peter Carey. Peter Cairns berthed aboard it as spare harpooner. In 1883, the ship picked up a man from an abandoned yacht in the North Sea. *The Adventure of Black Peter*, II, 400.

SELDEN: The Notting Hill murderer. Watson writes: "I remembered the case well, for it was one in which Holmes had taken an interest on account of the peculiar ferocity of the crime and the wanton brutality which had marked all the actions of the assassin. The commutation of his death sentence had been due to some doubts as to his complete sanity, so atrocious was his conduct." He escaped from Princetown prison, and later hid on the moor near Baskerville Hall. He died a horrible death at the jaws of the "enormous hound" of the Baskerville legend. *The Hound of the Baskervilles*, II, 39, 66.

SENEGAMBIA: Holmes felt that the murder of Batholomew Sholto was paralleled by cases from India and Senegambia. *The Sign of the Four*, I, 638.

SERGIUS: The real name of the man who gave the name of "Professor Coram" was Sergius. *The Adventure of the Golden Pince-Nez*, II, 352, 364.

SERPENTINE: Lestrade had been dragging the Serpentine for the body of Lady St. Simon (Hatty Doran), who had mysteriously disappeared. *The Adventure of the Noble Bachelor*, I, 292.

SERPENTINE AVENUE: Irene Adler's residence was Briony Lodge, Serpentine Avenue, St. John's Wood. It was in the Serpentine Mews that Holmes, dressed as an unemployed groom, gained the information by which he hoped to obtain the compromising photo of Adler and the hereditary King of Bohemia. It was also in the Avenue, outside the house, that Holmes staged the little play that gained him access to her sitting-room. *A Scandal in Bohemia*, I, 355, 357.

SEVERN: After "passing through the beautiful Stroud Valley and over the broad and gleaming Severn," Holmes and Watson found themselves at Ross, where they were to investigate the facts in the brutal slaying of Charles McCarthy. *The Boscombe Valley Mystery*, II, 140.

SHAFTER, ETTIE: She helped run her father's boarding-house on Sheridan Street in Vermissa, where Jack McMurdo stayed. They fell in love. *The Valley of Fear*, I, 525.

SHAFTER, JACOB: He ran a boarding-house on Sheridan Street in Vermissa. Jack McMurdo stayed there but was asked to leave when he became active in the Ancient Order of Freemen (the Scowrers). *The Valley of Fear*, I, 523.

SHERMAN: A bird-stuffer, who lived at NO. 3 Pinchin Lane, Lambeth. His sleuth-hound, Toby, assisted Holmes in *The Sign of the Four*. *The Sign of the Four*, I, 643.

SHLESSINGER, DR.: Supposedly a missionary from South America who was recuperating at the Englischer Hof in Baden from a disease caught in carrying out his apostolic duties. "He was preparing a map of the Holy Land, with special reference to the kingdom of the Midianites, upon which he was writing a monograph." While at Baden, he made the acquaintance of the Lady Frances Carfax, and he and his supposed wife left in her company for London. His left ear was jagged or torn, which revealed to Holmes his real identity: he was the notorious Holy Peters. *The Disappearance of Lady Frances Carfax*, II, 659, 662.

SHLESSINGER, MRS.: The alias used by Annie Fraser to dupe the Lady Frances Carfax. *The Disappearance of Lady Frances Carfax*, II, 659.

SHOLTO, BARTHOLOMEW: Brother of Thaddeus Sholto, he spent

much time and expense to rediscover the great Agra treasure, which indirectly led to his murder. *The Sign of the Four*, i, 635.

SHOLTO, MAJOR JOHN: Of the 34th Bombay Infantry, retired. He lived at Pondicherry Lodge, Upper Norwood. Once a close friend of Captain Arthur Morstan, who mysteriously disappeared in December, 1878, Sholto's death some four years later was part of a number of sensational events which involved Holmes. *The Sign of the Four*, i, 617, 627.

SHOLTO, THADDEUS: "A small man with a very high head, a bristle of red hair round the fringe of it, and a bald, shining scalp which shot out from among it like a mountain-peak from fir-trees. He writhed his hands together as he stood, and his features were in a perpetual jerk— now smiling, now scowling, but never for an instant in repose. Nature had given him a pendulous lip, and a too visible line of yellow and irregular teeth, which he strove feebly to conceal by constantly passing his hand over the lower part of his face. In spite of his obtrusive baldness, he gave the impression of youth. In point of fact, he had just turned his thirtieth year." His anonymous kindness to, and mysterious summons of, Mary Morstan led to the introduction of Holmes and Watson into the case of *The Sign of the Four*. His house was "an oasis of art in the howling desert of South London." *The Sign of the Four*, i, 624-25.

SHOSCOMBE OLD PLACE: Residence of Sir Robert Norberton and Lady Beatrice Falder, who had the earnings from the estate, in Berkshire. Lady Beatrice held the estate only as a "life interest" which would revert to her late husband's brother, Sir Robert, on her death. *The Adventure of Shoscombe Old Place*, ii, 631.

SHOSCOMBE PRINCE: Racehorse that Sir Robert Norberton ran in the Derby and which won the race. Sir Robert had been taking the Prince's half-brother, who was much slower on the track, out for spins in order to fool the touts. Shoscombe Prince was the favorite of Lady Beatrice Falder, but recently she had been paying him no attention. *The Adventure of Shoscombe Old Place*, ii, 632.

SHOSCOMBE SPANIELS: "You hear of them at every dog show. The most exclusive breed in England. They are the special pride of the lady of Shoscombe Old Place," Lady Beatrice Falder. When Sir Robert Norberton gave away her pet spaniel, it aroused the suspicions of John

Mason, who came to Holmes with the problem. *The Adventure of Shoscombe Old Place*, II, 631.

SHUMAN: He sold his Vermissa Valley ironworks to the West Wilmerton General Mining Company. *The Valley of Fear*, I, 543.

SIAM: With conditions as they were in Siam, it was awkward that Mycroft Holmes should be away from the Foreign Office. But, even so, he came around to Sherlock's rooms to press him for his aid in solving the death of Arthur Cadogan West on the tracks of the London Underground. *The Adventure of the Bruce-Partington Plans*, II, 435.

SIBERIA: After Sergius betrayed his Nihilist comrades in Russia, many of those latter were sent to Siberia to work in the salt mines. *The Adventure of the Golden Pince-Nez*, II, 365.

SIGERSON: After his supposed death at the Reichenbach Fall, Sherlock Holmes traveled for two years in Tibet. His explorations were so remarkable that news of them reached London, but—as Holmes had been posing as a Norwegian named Sigerson—Watson had never known that he was receiving news of the friend he thought dead. *The Adventure of the Empty House*, II, 337.

SILVER BLAZE: Racehorse from Colonel Ross's stable, King's Pyland, who disappeared mysteriously before he ran the Wessex Cup, in which he was heavily favored. His trainer was found murdered. *Silver Blaze*, II, 264.

SILVESTER'S: The Lady Frances Carfax banked at Silvester's. Holmes glanced through her account in an effort to discover any clues as to her whereabouts. "Single ladies must live, and their pass-books are compressed diaries." *The Disappearance of Lady Frances Carfax*, II, 657.

SIMPSON: A "small street Arab," he kept a watch on Henry Wood's lodgings for Sherlock Holmes. *The Crooked Man*, II, 234.

SIMPSON, "BALDY": In the Boer War, Simpson was in the same squadron as Godfrey Emsworth and James Dodd. However, during the morning fight at Buffelsspruit, outside Pretoria, Emsworth, Simpson, and one Anderson had gotten separated from their mates, and the latter two were killed. *The Adventure of the Blanched Soldier*, II, 718.

SIMPSON, FITZROY: He had been arrested upon circumstantial, but convincing, evidence for the murder of Silver Blaze's trainer, John Straker. Simpson "was a man of excellent birth and education, who had squandered a fortune upon the turf, and who lived now by doing a little quiet and genteel bookmaking in the sporting clubs of London." *Silver Blaze*, II, 266, 268.

SIMPSON'S: "When we have finished at the police-station I think that something nutritious at Simpson's would not be out of place," said Holmes to Watson. *The Adventure of the Dying Detective*, I, 450; see also *The Adventure of the Illustrious Client*, II, 675.

SINCLAIR, ADMIRAL: Admiral Sinclair entertained Sir James Walter at the former's house at Barclay Square during the whole of the evening when the theft of the Bruce-Partington plans occurred. *The Adventure of the Bruce-Partington Plans*, II, 436.

SINGH, MAHOMET: A Sikh trooper, he was one of the men bound by the sign of the four. *The Sign of the Four*, I, 676.

SINGLEFORD, LORD: He ran Rasper against Silver Blaze for the Wessex Cup. *Silver Blaze*, II, 278.

SINGLESTICK: In Watson's famous catalogue of "Sherlock Holmes — his limits," he noted that the Great Detective was "an expert singlestick player, boxer, and swordsman," *A Study in Scarlet*, I, 156; see also *The Adventure of the Illustrious Client*, II, 683.

SKIBBAREEN: Holmes, in disguise, gave serious trouble to the constabulary at Skibbareen. *His Last Bow*, II, 801.

SLANEY, ABE: "The most dangerous crook in Chicago," his great love for Elsie Patrick drove him to follow her to England. *The Adventure of the Dancing Men*, II, 542.

SLATER: A stonemason who, while walking from Forest Row about one o'clock in the morning, stopped as he passed Peter Carey's cabin at Woodman's Lee and saw the shadow of a strange man outlined against the light in the window. *The Adventure of Black Peter*, II, 401.

SLOANE, HANS: A noted English collector and benefactor of the seventeenth and eighteenth centuries, he was the exemplar of reclusive collector Nathan Garrideb. *The Adventure of the Three Garridebs*, II, 648.

SMALL, JONATHAN: One of the men bound by the sign of the four, he was responsible for the deaths of Major John Sholto and Bartholomew Sholto. Without seeing him, Holmes correctly deduced that Small was "a poorly educated man, small, active, with his right leg off, and wearing a wooden stump which is worn away upon the inner sole.... He is a middle-aged man, much sunburned, and has been a convict." *The Sign of the Four*, I, 629, 641, 668.

SMITH, CULVERTON: Of 13 Lower Burke Street. A planter and well-known resident of Sumatra, he was unmatched in his knowledge of the tropical disease that appeared to have struck down Sherlock Holmes. *The Adventure of the Dying Detective*, I, 443, 445.

SMITH, JACK: Son of Mordecai Smith of the *Aurora*, he was "a curly-headed lad of six." *The Sign of the Four*, I, 650.

SMITH, JAMES: Deceased father of Violet Smith, "the solitary cyclist of Charlington," he had conducted the orchestra at the old Imperial Theatre. *The Adventure of the Solitary Cyclist*, II, 383–85.

SMITH, JIM: Eldest son of Mr. and Mrs. Mordecai Smith, he accompanied his father on their steam launch, *Aurora*, which had been chartered by Jonathan Small. *The Sign of the Four*, I, 651.

SMITH, JOSEPH: One of the young Mormons who first spoke to John Ferrier identified himself as one of "the persecuted children of God.... We are of those who believe in those sacred writings, drawn in Egyptian letters on plates of beaten gold, which were handed unto the holy Joseph Smith at Palmyra." The migrant Mormon band was led by Brigham Young, who "spoke with the voice of Joseph Smith, which is the voice of God." *A Study in Scarlet*, I, 202.

SMITH, MORDECAI: Of Smith's Wharf. He was the owner of the steam launch *Aurora*, which was hired by Jonathan Small. *The Sign of the Four*, I, 650ff.

SMITH, MRS. MORDECAI: Wife of Mr. Mordecai Smith of the *Aurora*. She shared Holmes's concern over her husband's disappearance. *The Sign of the Four*, I, 650.

SMITH, RALPH: Uncle of Miss Violet Smith, "the solitary cyclist of Charlington," he had gone to Africa twenty-five years prior to the death of James Smith, his brother and Violet's father, and Violet and her mother had never had a word from him since. Thus, they were greatly surprised when, after answering an advertisement in *The Times* inquiring for their whereabouts, they were met by two men who claimed that Ralph Smith's dying wish had been that his sister-in-law and niece should experience no want, if the men could help it. Further, the men, Carruthers and Woodley by name, contended that Violet's Uncle Ralph had died in poverty. *The Adventure of the Solitary Cyclist*, ii, 385ff.

SMITH, MISS VIOLET: "The solitary cyclist of Charlington," she was a "young and beautiful woman, tall, graceful, and queenly, who presented herself at Baker Street late [one] evening and implored [Holmes's] assistance and advice." It seemed that Miss Smith, a music teacher, found herself beset by several persons, the most bizarre of whom was a "middle-aged man, with a short, dark beard" who rode after her whenever she went cycling. Holmes took on her case, even though he believed, at first, that her problem was nothing more than "some secretive lover." He was quick to discern, however, that there was "some deep intrigue going on round" Violet Smith. *The Adventure of the Solitary Cyclist*, ii, 383ff.

SMITH, WILLOUGHBY: The third secretary retained by Professor Coram, Willoughby Smith had "nothing against him either as a boy at Uppingham or as a young man at Cambridge." He was "a decent, quiet, hard-working fellow, with no weak spot in him at all." Thus, there seemed to be "no reason on earth why anyone should wish him harm." Yet Smith had been fatally stabbed in the neck with a small sealing-wax knife. *The Adventure of the Golden Pince-Nez*, ii, 352, 353.

SMITH-MORTIMER: One of the many cases Sherlock Holmes handled in 1894 was the famous Smith-Mortimer succession case. *The Adventure of the Golden Pince-Nez*, ii, 350.

SOAMES, HILTON: Tutor and lecturer at the College of St. Luke's in one of the great university towns, he came to Holmes with a painful problem concerning the Fortescue Scholarship examination. *The Adventure of the Three Students*, ii, 368.

SOAMES, SIR CATHCART: He entrusted his son to Dr. Thorneycroft Huxtable's care at the Priory School in Hallamshire. *The Adventure of the Priory School*, ii, 609.

SOMERTON, DR.: "A fast, sporting young chap," he was the surgeon at the penal colony at Blair Island, where Jonathan Small was imprisoned. His card parties managed to get Major Sholto and Captain Morstan hopelessly in debt. *The Sign of the Four*, I, 682.

SOPHY ANDERSON: "The year '87 furnished us with a long series of cases of greater or less interest, of which I retain the records." One of the cases during the twelve-month period concerned the facts connected with the loss of the British barque *Sophy Anderson*. *The Five Orange Pips*, I, 389.

SOTHEBY'S: Reclusive collector Nathan Garrideb seldom left his room, except to drive down to Sotheby's or Christie's sales rooms. *The Adventure of the Three Garridebs*, II, 648.

SOUTH AFRICA: Sir Charles Baskerville, whose mysterious death prompted an investigation by Sherlock Holmes, had made his fortune in South African speculation before returning to England and retiring to the family estate, Baskerville Hall, in Devonshire. *The Hound of the Baskervilles*, II, II; see also *The Adventure of the Solitary Cyclist*, II, 383, 387, 396; *The Adventure of the Three Students*, II, 381; *The Disappearance of Lady Frances Carfax*, II, 661, 662; *The Adventure of the Blanched Soldier*, II, 707; *The Adventure of the Dancing Men*, II, 527.

SOUTH AMERICA: Selden, the Notting Hill murderer, planned to escape to South America. *The Hound of the Baskervilles*, II, 69; see also *The Cardboard Box*, II, 199; *The Disappearance of Lady Frances Carfax*, II, 659.

SOUTH AUSTRALIA: Mary Fraser was brought up in the free atmosphere of Adelaide, in South Australia. *The Adventure of the Abbey Grange*, II, 493.

SOUTH BRIXTON: Mrs. Merrilow, Eugenia Ronder's landlady, kept her house in South Brixton. *The Adventure of the Veiled Lodger*, II, 454.

SOUTH DOWNS: Watson said, "But you had retired, Holmes. We heard of you as living the life of a hermit among your bees and your books in a small farm upon the South Downs." *His Last Bow*, II, 800.

SOUTHAMPTON: Mr. Fowler and Alice Rucastle were married there by special license on the day after he rescued her from the Copper Beeches. *The Adventure of the Copper Beeches*, II, 132; see also *The Adventure of the Abbey Grange*, II, 502; *The Adventure of the Blanched Soldier*, II, 708.

SOUTHERTON, LORD: The woods that surrounded the Copper Beeches on three sides were part of Lord Southerton's preserves. *The Adventure of the Copper Beeches*, II, 123.

SPAULDING, VINCENT: Pawnbroker Jabez Wilson's eager young assistant, he brought the offer of the Red-Headed League to Wilson's attention. After hearing of some of Spaulding's actions, Holmes did some digging himself, and unearthed the fact that Spaulding was, in reality, the dangerous criminal John Clay. *The Red-Headed League*, I, 427.

SPECKLED BAND, THE: Julia Stoner's last words were: "O, my God! Helen! It was the band! The speckled band!" Helen Stoner speculated to Holmes, "Sometimes I have thought that it was merely the wild talk of delirium, sometimes that it may have referred to some band of people, perhaps to these very gipsies in the plantation. I do not know whether the spotted handkerchiefs which so many of them wear over their heads might have suggested the strange adjective which she used." *The Adventure of the Speckled Band*, I, 243, 248, 249.

SPENCER JOHN GANG, THE: Steve Dixie, Barney Stockdale, and Susan Stockdale were members of this gang, which specialized in assaults, intimidation, and the like. *The Adventure of the Three Gables*, II, 723.

SPENDER, ROSE: Henry Peters and Annie Fraser brought her from the Brixton Workhouse Infirmary to their home, where she died three days later of senile decay. They claimed that she was an old nurse of Annie Fraser's, who posed as Peters's wife. *The Disappearance of Lady Frances Carfax*, II, 667.

SPLUGEN PASS: Holmes was sure that Baron Adelbert Gruner had killed his wife "when the so-called 'accident' happened in the Splügen Pass." *The Adventure of the Illustrious Client*, II, 672.

STACKHURST, HAROLD: His well-known coaching establishment, The Gables, was half a mile from Sherlock Holmes's retirement villa in Sussex. "Stackhurst himself was a well-known rowing Blue [letterman] in his day, and an excellent all-round scholar." He was also the one man in the vicinity who was on such friendly terms with Holmes that they "could drop in on each other in the evenings without an invitation." *The Adventure of the Lion's Mane*, II, 776.

STAMFORD: Dr. John H. Watson, recently invalided home from the second Afghan War, fortuitously ran into young Stamford, his former dresser at Barts, in the Criterion Bar. "The sight of a friendly face in the great wilderness of London is a pleasant thing indeed to a lonely man. In old days Stamford had never been a particular crony of mine, but now I hailed him with enthusiasm, and he, in his turn, appeared delighted to see me." Watson was looking for lodgings cheaper than his hotel room in the Strand, and Stamford introduced him to Sherlock Holmes, who needed someone with whom to share a suite in Baker Street. *A Study in Scarlet,* I, 145, 151.

STAMFORD, ARCHIE: Sherlock Holmes felt that the area near Farnham, on the borders of Surrey, was "a beautiful neighbourhood, and full of the most interesting associations." Prior to *The Adventure of the Solitary Cyclist,* Holmes's most memorable association with Farnham was that it was near there that he and Watson took Archie Stamford, the forger. *The Adventure of the Solitary Cyclist,* II, 384.

STAMFORD'S: Holmes had sent down to Stamford's for an Ordnance map of Devonshire. His spirit had "hung over it all day" as he mentally reconnoitered the scene of the mysterious death of Sir Charles Baskerville. *The Hound of the Baskervilles,* II, 18.

STANGER, JAMES: Outspoken editor of the Vermissa *Herald,* he was beaten by the Scowrers because of his editorial attacks on their Lodge. *The Valley of Fear,* I, 544-45.

STANGERSON, ELDER: One of the four principal Mormon elders, he was assigned the task of teaching Mormonism to John Ferrier by Brigham Young. *A Study in Scarlet,* I, 202, 203.

STANGERSON, JOSEPH: As a Mormon youth, with "a long, pale face," he had vied with Enoch J. Drebber for the hand of Lucy Ferrier. When Lucy and her adoptive father fled their home rather than have her marry either one of these suitors, Stangerson and Drebber, as members of the Avenging Angels, pursued them, and Stangerson shot Lucy's parent. *A Study in Scarlet,* I, *passim.*

STAPHOUSE FAMILY: They were blown up by the Scowrers. *The Valley of Fear,* I, 560.

STAPLES: The "solemn" butler of Mr. Culverton Smith. *The Adventure of the Dying Detective,* I, 445.

STAPLETON, BERYL: Supposed sister of Jack Stapleton, Merripit

House, in Devonshire. She tried to warn Sir Henry Baskerville away from the moor, where he lay under the curse of the Hound of the Baskervilles. He fell in love with her. *The Hound of the Baskervilles*, ii, 49, 106.

STAPLETON, JACK: Of Merripit House, in Devonshire, "he was a small, slim, clean-shaven, prim-faced man, flaxen-haired and lean-jawed, between thirty and forty years of age, dressed in a grey suit and wearing a straw hat." Holmes remarked, "I said it in London, Watson, and I say it again now, that never yet have we helped to hunt down a more dangerous man...." *The Hound of the Baskervilles*, ii, 45, 105.

STARK, COLONEL LYSANDER ("FRITZ"): Of Eyford, in Berkshire. He employed Victor Hatherley to come at an unusual hour for a large fee to repair his hydraulic press. Hatherley then lost his thumb under unusual circumstances, and this brought Sherlock Holmes into the case. *The Adventure of the Engineer's Thumb*, ii, 212.

STARR, DR. LYSANDER: When speaking to a man who claimed to have been "in the law at Topeka," Sherlock Holmes mentioned that he used to have a correspondent in that city, "old Dr. Lysander Starr, who was Mayor in 1890." The supposed lawyer replied that Dr. Starr's "name [was] still honoured" — a very revealing comment in light of the fact that Holmes "never knew a Dr. Lysander Starr of Topeka." *The Adventure of the Three Garridebs*, ii, 645, 646.

STATE AND MERTON COUNTY RAILROAD COMPANY: Ran the railroad that went through the Vermissa Valley, and owned several mines there. *The Valley of Fear*, i, 542.

STAUNTON, ARTHUR H.: The volume of Sherlock Holmes's commonplace book devoted to persons and things whose names began with the letter S was a "mine of varied information." One of the persons therein was "Arthur H. Staunton, the rising young forger." *The Adventure of the Missing Three-Quarter*, ii, 476.

STAUNTON, GODFREY: "The crack three-quarter, Cambridge, Blackheath, and five Internationals," Staunton was "the hinge that the whole [Cambridge rugger] team [turned] on." Accordingly, when Staunton mysteriously vanished just before Cambridge's important match with Oxford, his team's captain, Cyril Overton, rushed to Scotland Yard, and then to Sherlock Holmes, hoping that Staunton could be retrieved in time to play. Owing to such obstacles as Staunton's uncle, the parsimonious Lord Mount-James, and a certain Dr. Leslie Armstrong of Cambridge, Holmes failed to find the star athlete within the prescribed time; and in turn, Cambridge lost the match — a "defeat...entirely attributed to the unfortunate absence of the crack International, Godfrey Staunton, whose want was felt at every instant of the game." Eventually, however, the detective discovered both Staunton and the reason the athlete had abandoned his teammates in their moment of need. *The Adventure of the Missing Three-Quarter*, II, *passim*.

STAUNTON, HENRY: The volume of Sherlock Holmes's commonplace book devoted to persons and things whose names began with the letter *S* was a "mine of varied information." One of the persons therein was "Henry Staunton, whom [Holmes] helped to hang." *The Adventure of the Missing Three-Quarter*, II, 476.

STEILER, PETER, THE ELDER: He managed the Englischer Hof in Meiringen, where Holmes and Watson put up on May 3, 1891. He was "an intelligent man, and spoke excellent English, having served for three years as waiter at the Grosvenor Hotel in London. At his advice, upon the afternoon of the 4th we set off together with the intention of crossing the hills and spending the night at the Hamlet of Rosenlaui," by way of the Fall of Reichenbach. *The Final Problem*, II, 312.

STEINER: An agent of the German spy Von Bork, he was captured before World War I. *His Last Bow*, II, 798.

STENDALS, THE: Murdered by the Scowrers. *The Valley of Fear*, I, 560.

STEPHENS: Butler at Shoscombe Old Place. He and the head trainer, John Mason, observed the strange actions of Sir Robert Norberton. Mason sought out Holmes's aid. *The Adventure of Shoscombe Old Place*, II, 633.

STEPNEY: Gelder & Co., which had supplied both Morse Hudson and Harding Brothers with their plaster casts of the head of Napoleon, was located in Church Street, Stepney. It was "a river-side city of a hundred thousand souls, where the tenement houses swelter and reek with the outcasts of Europe." *The Adventure of the Six Napoleons*, II, 578, 579.

STERNDALE, DR. LEON: The great lion-hunter and explorer had a huge body, a "craggy and deeply-seamed face with...fierce eyes and hawk-like nose," grizzled hair, and a beard which was "golden at the fringes and white near the lips, save for the nicotine stain from his perpetual cigar." On his Cornish mother's side, he could be called cousin to the Tregennis family. He had spent so much of his life outside the law that he had "come at last to be a law to" himself. *The Adventure of the Devil's Foot*, II, 515ff.

STEVENS, BERT: A "terrible murderer" who had wanted Holmes and Watson to get him off in '87, his name was recalled by Holmes when Watson made the dangerous argument that a man's appearance could be used as a valid determinant of his innocence or guilt. Watson quickly recognized the weakness of his argument when Holmes reminded him that Bert Stevens had been a most "mild-mannered, Sunday-school young man." *The Adventure of the Norwood Builder*, II, 424.

STEVENSON: One of the two men on the Cambridge varsity rugger team who was being considered as a replacement for Godfrey Staunton, the crack three-quarter. *The Adventure of the Missing Three-Quarter*, II, 476–77.

STEWART, JANE: Housemaid at Lachine, the Barclays' villa in Aldershot, she overheard the argument which took place between Colonel Barclay and his wife shortly before he was found dead, and she unconscious, in their locked morning-room. *The Crooked Man*, II, 228.

STEWART, MRS.: A resident of Lauder, she had been killed in 1887. Holmes was sure Colonel Sebastian Moran was at the bottom of it; "but nothing could be proved." *The Adventure of the Empty House*, II, 347.

STIMSON & CO.: Undertakers, of the Kennington Road. Henry Peters and Annie Fraser hired them to carry out the funeral of Rose Spender. *The Disappearance of Lady Frances Carfax*, II, 667.

STOCKDALE, BARNEY: Steve Dixie's boss in the Spencer John gang. *The Adventure of the Three Gables*, II, 723.

STOCKDALE, SUSAN: A maid at Mrs. Maberley's home, The Three Gables, and a member of the Spencer John gang, she was also the wife of Barney Stockdale. *The Adventure of the Three Gables*, II, 725.

STOKE MORAN: Site of the ancestral home of the Roylotts, in western Surrey. *The Adventure of the Speckled Band*, I, 253.

STONE, REV. JOSHUA: His large house, Nether Walsling, lay near

Aloysius Garcia's Wisteria Lodge, in Surrey. *The Adventure of Wisteria Lodge*, II, 246.

STONER, HELEN: Daughter of Major-General and Mrs. Stoner, she consulted Holmes in *The Adventure of the Speckled Band*, when she feared that she would suffer the same horrible fate as her twin sister. *The Adventure of the Speckled Band*, I, 244.

STONER, JULIA: The twin sister of Helen Stoner, she died under mysterious circumstances in 1881. Her last words were: "O, my God! Helen! It was the band! The speckled band!" *The Adventure of the Speckled Band*, I, 248.

STONER, MAJOR-GENERAL: Of the Bengal Artillery, he died in India, leaving a young widow and two infant daughters. *The Adventure of the Speckled Band*, I, 245.

STONER, MRS.: Widow of Major-General Stoner, she married Dr. Grimesby Roylott. She had had twin daughters, Helen and Julia, by her first marriage. Helen said, "When Dr. Roylott was in India he married my mother, Mrs. Stoner, the young widow of Major-General Stoner, of the Bengal Artillery. My sister Julia and I were twins, and we were only two years old at the time of my mother's re-marriage.... Shortly after our return to England my mother died — she was killed eight years ago in a railway accident near Crewe." *The Adventure of the Speckled Band*, I, 245-46.

STOPER, MISS: She managed Westaway's employment agency for governesses in the West End, to which Miss Violet Hunter applied. *The Adventure of the Copper Beeches*, II, 116.

STRADIVARIUS: "We had a pleasant little meal together, during which Holmes would talk about nothing but violins, narrating with great exultation how he had purchased his Stradivarius, which was worth at least five hundred guineas, at a Jew broker's in Tottenham Court Road for fifty-five shillings." *The Cardboard Box*, II, 200; see also *A Study in Scarlet*, I, 166; *The Sign of the Four*, I, 662.

STRAKER, JOHN: The trainer of the racehorse Silver Blaze, at Colonel Ross's King's Pyland, in Dartmoor. Straker was found horribly murdered, his head shattered by a savage blow. He was "a retired jockey, who rode in Colonel Ross's colours before he became too heavy for the weighing chair. He has served the Colonel for five years as jockey, and for seven as trainer, and has always shown himself to be a zealous and honest servant." *Silver Blaze*, ii, 264.

STRAKER, MRS.: Wife of Silver Blaze's trainer, who had been found dead on the moor. *Silver Blaze*, ii, 272.

STRAND, THE: Dr. John H. Watson, upon his return to London, "that great cesspool," after being invalided home during the second Afghan War, "stayed for some time at a private hotel in the Strand, leading a comfortless, meaningless existence, and spending such money as I had, considerably more freely than I ought." *A Study in Scarlet*, i, 145, 169; *The Red-Headed League*, i, 430; *The Resident Patient*, i, 267; *The Final Problem*, ii, 307; *The Adventure of the Missing Three-Quarter*, ii, 475, 477.

STRASBOURG: After spending two days in Brussels, Holmes and Watson pushed on to Strasbourg. There, Holmes received word that, although Professor Moriarty's gang had been rounded up in London, the evil genius himself had escaped the police. Almost immediately, Holmes and Watson left for Geneva. *The Final Problem*, ii, 310.

STRAUBENZEE: An arms manufacturer who lived in the Minories. He had made the air-gun — "a pretty bit of work, as I understand" — which Count Negretto Sylvius used in an attempt to persuade Holmes to stay off the case of the stolen Crown diamond. *The Adventure of the Mazarin Stone*, ii, 738.

STRAUSS, HERMAN: Jack McMurdo thought that the murderers Lawler and Andrews might be after Strauss. *The Valley of Fear*, i, 556.

STREATHAM: The southern suburb of London where Fairbank, the modest residence of the great financier, Alexander Holder, was located. *The Adventure of the Beryl Coronet*, ii, 286.

SUDBURY: A student at Harold Stackhurst's well-known coaching establishment, The Gables, he was one of the persons who discovered the carcass of Fitzroy McPherson's Airedale terrier on the very edge of the pool where its master had received a killing blow. *The Adventure of the Lion's Mane*, ii, 776, 784.

SUMATRA: Holmes apparently contracted a coolie disease from Sumatra in *The Adventure of the Dying Detective*. Culverton Smith, who also appears in that tale, was a well-known resident of that island. *The Adventure of the Dying Detective*, i, 440, 443.

SUMNER: A shipping agent in the Ratcliff Highway. Captain Basil (Sherlock Holmes in disguise) had sent for three harpooners to report to him at Baker Street from Sumner's office. *The Adventure of Black Peter*, II, 408.

SUNG DYNASTY: During the research into Chinese pottery he had undertaken at Holmes's request, Watson learned of the glories of the primitive period of the Sung and the Yüan dynasties. *The Adventure of the Illustrious Client*, II, 684.

SURREY: Holmes possessed a ravenous appetite upon his return to Baker Street after his investigation of the missing naval treaty, for he had just "breathed thirty miles of Surrey air." *The Naval Treaty*, II, 189; see also *The Man with the Twisted Lip*, I, 378; *The Adventure of the Speckled Band*, I, 243; *The Adventure of the Solitary Cyclist*, II, 383, 384, 392; *The Adventure of the Retired Colourman*, II, 553.

SURREY CONSTABULARY: Inspector Baynes, whom Holmes thought would rise high in his profession, was a member of the Surrey Constabulary. *The Adventure of Wisteria Lodge*, II, 240.

SUSSEX: Sherlock Holmes retired to a little home in Sussex, where he gave himself "up entirely to that soothing life of Nature for which [he] had so often yearned during the long years spent amid the gloom of London.... My villa is situated upon the southern slope of the Downs, commanding a great view of the Channel." Also, Holmes characterized Anderson, the constable of the neighboring village, as being of "solid Sussex breed — a breed which covers much good sense under a heavy, silent exterior." *The Adventure of the Lion's Mane*, II, 776, 779; see also *The Five Orange Pips*, I, 392; *The Adventure of the Sussex Vampire*, II, 463; *The Musgrave Ritual*, I, 126; *The Adventure of the Second Stain*, I, 301.

SUTHERLAND, MISS MARY: She came to Holmes with the perplexing problem of the disappearance of her husband-to-be, Mr. Hosmer Angel, almost on the church steps. Holmes felt that "there was never any mystery in the matter, though, as I said yesterday, some of the details are of interest." *A Case of Identity*, I, 406, 411, 413, 416.

SUTRO, MR.: Mrs. Mary Maberley's lawyer. *The Adventure of the Three Gables*, II, 725, 729.

SUTTON: A member of the Worthingdon bank gang. They made away with seven thousand pounds from the Worthingdon bank in 1875, but the bank's caretaker was murdered. Sutton turned state's evidence when they were arrested, and thus secured the execution of one of the gang, Cartwright, and fifteen years for the rest. *The Resident Patient*, I, 279.

SWAIN, JOHN: Elias Openshaw's notebook for March, 1869, read, "7th. Set the pips on McCauley, Paramore, and Swain of St. Augustine .... 10th. John Swain cleared." *The Five Orange Pips*, I, 397.

SWINDON: On their way to Ross to investigate the facts surrounding the death of Charles McCarthy, Holmes and Watson's train stopped at Swindon for lunch. *The Boscombe Valley Mystery*, II, 140.

SWINDON, ARCHIE: He sold out and left the Vermissa Valley rather than pay protection money to the Scowrers. *The Valley of Fear*, I, 542.

SWITZERLAND: On their Continental journey, Holmes and Watson made their way at their leisure into Switzerland, via Luxembourg and Basel. *The Final Problem*, II, 310.

SWORDS: In Watson's famous catalogue of "Sherlock Holmes — his limits," he noted that the Great Detective was "an expert singlestick player, boxer, and swordsman." *A Study in Scarlet*, I, 156.

SYDENHAM: The Lewisham gang of robbers, the Randalls, pulled a job at Sydenham a fortnight before the brutal slaying of Sir Eustace Brackenstall of which they were suspected. Captain Jack Croker, of the *Bass Rock*, lived in Sydenham. *The Adventure of the Abbey Grange*, II, 492, 502.

SYLVIUS, COUNT NEGRETTO: He had stolen the great Crown diamond and hoped to persuade Holmes to stay out of the case — which led to his own undoing. Holmes respected his bravery, though: "A man of nerve. Possibly you have heard of his reputation as a shooter of big game. It would indeed be a triumphant ending to his excellent sporting records if he added me to his bag." *The Adventure of the Mazarin Stone*, II, 738, 739.

T

TANGEY: Commissionaire at the Foreign Office. On the night that the top-secret naval treaty disappeared from Percy Phelps's office there, Tangey had been asleep at his post—a shameful dereliction of duty by an old soldier who had been in the Coldstream Guards. *The Naval Treaty*, II, 177.

TANGEY, MRS.: The commissionaire's wife, she did the cleaning at the Foreign Office. The night that the top-secret naval treaty disappeared from Percy Phelps's office, she had taken his order for coffee and then left quickly for home. A policeman had recognized her shortly thereafter as a tall and elderly woman with a Paisley shawl. *The Naval Treaty*, II, 172, 174, 181.

TANKERVILLE CLUB: One of Colonel Sebastian Moran's clubs. *The Adventure of the Empty House*, II, 347.

TANKERVILLE CLUB SCANDAL: John Openshaw had heard of Holmes from Major Prendergast, whom Holmes had saved in the Tankerville Club Scandal. Prendergast was wrongfully accused of cheating at cards. *The Five Orange Pips*, I, 392.

TAPANULI FEVER: Said Holmes to Watson, "What do you know, pray, of Tapanuli fever? What do you know of the black Formosa corruption?"

"I have never heard of either," replied the good Doctor. *The Adventure of the Dying Detective*, I, 441.

TARLETON MURDERS: One of Holmes's untold cases. *The Musgrave Ritual*, I, 124.

TARLTON, SUSAN: A maid at Yoxley Old Place, she was "the only person who [could] say anything positive" about the immediate circumstances surrounding the murder of Willoughby Smith. *The Adventure of the Golden Pince-Nez*, II, 352, 353.

TAVERNIER: The French modeler who made the wax image of Holmes which was used to fool Count Negretto Sylvius. *The Adventure of the Mazarin Stone*, II, 739.

TAVISTOCK: It was there that Inspector Gregory and Colonel Ross met

Holmes and Watson's train. They proceeded to the King's Pyland stables to investigate the disappearance of the racehorse, Silver Blaze, and the death of his trainer, John Straker. A cluster of small villas about a half a mile to the north of the stables had been built by a Tavistock contractor for the use of invalids and others who wished to enjoy the pure Dartmoor air. The city itself lay two miles to the west of King's Pyland. *Silver Blaze*, ii, 264, 269.

TEDDY: Henry Wood's pet mongoose, whom he had trained to catch a defanged cobra to entertain the soldiers nightly in their canteens. *The Crooked Man*, ii, 237.

TERAI: Young Victor Trevor, heartbroken over the disclosures of his father, went out to the Terai tea planting, where Holmes had heard that he was doing well. *The "Gloria Scott"*, i, 122.

THOR BRIDGE: Maria Pinto Gibson, the wife of Neil Gibson, the Gold King, was found shot to death on Thor Bridge on their Hampshire estate. "This bridge — a single broad span of stone with balustraded sides — carries the drive over the narrowest part of a long, deep, reed-girt sheet of water. Thor Mere it is called. In the mouth of the bridge lay the dead woman." *The Problem of Thor Bridge*, ii, 591.

THOR PLACE: Neil Gibson's Hampshire estate. *The Problem of Thor Bridge*, ii, 597.

THOREAU, HENRY DAVID: "Circumstantial evidence is occasionally very convincing, as when you find a trout in milk, to quote Thoreau's example," said Holmes. *The Adventure of the Noble Bachelor*, i, 291.

THORSLEY: James Mortimer, who sought Holmes's aid in *The Hound of the Baskervilles*, was Medical Officer for the parishes of Grimpen, Thorsley, and High Barrow. *The Hound of the Baskervilles*, ii, 5.

THREADNEEDLE STREET: A little distance down Threadneedle Street, where there was a small angle in the wall, the wretched beggar Hugh Boone took his daily post. *The Man with the Twisted Lip*, i, 376; see also *The Adventure of the Beryl Coronet*, ii, 283.

THREE GABLES, THE: Mrs. Mary Maberley's residence in Harrow Weald. It was "a brick and timber villa, standing in its own acre of undeveloped grassland. Three small projections above the upper windows made a feeble attempt to justify its name. Behind was a grove of melancholy, half-grown pines, and the whole aspect of the place was poor and depressing." *The Adventure of the Three Gables*, ii, 724.

THREE MONTHS IN THE JUNGLE: One of Colonel Sebastian Moran's publications was *Three Months in the Jungle*, 1884. *The Adventure of the Empty House*, ii, 346.

THROGMORTON STREET: James M. Dodd's card showed Sherlock Holmes that Dodd was "a stockbroker from Throgmorton Street." *The Adventure of the Blanched Soldier*, ii, 708.

THUCYDIDES: A chapter of Thucydides was to be given as the first examination paper in the competition for the Fortescue Scholarship. *The Adventure of the Three Students*, ii, 369.

THURSTON: Watson's billiards partner at his club, Thurston offered to share his option on some South African securities with Watson. *The Adventure of the Dancing Men*, ii, 528.

TIBET: Knowing that two of the most dangerous members of the Moriarty gang were still at liberty following his supposed death at the Reichenbach Fall (and that they knew he was still alive), Sherlock Holmes traveled for two years in Tibet and amused himself by visiting Lhassa and spending some days with the "head Llama." *The Adventure of the Empty House*, ii, 337.

TIMES, THE: It was in *The Times* that Violet Smith and her mother saw an advertisement inquiring about their whereabouts. As they were very poor then, they became quite excited, for they thought that someone had left them a fortune. *The Adventure of the Solitary Cyclist*, ii, 385.

TIRED CAPTAIN, THE ADVENTURE OF THE: One of the cases which took place in the July preceding Watson's marriage, and in which he "had the privilege of being associated with Sherlock Holmes, and of studying his methods." *The Naval Treaty*, ii, 167.

TIRES: Holmes was familiar with forty-two different impressions left by tires. This knowledge was instrumental in solving the mysterious disappearance of a young lord. *The Adventure of the Priory School*, ii, 617.

TOBACCO: Holmes, outlining his faults to Watson upon their first meeting, asked, "You don't mind the smell of strong tobacco, I hope."
"I always smoke 'ship's' myself," replied Watson. *A Study in Scarlet*, i,

151; see also *The Hound of the Baskervilles*, II, 18; *The Adventure of the Mazarin Stone*, II, 737.

TOBIN: The caretaker in "the great Worthingdon bank business" who lost his life. *The Resident Patient*, I, 279.

TOBY: Mr. Sherman's sleuth-hound, who assisted Holmes in trailing the murderers of Bartholomew Sholto. "Toby proved to be an ugly, long-haired, lop-eared creature, half spaniel and half lurcher, brown and white in colour, with a very clumsy, waddling gait." *The Sign of the Four*, I, 644.

TODMAN: Sold his Vermissa Valley mine to the State and Merton County Railroad Company. *The Valley of Fear*, I, 542

TOLLER: Groom at the Copper Beeches in Hampshire, he was the only person in the household who could handle the savage mastiff, Carlo. *The Adventure of the Copper Beeches*, II, 124.

TOLLER, MRS.: A servant at the Copper Beeches in Hampshire. *The Adventure of the Copper Beeches*, II, 124.

TONGA: The Andaman Islander who was the loyal companion of Jonathan Small, who had once saved his life. *The Sign of the Four*, I, 667.

TOPEKA: The man who claimed to be John Garrideb also claimed to have been "in the law at Topeka." What's more, when Sherlock Holmes mentioned "old Dr. Lysander Starr, who was Mayor [of Topeka] in 1890," the man claimed that Starr's name was "still honoured" in the town. That last claim convinced Holmes that the man was not what he said he was, for Holmes "never knew a Dr. Lysander Starr of Topeka." *The Adventure of the Three Garridebs*, II, 645, 646.

TORQUAY TERRACE: Madame Charpentier's boarding-house, where the late Enoch J. Drebber had stayed, was in Torquay Terrace, Camberwell. *A Study in Scarlet*, I, 184.

TORRINGTON LODGE: Situated in the London suburb of Blackheath, it was the residence which John Hector McFarlane, accused murderer of Jonas Oldacre, shared with his parents. *The Adventure of the Norwood Builder*, II, 417.

TOSCA, CARDINAL: The year 1895 contained a number of memorable cases, one of which was Holmes's "famous investigation of the sudden death of Cardinal Tosca — an inquiry which was carried out by him at the express desire of his Holiness the Pope...." *The Adventure of Black Peter*, II, 398.

TOTTENHAM COURT ROAD: The late Mr. Sutherland had his plumber's business in Tottenham Court Road. *A Case of Identity*, I, 407; see also *The Cardboard Box*, II, 200; *The Adventure of the Red Circle*, II, 695.

TRAFALGAR SQUARE: John Clayton picked up a fare in Trafalgar Square who paid him to shadow two men, Sir Henry Baskerville and Dr. James Mortimer. *The Hound of the Baskervilles*, II, 34; see also *The Adventure of the Noble Bachelor*, I, 293.

TRANSYLVANIA: Holmes had an entry under "Vampires in Transylvania" in his great index volume. *The Adventure of the Sussex Vampire*, II, 463.

TREDANNICK WARTHA: The house of the Tregennis family, it was situated outside the Cornish hamlet of Tredannick Wollas, "near the old stone cross upon the moor." *The Adventure of the Devil's Foot*, II, 510, 513.

TREDANNICK WOLLAS: The Cornish hamlet nearest the small cottage to which, in the spring of 1897, Sherlock Holmes had adjourned for "a complete change of scene and air." *The Adventure of the Devil's Foot*, II, 508, 509.

TREGELLIS, JANET: Daughter of the head gamekeeper at Hurlstone, the ancestral home of a branch of the Musgrave family, in Western Sussex, she was the last lover of the butler, Richard Brunton. *The Musgrave Ritual*, I, 128.

TREGENNIS, BRENDA: Found dead of fright the morning after she had played cards with her three brothers, she "had been a very beautiful girl, though [at the time of her death] verging upon middle age. Her dark, clear-cut face was handsome, even in death, but there [yet] lingered upon it something of that last convulsion of horror which had been her last human condition." *The Adventure of the Devil's Foot*, II, 513.

TREGENNIS, GEORGE: On a certain spring evening in 1897, he sat down, "in excellent health and spirits," to play cards with his brothers and sister. On the following morning, however, he and his brother Owen were found "laughing, shouting, and singing, the senses stricken clean out of them," while their sister lay dead. His face was "an expression of the utmost horror — a convulsion of terror which was dreadful to look upon." Shortly thereafter, George and Owen were removed to the Helston asylum. *The Adventure of the Devil's Foot*, 11, 510ff.

TREGENNIS, MORTIMER: "An independent gentleman" who rented rooms from the vicar of the parish centered in the Cornish hamlet of Tredannick Wollas, he was said to be "a sad-faced, introspective man ...brooding apparently upon his own affairs." Mortimer certainly had reason to be "sad-faced," for his sister had been killed and his two brothers driven insane. *The Adventure of the Devil's Foot*, 11, 510, 511.

TREGENNIS, OWEN: On a certain spring evening in 1897, he sat down, "in excellent health and spirits," to play cards with his brothers and sister. On the morning following, however, he and his brother George were found "laughing, shouting, and singing, the senses stricken clean out of them," while their sister lay dead. Upon his face, at that time, was "an expression of the utmost horror—a convulsion of terror which was dreadful to look upon." Shortly thereafter, Owen and George were removed to the Helston asylum. *The Adventure of the Devil's Foot*, 11, 510ff.

TREPOFF: At the time of *A Scandal in Bohemia*, Watson had from time to time heard some vague account of Holmes's doings, such as his summons to Odessa in the case of the Trepoff murder. *A Scandal in Bohemia*, 1, 347.

TREVELYAN, DR. PERCY: Of 403 Brook Street, he graduated from London University, occupied a research position at King's College Hospital, and won the Bruce Pinkerton Prize and Medal for his monograph on obscure nervous lesions. He came into a windfall in the person of a Mr. Blessington, who set him up in the Brook Street practice in return for three quarters of his earnings, his care, and rooms on the premises. Nevertheless, Mr. Blessington's strange behavior impelled Trevelyan to seek Holmes's advice. *The Resident Patient*, 1, 268, 269.

TREVOR, JUSTICE OF THE PEACE: Victor Trevor's father, he had been a pugilist, traveler, and gold digger. "Trevor senior was a widower. ... He was a man of little culture, but with a considerable amount of rude strength both physically and mentally. He knew hardly any books, but he had travelled far, had seen much of the world, and had remembered all that he had learned." In his younger days, he had had a checkered career, which came back to haunt him in the person of one Hudson. *The "Gloria Scott"*, 1, 108, 114.

TREVOR, VICTOR: The only friend Sherlock Holmes had made during his two years at college. His bull-terrier froze itself to Holmes's ankle one morning, and thus began the friendship. His invitation to Holmes to come down to his father's place at Donnithorpe, in Norfolk, involved Holmes in his first case. When the truth surrounding the case was fully disclosed, Trevor was heartbroken over the facts concerning his father, and went out to the Terai tea planting, where Holmes heard that he was doing well. *The "Gloria Scott"*, I, 107, 108, 122.

TRICHINOPOLY: Holmes reasoned that the murderer of Enoch J. Drebber had smoked a Trichinopoly cigar. "I gathered up some scattered ash from the floor. It was dark in colour and flakey — such an ash as is only made by a Trichinopoly. I have made a special study of cigar ashes — in fact, I have written a monograph upon the subject. I flatter myself that I can distinguish at a glance the ash of any known brand either of cigar or of tobacco." *A Study in Scarlet*, I, 173; see also *The Sign of the Four*, I, 612.

TRINCOMALEE: At the time of *A Scandal in Bohemia*, Watson had, from time to time, heard some vague account of Holmes's doings, such as his clearing up of the singular tragedy of the Atkinson brothers at Trincomalee. *A Scandal in Bohemia*, I, 347.

TRINITY COLLEGE: One of the colleges of Cambridge University, it was the residence of Jeremy Dixon, owner of the canine "detective" Pompey. Pompey worked in collaboration with Sherlock Holmes to discover the whereabouts of Godfrey Staunton, the missing star of Cambridge University's rugger team. Cyril Overton, who sent Holmes the inscrutable telegram that involved him in the case, was also of Trinity College. *The Adventure of the Missing Three-Quarter*, II, 475, 487, 488.

TRIPLE ALLIANCE (GERMANY, AUSTRIA-HUNGARY, ITALY): The naval treaty which disappeared from the unfortunate Percy Phelps's office "defined the position of Great Britain towards the Triple Alliance, and foreshadowed the policy this country would pursue in the event of the French fleet gaining a complete ascendency over that of Italy in the Mediterranean." *The Naval Treaty*, II, 172.

TRUMPINGTON: A village, south of Cambridge, where Sherlock Holmes finally found Godfrey Staunton, the missing star of Cambridge University's rugger team. *The Adventure of the Missing Three-Quarter*, ii, 487, 488.

TUNBRIDGE WELLS: After pinning Peter Carey to the wall of his cabin like a beetle on a card, the culprit walked ten miles to Tunbridge Wells, and there caught a train to London. *The Adventure of Black Peter*, ii, 412.

TURKEY, SULTAN OF: Holmes "had a commission from the Sultan of Turkey which called for immediate action, as political consequences of the gravest kind might [have arisen] from its neglect." *The Adventure of the Blanched Soldier*, ii, 715.

TURKISH BATH: Watson admitted that both he and Holmes had a weakness for the Turkish bath. "It was over a smoke in the pleasant lassitude of the drying-room that I have found him less reticent and more human than anywhere else." They lay together on two couches in the Northumberland Avenue establishment at the opening of one adventure. *The Adventure of the Illustrious Client*, ii, 671; see also *The Disappearance of Lady Frances Carfax*, ii, 656.

TURNER, ALICE: The daughter of John Turner, of Boscombe Valley Estate. James McCarthy had refused to propose to her, although there was an obvious attraction between the two young people. When James was arrested for the murder of his father, Alice felt that he was innocent and retained Inspector Lestrade to find out the truth. Lestrade consulted Holmes when the case seemed hopeless to him. *The Boscombe Valley Mystery*, ii, 140.

TURNER, JOHN: He had made his fortune in Australia and retired to the Boscombe Valley area, in Herefordshire, where he was found murdered. He let a farm on his estate to his old acquaintance, Charles McCarthy. In his younger days, he was known as Black Jack of Ballarat. *The Boscombe Valley Mystery*, ii, 135, 146, 149.

TURNER, MRS.: She appeared as Holmes's landlady during his battle of wits with Irene Adler. "When Mrs. Turner has brought in the tray I will make it clear to you." *A Scandal in Bohemia*, i, 361.

TUSON, SERGEANT: Of London's City Police. His alertness foiled the Beddingtons' daring robbery of Mawson & Williams'. *The Stockbroker's Clerk*, ii, 165–66.

TUXBURY OLD PARK: The Emsworth family's residence, near Bedford. *The Adventure of the Blanched Soldier*, ii, 709.

TYPE: "The detection of types is one of the most elementary branches of knowledge to the special expert in crime, though I confess that once when I was very young I confused the *Leeds Mercury* with the *Western Morning News*." Holmes correctly identified the letters of the warning message sent to Sir Henry Baskerville, as having been cut from a *Times* article. *The Hound of the Baskervilles*, II, 22–23.

TYPEWRITER: The typewriter provided a number of clues in Holmes's solution of the disappearance of Miss Mary Sutherland's fiancé on the way to their wedding. "It is a curious thing that a typewriter has really quite as much individuality as a man's handwriting. Unless they are quite new, no two of them write exactly alike. Some letters get more worn than others and some wear only on one side.... I think of writing another little monograph some of these days on the typewriter and its relation to crime. It is a subject to which I have devoted some little attention." *A Case of Identity*, I, 414.

U

UBANGI: Dr. Leon Sterndale had obtained his specimen of *radix pedis diaboli* in the Ubangi country of Central Africa. *The Adventure of the Devil's Foot*, II, 524.

UFFA: "The year of '87 furnished us with a long series of cases of greater or less interest, of which I retain the records." One of the cases during this twelve-month period concerned the singular adventures of the Grice Patersons in the island of Uffa. *The Five Orange Pips*, I, 389.

UNDERGROUND, THE: Arthur Cadogan West's dead body was discovered by a platelayer named Mason just outside Aldgate Station on the Underground system in London. *The Adventure of the Bruce-Partington Plans*, II, 434; see also *A Study in Scarlet*, I, 160; *The Red-Headed League*, I, 428.

UNDERWOOD, JOHN: The hat found beside the dead body of Enoch J. Drebber was made by John Underwood and Sons, 129 Camberwell Road. *A Study in Scarlet*, I, 187.

"UPON THE DISTINCTION BETWEEN THE ASHES OF THE VARIOUS TOBACCOS": Holmes told Watson, "I have been guilty of several monographs. They are all upon technical subjects. Here, for example, is one 'Upon the Distinction Between the Ashes of the Various Tobaccos.' In it I enumerate a hundred and forty forms of cigar, cigarette, and pipe tobacco, with coloured plates illustrating the difference in the ash. It is a point which is continually turning up in criminal trials, and which is sometimes of supreme importance as a clue." *The Sign of the Four*, I, 612.

"UPON THE POLYPHONIC MOTETS OF LASSUS": The day before the crucial denouement of the recovery of the stolen submarine plans, Holmes "lost himself in a monograph which he had undertaken upon the Polyphonic Motets of Lassus....which has since been printed for private circulation, and is said by experts to be the last word upon the subject." *The Adventure of the Bruce-Partington Plans*, II, 449, 452.

UPPER NORWOOD: Major Sholto's estate, Pondicherry Lodge, was situated there. *The Sign of the Four*, I, 617.

UPPER SWANDAM LANE: Site of the Bar of Gold opium den, where Watson once discovered both Isa Whitney and Sherlock Holmes. *The Man with the Twisted Lip*, I, 369.

UPPINGHAM: An ancient public school in Rutlandshire, it had been attended by Willoughby Smith prior to his going on to Cambridge. At both those institutions, Smith had had "nothing against him." *The Adventure of the Golden Pince-Nez*, II, 353.

UPWOOD, COLONEL: The full explanation of the adventure of *The Hound of the Baskervilles* had to wait until Holmes had concluded two cases "of the utmost importance." In the first, "he had exposed the atrocious conduct of Colonel Upwood in connection with the famous card scandal of the Nonpareil Club." *The Hound of the Baskervilles*, II, 105.

UTAH: There was not one of the Mormon band "who did not sink upon his knees in heartfelt prayer when they saw the broad valley of Utah bathed in the sunlight beneath them, and learned from the lips of their leader that this was the promised land, and that these virgin acres were to be theirs evermore." *A Study in Scarlet*, I, 203.

UTRECHT: The death of Enoch J. Drebber reminded Holmes "of the circumstances attendant on the death of Van Jansen in Utrecht, in the year '34," for, though no wound appeared on the body, great gouts and splashes of blood lay all around. *A Study in Scarlet*, I, 168.

V

v. r.: The initials of Queen Victoria (Victoria Regina). Watson said, "I have always held...that pistol practice should distinctly be an open-air pastime; and when Holmes in one of his queer humours would sit in an arm-chair, with his hair-trigger and a hundred Boxer cartridges, and proceed to adorn the opposite wall with a patriotic V. R. done in bullet-pocks, I felt strongly that neither the atmosphere nor the appearance of our room was improved by it." *The Musgrave Ritual*, I, 123.

vamberry: The case of Vamberry, the wine merchant, was one of Holmes's untold tales. *The Musgrave Ritual*, I, 124.

vampires: Sherlock Holmes's index contained "the record of old cases, mixed with the accumulated information of a lifetime." The great index volume devoted to the letter *V* was especially interesting: one of its items concerned "Vampires in Transylvania," another "Vampirism in Hungary." *The Adventure of the Sussex Vampire*, II, 463.

van deher: Sold his Vermissa Valley ironworks to the West Wilmerton General Mining Company. *The Valley of Fear*, I, 543.

van jansen: The death of Enoch J. Drebber reminded Holmes "of the circumstances attendant on the death of Van Jansen in Utrecht, in the year '34," for, though no wound appeared on the body, great gouts and splashes of blood lay all around. *A Study in Scarlet*, I, 168.

van seddar: Count Negretto Sylvius felt that Holmes knew nothing about Van Seddar, who was to convey the stolen Crown diamond to Amsterdam. *The Adventure of the Mazarin Stone*, II, 744.

van shorst: Apparently murdered by the Scowrers in the Vermissa Valley. *The Valley of Fear*, I, 528.

VANDELEUR: Assumed name of Rodger and Beryl Baskerville when they ran a school in the east of Yorkshire. Mr. Vandeleur had a great interest in entomology, and "the name of Vandeleur had been permanently attached to a certain moth which he had, in his Yorkshire days, been the first to describe." *The Hound of the Baskervilles*, II, 106, 107.

VANDERBILT AND THE YEGGMAN: Sherlock Holmes's "good old index" contained "the record of old cases, mixed with the accumulated information of a lifetime." The volume devoted to the letter *V* was especially interesting: one of its items concerned "Vanderbilt and the Yeggman." *The Adventure of the Sussex Vampire*, II, 463.

VATICAN CAMEOS: Holmes had been preoccupied with the little affair of the Vatican cameos at the time of the newspaper reports of the mysterious death of Sir Charles Baskerville. Thus, he had not followed up on the Baskerville case immediately. *The Hound of the Baskervilles*, II, 12.

VENNER & MATHESON: A well-known engineering firm of Greenwich. Victor Hatherley had been apprenticed to them for seven years and had picked up considerable experience before he went into business for himself. *The Adventure of the Engineer's Thumb*, II, 212.

VENOMOUS LIZARD OR GILA: Sherlock Holmes's "good old index" contained "the record of old cases, mixed with the accumulated information of a lifetime." The volume devoted to *V* was especially interesting: one of its items concerned a "venomous lizard or gila" which had featured in a case which Holmes thought "remarkable." *The Adventure of the Sussex Vampire*, II, 463.

VENUCCI, LUCRETIA: Maid of the Princess of Colonna, she had been suspected of stealing the famous black pearl of the Borgias from the princess's bedroom at the Dacre Hotel. *The Adventure of the Six Napoleons*, II, 586.

VENUCCI, PIETRO: "One of the greatest cut-throats in London," Venucci was from Naples and had ties with the Mafia. He was found brutally murdered on the doorstep of Horace Harker's residence. *The Adventure of the Six Napoleons*, II, 576, 581.

VERE STREET: As Holmes walked down Vere Street, a brick came down from the roof of one of the houses, and was shattered to fragments at his feet. This was the second of Professor Moriarty's promised attacks upon Holmes's life. *The Final Problem*, II, 306.

VERMISSA: The central township which lies at the head of the Vermissa Valley, known for its coal and iron production. *The Valley of Fear*, I, 521.

VERNER: Following his epic struggle with Professor Moriarty above the Reichenbach Fall and his subsequent travels, Sherlock Holmes returned to his lodgings on Baker Street. After he had been back for some months, he asked that Watson sell his small Kensington practice and return to share the old quarters. Watson was astounded when a young doctor named Verner purchased his practice, giving "with astonishingly little demur the highest price that [Watson] ventured to ask — an incident which only explained itself some years later, when [Watson] found that Verner was a distant relative of Holmes, and that it was [his] friend who had really found the money." *The Adventure of the Norwood Builder*, II, 414.

VERNET, EMILE JEAN HORACE: A distinguished French artist, his sister was the grandmother of Sherlock Holmes, who felt that his own faculty for observation and his facility for deduction were inherited through the Vernet line, for "art in the blood is liable to take the strangest forms." *The Greek Interpreter*, I, 590.

VERNON LODGE: Near Kingston, residence of the notorious Baron Adelbert Gruner. *The Adventure of the Illustrious Client*, II, 674, 686.

VIBART, JULES: The fiancé of Marie Devine, he connected the sudden departure of her mistress, the Lady Frances Carfax, "with the visit to the hotel a day or two before of a tall, dark, bearded man." *The Disappearance of Lady Frances Carfax*, II, 658.

VICTORIA STATION: The train on which Holmes, Watson, and Colonel Ross were returning, after the successful conclusion of *Silver Blaze*, arrived in London at Victoria Station. *Silver Blaze*, II, 281; see also *The Adventure of the Sussex Vampire*, II, 467.

VICTORIA STREET: Victor Hatherley, hydraulic engineer, had his office at 16A Victoria Street. He came to Watson with one thumb cut off. *The Adventure of the Engineer's Thumb*, II, 210.

VIE DE BOHEME: As Holmes went out to pursue the elusive Mrs. Sawyer, Watson passed the time "skipping over the pages of Henri Murger's *Vie de Bohème*." *A Study in Scarlet*, I, 182.

VIGOR: Sherlock Holmes's "good old index" contained "the record of old cases, mixed with the accumulated information of a lifetime." The volume devoted to the letter *V* was especially interesting: one of its items concerned "Vigor, the Hammersmith wonder." *The Adventure of the Sussex Vampire*, ii, 463.

VIOLIN: In Watson's famous catalogue of "Sherlock Holmes—his limits," he noted that the Great Detective played "the violin well," although he also had other things to say about his newly acquired companion's skills on that instrument: "These were very remarkable, but as eccentric as all his other accomplishments. That he could play pieces, and difficult pieces, I knew well, because at my request he has played me some of Mendelssohn's Lieder, and other favourites. When left to himself, however, he would seldom produce any music or attempt any recognized air. Leaning back in his arm-chair of an evening, he would close his eyes and scrape carelessly at the fiddle which was thrown across his knee. Sometimes the chords were sonorous and melancholy. Occasionally they were fantastic and cheerful. Clearly they reflected the thoughts which possessed him, but whether the music aided those thoughts, or whether the playing was simply the result of a whim or fancy, was more than I could determine. I might have rebelled against these exasperating solos had it not been that he usually terminated them by playing in quick succession a whole series of my favorite airs as a slight compensation for the trial upon my patience." *A Study in Scarlet*, i, 156, 158; see also *The Sign of the Four*, i, 655; *The Red-Headed League*, i, 431; *The Adventure of the Illustrious Client*, ii, 675.

VIPERS: Sherlock Holmes's "good old index" contained "the record of old cases, mixed with the accumulated information of a lifetime." The volume devoted to the letter *V* was especially interesting: one of its items concerned "vipers." *The Adventure of the Sussex Vampire*, ii, 463.

VITTORIA: Another item under the heading *V* in Sherlock Holmes's "good old index" concerned "Vittoria, the circus belle." *The Adventure of the Sussex Vampire*, ii, 463.

VIXEN TOR: "The sun was already sinking when I reached the summit of the hill, and the long slopes beneath me were all golden-green on one side and grey shadow on the other. A haze lay upon the farthest skyline, out of which jutted the fantastic shapes of Belliver and Vixen Tor." This was the setting in which Watson sought the hidden lair of the mysterious man on the tor. *The Hound of the Baskervilles*, ii, 80.

VON BISCHOFF: Holmes was jubilant over his discovery of "an infallible test for blood stains." Said he, "There was the case of Von Bischoff at Frankfort last year. He would certainly have been hung had this test been in existence." *A Study in Scarlet*, I, 150, 151.

VON BORK: A German agent whom Holmes beat in a battle of wits just preceding the First World War. He was "a man who could hardly be matched among all the devoted agents of the Kaiser. It was his talents which had first recommended him for the English mission, the most important mission of all, but since he had taken it over, those talents had become more and more manifest to the half-dozen people in the world who were really in touch with the truth." Von Bork gathered his information under the guise of a sportsman, associating with British officers and Cabinet Ministers. Although Von Bork was a spy, his English servant, Martha, thought that "according to his lights he [had] been a kind master." Before Holmes became involved with him, he had had dealings with Von Bork's cousin and uncle. *His Last Bow*, II, 792, 793, 800, 802.

VON HERDER: "The blind German mechanic, who constructed [a powerful air-gun] to the order of...Professor Moriarty." The air-gun, "noiseless and of tremendous power," fired soft revolver bullets. *The Adventure of the Empty House*, II, 331, 344.

VON HERLING, BARON: Chief Secretary of the German legation in London, he was privy to the operations in England of the German spy, Von Bork. *His Last Bow*, II, 792.

VON KRAMM, COUNT: The hereditary King of Bohemia, Wilhelm Gottsreich Sigismond von Ormstein, came to Holmes disguised as the Count von Kramm, a Bohemian nobleman. *A Scandal in Bohemia*, I, 352.

VON ORMSTEIN, WILHELM GOTTSREICH SIGISMOND, GRAND DUKE OF CASSEL-FALSTEIN, AND HEREDITARY KING OF BOHEMIA: He had become romantically involved with Irene Adler at an early date. Now that his marriage was approaching, he sought to recover a compromising photograph which she refused to give up. Von Ormstein sought Holmes's aid in recovering the photo. *A Scandal in Bohemia*, I, 351-52.

VON SAXE-MENINGEN, CLOTILDE LOTHMAN: The hereditary King

of Bohemia's marriage to Clotilde Lothman von Saxe-Meningen, second daughter of the King of Scandinavia, was threatened by a compromising photograph in Irene Adler's possession. *A Scandal in Bohemia*, I, 354.

VON WALDBAUM, FRITZ: Watson retained an almost verbatim report of Holmes's interview with Monsieur Dubuque, of the Paris police, and Fritz von Waldbaum, the well-known specialist of Danzig, in the matter of the Adventure of the Second Stain. *The Naval Treaty*, II, 167.

VOODOOISM AND THE NEGROID RELIGIONS: Written by Eckermann. Holmes spent a morning in the British Museum reading it in order to determine the significance of the torn bird, the pail of blood, and the charred bones found in the "weird kitchen" of Wisteria Lodge. *The Adventure of Wisteria Lodge*, II, 259.

W

WAGNER, RICHARD: Sherlock Holmes so enjoyed the musical compositions of this German composer that, at the conclusion of *The Adventure of the Red Circle*, he asked Watson to join him at a Wagner night at Covent Garden, even though he knew that they had already missed the first act. *The Adventure of the Red Circle*, II, 704.

WAINWRIGHT: "A complex mind," said Holmes of the notorious Baron Adelbert Gruner. "All great criminals have that. My old friend Charlie Peace was a violin virtuoso. Wainwright was no mean artist. I could quote many more." *The Adventure of the Illustrious Client*, II, 675.

WALDRON: Rodger Prescott, "the greatest counterfeiter London [had ever seen]," used this alias to rent the rooms later occupied by Nathan Garrideb. A tall, dark man with a beard, Prescott was shot to death in 1895, and Waldron was remembered as "a tall, bearded man with very dark features" who had suddenly vanished at exactly the same time of Prescott's death. *The Adventure of the Three Garridebs*, II, 652, 654.

WALES: The Duke of Holdernesse had mineral holdings in Wales and sometimes resided at Carston Castle, Bangor, Wales. *The Adventure of the Priory School*, II, 608; see also *The Adventure of the Missing Three-Quarter*, II, 476.

WALKER BROTHERS: Sent in a hundred dollars to the Scowrers for protection, but five hundred was demanded. *The Valley of Fear*, I, 542.

WALLINGTON: Sarah Cushing lived in New Street, Wallington. *The Cardboard Box*, II, 200.

WALSALL: "As to Miss Violet Hunter, my friend Holmes, rather to my disappointment, manifested no further interest in her when once she had ceased to be the centre of one of his problems, and she is now the head of a private school at Walsall, where I believe that she has met with considerable success." *The Adventure of the Copper Beeches*, II, 132.

WALTER, COLONEL VALENTINE: The younger brother of Sir James Walter, he was a very tall, handsome, light-bearded man of fifty whose "wild eyes, stained cheeks, and unkempt hair" all spoke of the sorrow he felt at his brother's death. *The Adventure of the Bruce-Partington Plans*, II, 441.

WALTER, SIR JAMES: The actual official guardian of the stolen Bruce-Partington submarine plans, he was a famous Government expert whose "decorations and sub-titles [filled] two lines of a book of reference." One of the two men who had a key to the safe in which the precious plans were kept, he was so proud that it broke his heart to think of the thief's identity. *The Adventure of the Bruce-Partington Plans*, II, 436.

WALTERS, CONSTABLE: The policeman in the Surrey Constabulary who was left in possession of Wisteria Lodge, the house of the recently murdered Aloysius Garcia. *The Adventure of Wisteria Lodge*, II, 247.

WANDSWORTH COMMON: Mr. Melas, after his strange, late-night experience with Harold Latimer, was let off from a closed carriage at Wandsworth Common. *The Greek Interpreter*, I, 600.

WARBURTON, COLONEL: Watson was instrumental in introducing two cases to Sherlock Holmes, that of Mr. Hatherley's thumb and that of Colonel Warburton's madness. "Of these the latter may have afforded a finer field for an acute and original observer...." *The Adventure of the Engineer's Thumb*, II, 209.

WARDLAW, COLONEL: Ran Pugilist for the Wessex Cup against Silver Blaze. *Silver Blaze*, II, 278.

WARNER, JOHN: Ex-gardener of High Gable, who had been "sacked in a moment of temper by his imperious employer," Mr. Henderson. Holmes used Warner to gain information concerning the staff and layout of the establishment. Warner was also responsible for rescuing Miss Burnett from her employer. *The Adventure of Wisteria Lodge*, II, 253.

WARREN, MR.: A timekeeper at Morton & Waylight's, in Tottenham Court Road, he was the husband of the woman who complained to Sherlock Holmes about the unusual habits of one of their lodgers. Even though the husband was as nervous over it as his wife, he quickly became the more nervous "when two men came up behind him, threw a coat over his head, and bundled him into a cab that was beside the kerb," finally tossing him out onto Hampstead Heath. *The Adventure of the Red Circle*, II, 695.

WARREN, MRS.: A landlady, she brought her problem to Holmes because he had arranged an affair for a lodger of hers the year previous. Although the detective rebuffed her initially, Mrs. Warren drew upon "the pertinacity, and also the cunning, of her sex" in order to get Holmes to take her case. It is doubtful that the detective realized at the outset, however, that Mrs. Warren's uneasiness about the unusual activities of one of her lodgers would lead Holmes to the murder of "a devil and a monster." *The Adventure of the Red Circle*, II, 691ff.

WARRENDER, MISS MINNIE: Holmes had all the facts concerning the life history of Miss Minnie Warrender in a squat notebook. *The Adventure of the Mazarin Stone*, II, 741.

WARSAW: During a visit to Warsaw, the King of Bohemia made the acquaintance of Irene Adler, onetime prima donna of the Imperial Opera there. *A Scandal in Bohemia*, I, 353, 354.

WATERBEACH: One of the villages on the north side of Cambridge, it had been "explored, and...[found] disappointing" by Sherlock Holmes in his search for Godfrey Staunton. *The Adventure of the Missing Three-Quarter*, II, 487.

WATERLOO BRIDGE: Jefferson Hope trailed Enoch Drebber's cab "across Waterloo Bridge and through miles of streets, until, to my astonishment, we found ourselves back in the terrace in which he had boarded." *A Study in Scarlet*, i, 226; see also *The Five Orange Pips*, i, 398, 401.

WATERLOO STATION: John Openshaw intended to return to his Horsham estate from Waterloo Station, but instead he met his death near Waterloo Bridge. *The Five Orange Pips*, i, 398, 401; see also *The Crooked Man*, ii, 225; *The Naval Treaty*, ii, 169; *The Hound of the Baskervilles*, ii, 34; *The Adventure of the Solitary Cyclist*, ii, 388.

W[ATSON]., H.: Holmes deduced a number of remarkable things concerning Dr. Watson's elder brother from their father's watch, which had been in the elder brother's possession for some time, but which now belonged to Holmes's companion. "He was a man of untidy habits — very untidy and careless. He was left with good prospects, but he threw away his chances, lived for some time in poverty with occasional short intervals of prosperity, and, finally, taking to drink, he died. That is all I can gather." *The Sign of the Four*, i, 614.

[WATSON], JAMES: Kate Whitney had come to seek Mrs. Watson's aid, for her husband was "much addicted to opium," and had not been home for two days. Mrs. Watson offered, "Should you rather that I sent James off to bed?" Dr. John H. Watson went out looking for the errant man, knowing — one hopes — why his wife had called him "James" instead of "John," or, perhaps, who the other individual in the Watson family was. *The Man with the Twisted Lip*, i, 369.

WATSON, JOHN H., M.D.; BIOGRAPHY: "In the year 1878 I took my degree of Doctor of Medicine of the University of London, and proceeded to Netley to go through the course prescribed for surgeons in the army. Having completed my studies there, I was duly attached to the Fifth Northumberland Fusiliers as Assistant Surgeon. The regiment was stationed in India at the time, and before I could join it, the second Afghan War had broken out. On landing at Bombay, I learned that my corps had advanced through the passes, and was already deep in the enemy's country. I followed, however, with many other officers who were in the same situation as myself, and succeeded in reaching Candahar in safety, where I found my regiment, and at once entered upon my new duties.

"The campaign brought honours and promotion to many, but for me it had nothing but misfortune and disaster. I was removed from my brigade and attached to the Berkshires, with whom I served at the fatal battle of Maiwand. There I was struck on the shoulder by a Jezail bullet, which shattered the bone and grazed the subclavian artery. I should have fallen into the hands of the murderous Ghazis had it not been for the devotion and courage shown by Murray, my orderly, who threw me across a packhorse, and succeeded in bringing me safely to the British lines.

"Worn with pain, and weak from the prolonged hardships which I had undergone, I was removed, with a great train of wounded sufferers, to the base hospital at Peshawur. Here I rallied, and had already improved so far as to be able to walk about the wards, and even to bask a little upon the verandah, when I was struck down by enteric fever, that curse of our Indian possessions. For months my life was despaired of, and when at last I came to myself and became convalescent, I was so weak and emaciated that a medical board determined that not a day should be lost in sending me back to England. I was despatched, accordingly, in the troopship *Orontes*, and landed a month later on Portsmouth jetty, with my health irretrievably ruined, but with permission from a paternal government to spend the next nine months in attempting to improve it.

"I had neither kith nor kin in England, and was therefore as free as air — or as free as an income of eleven shillings and sixpence a day will permit a man to be. Under such circumstances I naturally gravitated to London, that great cesspool into which all the loungers and idlers of the Empire are irresistibly drained. There I stayed for some time at a private hotel in the Strand, leading a comfortless, meaningless existence, and spending such money as I had, considerably more freely than I ought. So alarming did the state of my finances become, that I soon realized that I must either leave the metropolis and rusticate somewhere in the country, or that I must make a complete alteration in my style of living. Choosing the latter alternative, I began by making up my mind to leave the hotel, and to take up my quarters in some less pretentious and less expensive domicile.

"On the very day that I had come to this conclusion, I was standing at the Criterion Bar, when someone tapped me on the shoulder, and turning round I recognized young Stamford, who had been a dresser under me at Barts. The sight of a friendly face in the great wilderness of London is a pleasant thing indeed to a lonely man. In old days Stamford had never been a particular crony of mine, but now I hailed him with enthusiasm, and he, in his turn, appeared to be delighted to see me. In the exuberance of my joy, I asked him to lunch with me at the Holborn, and we started off together in a hansom.

"'Whatever have you been doing with yourself, Watson?' he asked in undisguised wonder, as we rattled through the crowded London streets. 'You are as thin as a lath and as brown as a nut.'

"I gave him a short sketch of my adventures, and had hardly concluded it by the time that we reached our destination.

"'Poor devil!' he said commiseratingly, after he had listened to my misfortunes. 'What are you up to now?'

"'Looking for lodgings,' I answered. 'Trying to solve the problem as to whether it is possible to get comfortable rooms at a reasonable price.'

"'That's a strange thing,' remarked my companion, 'you are the second man today that has used that expression to me.'

"'And who was the first?' I asked.

"'A fellow who is working at the chemical laboratory up at the hospital. He was bemoaning himself this morning because he could not get someone to go halves with him in some nice rooms which he had found, and which were too much for his purse.'

"'By Jove!' I cried; 'if he really wants someone to share the rooms and the expense, I am the very man for him. I should prefer having a partner to being alone.'

"'Young Stamford looked rather strangely at me over his wine-glass. 'You don't know Sherlock Holmes yet,' he said; 'perhaps you would not care for him as a constant companion.'" *A Study in Scarlet*, I, 143-48.

Dr. Watson identified himself, in his conversation with Dr. Percy Trevelyan, as "a retired Army surgeon." *The Resident Patient*, I, 268.

During his school days, Watson had been "intimately associated with a lad named Percy Phelps, who was of much the same age as myself, though he was two classes ahead of me." "Tadpole" Phelps had been in the fifth form when Watson was in the third. *The Naval Treaty*, II, 167, 168.

In some manner, Holmes, during his wanderings after his supposed death above the Fall of Reichenbach, had learned of Dr. Watson's "sad bereavement, and his sympathy was shown in his manner rather than in his words. 'Work is the best antidote to sorrow, my dear Watson,' said he, 'and I have a piece of work for us both to-night which, if we can bring it to a successful conclusion, will in itself justify a man's life on this planet.'" *The Adventure of the Empty House*, II, 337.

At the time of his work for Holmes in *His Last Bow*, Watson was about to join the war effort in his "old service." *His Last Bow*, II, 803.

Dr. Watson was living in his own rooms in Queen Anne Street at the time of *The Adventure of the Illustrious Client*. *The Adventure of the Illustrious Client*, II, 672.

Watson had played rugby for Blackheath when Big Bob Ferguson was three-quarter for Richmond. In one of their athletic confrontations, Ferguson threw Watson "over the ropes into the crowd at the Old Deer Park." *The Adventure of the Sussex Vampire*, II, 465.

Sir Robert Norberton lived at Shoscombe Old Place, in Berkshire, and Watson "knew it well, for my summer quarters were down there once." Later, Holmes asked his friend, "By the way, Watson, you know something of racing?"

"I ought to. I pay for it with about half my wound pension." *The Adventure of Shoscombe Old Place*, II, 630.

WATSON, JOHN H., M.D.; AS AUTHOR: "I know, my dear Watson, that you share my love of all that is bizarre and outside the conventions and humdrum routine of everyday life. You have shown your relish for it by the enthusiasm which has prompted you to chronicle, and, if you will excuse my saying so, somewhat to embellish so many of my own little adventures."

"Your cases have indeed been of the greatest interest to me," Watson observed. *The Red-Headed League*, I, 418.

Mycroft Holmes greeted Dr. Watson upon their first meeting, "'I'm glad to meet you, sir,' said he, putting out a broad, flat hand, like the flipper of a seal. 'I hear of Sherlock everywhere since you became his chronicler.'" *The Greek Interpreter*, I, 594.

Stanley Hopkins had figured in seven of Holmes's cases, and these all were chronicled by Dr. Watson. Holmes admitted to Watson that "you have some power of selection which atones for much which I deplore in your narratives. Your fatal habit of looking at everything from the point of view of a story instead of as a scientific exercise has ruined what might have been an instructive and even classical series of demonstrations. You slur over work of the utmost finesse and delicacy in order to dwell upon sensational details which may excite but cannot possibly instruct the reader." *The Adventure of the Abbey Grange*, II, 491.

Dr. Watson had intended *The Adventure of the Abbey Grange* to be the last of the exploits of Sherlock Holmes that he would narrate. "This resolution of mine was not due to any lack of material, since I have notes of many hundreds of cases to which I have never alluded, nor was it caused by any waning interest on the part of my readers in the singular personality and unique methods of this remarkable man. The real reason lay in the reluctance which Mr. Holmes has shown to the continued publication of his experiences." *The Adventure of the Second Stain*, I, 301.

"Somewhere in the vaults of the bank of Cox & Co., at Charing Cross, there is a travel-worn and battered tin dispatch-box with my name, John H. Watson, M.D., Late Indian Army, painted upon the lid. It is crammed with papers, nearly all of which are records of cases to illustrate the curious problems which Mr. Sherlock Holmes had at various times to examine." *The Problem of Thor Bridge*, II, 588.

"When one considers that Mr. Sherlock Holmes was in active practice for twenty-three years, and that during seventeen of these I was allowed to co-operate with him and to keep notes of his doings, it will be clear that I have a mass of material at my command. The problem has always been, not to find, but to choose. There is the long row of year-books which fill a shelf, and there are the dispatch-cases filled with documents, a perfect quarry for the student, not only of crime, but of the social and official scandals of the late Victorian era." *The Adventure of the Veiled Lodger*, II, 453.

WATSON, JOHN H., M.D.; DETECTIVE POWERS: Holmes commented on Watson's impression of Miss Mary Sutherland, who had just paid them a visit at 221B Baker Street: "'Pon my word, Watson, you are coming along wonderfully. You have really done very well indeed. It is true that you have missed everything of importance, but you have hit upon the method, and you have a quick eye for colour. Never trust to general impressions, my boy, but concentrate yourself upon details." *A Case of Identity*, I, 411.

Even though he thought Holmes had perished in the thundering Fall of Reichenbach, Watson kept alive his memory by his own interest in crime. "It can be imagined that my close intimacy with Sherlock Holmes had interested me deeply in crime, and that after his disappearance I never failed to read with care the various problems which came before the public, and I even attempted more than once for my own private satisfaction to employ his methods in their solution, though with indifferent success." *The Adventure of the Empty House*, II, 329.

According to Holmes, Watson had some remarkable characteristics. Indeed, Holmes thought Watson "an ideal helpmate" because, to the latter, each development came as a perpetual surprise, and the future was always a closed book. *The Adventure of the Blanched Soldier*, II, 707.

Holmes said, "The same old Watson! You never learn that the gravest issues may depend upon the smallest things." *The Adventure of the Creeping Man*, II, 752.

WATSON, JOHN H., M.D.; HIS HABITS: Holmes and Watson outlined their mutual faults, upon their first meeting. Holmes queried, "What have you to confess now? It's just as well for two fellows to know the worst of one another before they begin to live together."

"I keep a bull pup," Watson replied, "and I object to rows, because my nerves are shaken, and I get up at all sorts of ungodly hours, and I am extremely lazy. I have another set of vices when I'm well, but those are the principal ones at present." *A Study in Scarlet*, I, 151.

Dr. Watson was somewhat piqued with Holmes's personal sloppiness on the winter's night that the Great Detective sidetracked him with the story of *The Musgrave Ritual*. "Not that I am in the least conventional in that respect myself," claimed Watson. "The rough-and-tumble work in Afghanistan, coming on top of a natural Bohemianism of disposition, has made me rather more lax than befits a medical man. But with me there is a limit...." *The Musgrave Ritual*, I, 123.

Holmes said to Watson, "Hum! you still smoke the Arcadia mixture of your bachelor days, then! There's no mistaking that fluffy ash upon your coat. It's easy to tell that you've been accustomed to wear a uniform, Watson; you'll never pass as a pure-bred civilian as long as you keep that habit of carrying your handkerchief in your sleeve." *The Crooked Man*, II, 225.

In their running pursuit of Violet Smith's empty dog-cart, Watson's "sedentary life began to tell upon me, and I was compelled to fall behind." *The Adventure of the Solitary Cyclist*, II, 392.

Watson claimed that he never broke his word of honor in his life. *The Adventure of Charles Augustus Milverton*, II, 564.

Though Sherlock Holmes was expert in many subjects, he sometimes trusted Watson's opinion above his own in matters relating to women, saying "the fair sex is [Watson's] department." *The Adventure of the Second Stain*, I, 310.

Watson, in his latter years, posed as the chauffeur of the Irish-American spy, Altamont. At that time, Watson appeared as a "heavily built, elderly man, with a grey moustache." *His Last Bow*, II, 796.

Holmes said, "Good old Watson! You are the one fixed point in a changing age." *His Last Bow*, II, 803.

WATSON, JOHN H., M.D.; MEDICAL PRACTICE: Watson thought he could join Holmes in an afternoon outing to St. James's Hall to hear Sarasate, for he had "nothing to do today. My practice is never very absorbing." *The Red-Headed League*, I, 428.

Watson prefaced *The Adventure of the Engineer's Thumb* with these remarks: "It was in the summer of '89, not long after my marriage, that the events occurred which I am now about to summarize. I had returned to civil practice, and had finally abandoned Holmes in his Baker Street rooms, although I continually visited him, and occasionally even persuaded him to forgo his Bohemian habits so far as to come and visit us. My practice had steadily increased, and as I happened to live at no very great distance from Paddington Station, I got a few patients from among the officials." *The Adventure of the Engineer's Thumb*, II, 209.

"At the time of which I speak, Holmes had been back for some months, and I, at his request, had sold my practice and returned to share the old quarters in Baker Street. A young doctor, named Verner, had purchased my small Kensington practice, and given with astonishingly little demur the highest price that I ventured to ask — an incident which only explained itself some years later, when I found that Verner was a distant relation of Holmes, and that it was my friend who had really found the money." *The Adventure of the Norwood Builder*, II, 414.

When Watson traveled with Holmes to Camford to investigate the strange case of Professor Presbury, their sudden departure caused "frantic planning and hurrying on [Watson's] part, as my practice was by this time not inconsiderable." It was September of 1903. *The Adventure of the Creeping Man*, II, 758.

WATSON, JOHN H., M.D.; AND SHERLOCK HOLMES: Inviting Watson to join him in the investigation of the strange disappearance of Neville St. Clair, Holmes said, "Oh, a trusty comrade is always of use. And a chronicler still more so." Later, in the same case, Holmes again complimented his old friend, by saying, "You have a grand gift of silence, Watson. It makes you quite invaluable as a companion." *The Man with the Twisted Lip*, I, 372, 373.

Watson "had no keener pleasure than in following Holmes in his professional investigations, and in admiring the rapid deductions, as swift as intuitions, and yet always founded on a logical basis, with which he unravelled the problems which were submitted to him." *The Adventure of the Speckled Band*, I, 244.

Watson wrote, "It may be remembered that after my marriage, and my subsequent start in private practice, the very intimate relations which had existed between Holmes and myself became to some extent modified. He still came to me from time to time when he desired a companion in his investigations, but these occasions grew more and more seldom, until I find that in the year 1890 there were only three cases of which I retain any record." *The Final Problem*, II, 301.

"It was on a bitterly cold and frosty morning during the winter of '97 that I was wakened by a tugging at my shoulder. It was Holmes. The candle in his hand shone upon his eager, stooping face, and told me at a glance that something was amiss.

"'Come, Watson, come!' he cried. 'The game is afoot. Not a word! Into your clothes and come!'" *The Adventure of the Abbey Grange*, II, 491.

All his "years of humble but single-minded service culminated in that moment of revelation" when Holmes exclaimed, "You're not hurt, Watson? For God's sake, say that you are not hurt" by Killer Evans's near-fatal shot. *The Adventure of the Three Garridebs*, II, 653.

"It was one Sunday evening early in September of the year 1903 that I received one of Holmes's laconic messages: 'Come at once if convenient—if inconvenient come all the same.—s.h..' The relations between us in those latter days were peculiar. He was a man of habits, narrow and concentrated habits, and I had become one of them. As an institution I was like the violin, the shag tobacco, the old black pipe, the index books, and others perhaps less excusable. When it was a case of active work and a comrade was needed upon whose nerve he could place some reliance, my rôle was obvious. But apart from this I had uses. I was a whetstone for his mind. I stimulated him. He liked to think aloud in my presence. His remarks could hardly be said to be made to me — many of them would have been as appropriately addressed to his bed-stead — but none the less, having formed the habit, it had become in some way helpful that I should register and interject. If I irritated him by a certain methodical slowness in my mentality, that irritation served only to make his own flame-like intuitions and impressions flash up the more vividly and swiftly. Such was my humble rôle in our alliance." *The Adventure of the Creeping Man*, ii, 751.

During the time of Holmes's Sussex retirement, the good Doctor Watson had passed almost entirely beyond the ken of the Great Detective. "An occasional week-end visit was the most I ever saw of him." Thus, Holmes had to act as his own chronicler in some of the adventures of his retirement. *The Adventure of the Lion's Mane*, ii, 776.

WATSON, JOHN H., M.D.; MARRIAGE:
Watson had seen little of Holmes at the time of *A Scandal in Bohemia*. "My marriage had drifted us away from each other. My own complete happiness, and the home-centred interests which rise up around the man who first finds himself master of his own establishment, were sufficient to absorb all my attention...." Later, Holmes amazed Watson with some simple deductions concerning his friend's new state of life: "'Wedlock suits you,' he remarked. 'I think, Watson, that you have put on seven and a half pounds since I saw you.'

"'Seven,' I answered.

"'Indeed, I should have thought a little more. Just a trifle more, I fancy, Watson. And in practice again, I observe. You did not tell me that you intended to go into harness.'" *A Scandal in Bohemia*, i, 346, 348.

At the time of Holmes's investigation of the strange fate of the Boer War veteran, "The good Watson had at the time deserted me for a wife, the only selfish action which I can recall in our association. I was alone." It was January 1903. *The Adventure of the Blanched Soldier*, ii, 707.

WATSON, MRS.: Watson wrote, "One night — it was in June, '89 — there came a ring to my bell, about the hour when a man gives his first yawn, and glances at the clock. I sat up in my chair, and my wife laid her needlework down in her lap and made a little face of disappointment." The caller was Kate Whitney, an old schoolmate and friend of Mrs.

Watson's, seeking aid for her poor husband, who was "much addicted to opium." Watson commented knowingly that "folk who were in grief came to my wife like birds to a lighthouse." *The Man with the Twisted Lip*, I, 368.

"'Ah, my dear Watson,' said [Holmes], striding into the room, 'I am very delighted to see you. I trust Mrs. Watson has entirely recovered from all the little excitements connected with our adventure of the Sign of Four?'" With this amenity out of the way, Holmes proceeded to enlist Watson for the investigation of the strange tale of Hall Pycroft. *The Stockbroker's Clerk*, II, 153.

Holmes queried Dr. Watson as to whether Mrs. Watson was in. On receiving the reply that she was away on a visit, Holmes felt that it was easier for him "to propose that you should come away with me for a week on to the Continent." *The Final Problem*, II, 302. [See also Mary Morstan.]

WEISS & CO.: A London firm. The very delicate cataract knife that was found in John Straker's pocket was manufactured by Weiss & Co. *Silver Blaze*, II, 271.

WELBECK STREET: As Holmes passed the corner which leads from Bentinck Street on to the Welbeck Street crossing, a two-horse van, furiously driven, whizzed past him. He sprang for the footpath and only avoided sure death by a fraction of a second. *The Final Problem*, II, 306.

WELLINGTON STREET: On their way from Lee, in Kent, to the Bow Street police station to interview Hugh Boone, Holmes and Watson dashed up Wellington Street. *The Man with the Twisted Lip*, I, 382.

WESSEX CUP: Silver Blaze, who was the favorite for the running of the Wessex Cup, disappeared shortly before the race, and his trainer was found murdered. *Silver Blaze*, II, 261.

WEST, ARTHUR CADOGAN: Found dead just outside Aldgate Station on the Underground system in London, the twenty-seven-year-old West was an enigma. On the one hand, he had been a clerk at Woolwich Arsenal who, though hot-headed and impetuous, had been a straight, honest man with ten years of good work to his credit. On the other hand, however, some of the top-secret plans for the Bruce-Partington submarine were found on his dead body. Before Holmes could decide whether West had been either a spy or a good citizen, the detective had to solve yet another mystery, namely, what had impelled West to leave his fiancée, Miss Violet Westbury, standing in the fog on the evening prior to the discovery of the former's dead body? *The Adventure of the Bruce-Partington Plans*, ii, 437.

WEST SECTION COALING COMPANY: Had paid its annual contribution to the Scowrers for protection. *The Valley of Fear*, i, 542.

WEST WILMERTON GENERAL MINING COMPANY: Bought the Vermissa Valley ironworks of Manson, Shuman, Van Deher, and Atwood. *The Valley of Fear*, i, 543.

WESTAWAY'S: A well-known agency for governesses, managed by Miss Stoper. It was here that Miss Violet Hunter met her peculiar employer, Jephro Rucastle. *The Adventure of the Copper Beeches*, ii, 116.

WESTBURY, MISS VIOLET: She was the fiancée of young Arthur Cadogan West, who left her standing in the fog one night on their way to the theatre and was later found dead on the tracks of the London Underground with some of the stolen Bruce-Partington submarine plans in his pocket. She felt that he had been innocent. *The Adventure of the Bruce-Partington Plans*, ii, 434, 441.

WESTHOUSE & MARBANK: The great claret importers of Fenchurch Street. James Windibank was a commercial traveler for them. *A Case of Identity*, i, 410-11.

WESTMINSTER: Eduardo Lucas, the international spy, was "stabbed to the heart" at his residence, 16 Godolphin Street, Westminster. *The Adventure of the Second Stain*, i, 308.

WESTMINSTER STAIRS: A fast steam launch was to meet Holmes, Watson, and Athelney Jones at the Westminster Stairs. *The Sign of the Four*, i, 661.

WESTPHAIL, MISS HONORIA: Maiden sister of Mrs. Stoner and aunt of Helen and Julia Stoner. At Miss Westphail's home in Harrow, Julia met the half-pay major of Marines, to whom she became engaged. *The Adventure of the Speckled Band*, i, 247.

WESTVILLE ARMS: Holmes, Watson, and Inspector MacDonald all stayed at this hotel in the village of Birlstone, in Sussex, while investigating the horrible murder of John Douglas. *The Valley of Fear*, i, 489.

WHITAKER'S ALMANACK: This volume held the key to Fred Porlock's cipher message. *The Valley of Fear*, I, 475.

WHITE, ABEL: An indigo-planter in India, he took pity on Jonathan Small, who had lost a leg to a crocodile in the Ganges River. White offered Small a job as overseer on his plantation. White was later killed in the Indian Mutiny. *The Sign of the Four*, I, 674.

WHITE EAGLE TAVERN: Broderick and Nelson's large timber yard, to which Toby traced a second scent of creosote, lay just past the White Eagle tavern. *The Sign of the Four*, I, 649.

WHITE HART: On the night that Constable John Rance discovered the dead body of Enoch J. Drebber in a lonely suburban London apartment, he had investigated a fight at the White Hart tavern. *A Study in Scarlet*, I, 176.

WHITEHALL: Every morning Mycroft Holmes walked around the corner from his rooms in Pall Mall into Whitehall, where he was thought to hold a position auditing the books in some of the Government departments. *The Greek Interpreter*, I, 592; see also *The Naval Treaty*, II, 174; *The Adventure of the Bruce-Partington Plans*, II, 433; *The Adventure of the Mazarin Stone*, II, 741.

WHITEHALL TERRACE: The Right Honourable Trelawney Hope and his wife Lady Hilda kept a house in Whitehall Terrace. *The Adventure of the Second Stain*, I, 303.

WHITNEY, ELIAS: Doctor of Divinity and principal of the Theological College of St. George's. His brother, Isa Whitney, was "much addicted to opium," and it was on an errand of mercy to recover Isa from an opium den that Watson met Holmes under very strange circumstances. *The Man with the Twisted Lip*, I, 368.

WHITNEY, ISA: "Isa Whitney, brother of the late Elias Whitney, D.D., Principal of the Theological Seminary of St. George's, was much addicted to opium.... He found, as so many more have done, that the practice is easier to attain than to get rid of, and for many years he continued to be a slave to the drug, an object of mingled horror and pity to his friends and relatives," wrote Watson. One night, in June of 1889, Watson went on an errand of mercy at the request of Whitney's wife, to recover him from the Bar of Gold opium den, in Upper Swandam Lane.

Watson sent Isa home in a cab, but remained himself, for he had unexpectedly encountered Sherlock Holmes. *The Man with the Twisted Lip*, I, 368.

WHITNEY, KATE: When her husband, Isa, who was "much addicted to opium," had not been home for two days, she sought out the aid of her old friend and school companion, Mrs. Watson. The good Doctor offered to search out her husband, and that led to another tale. *The Man with the Twisted Lip*, I, 368.

WHITTINGTON, LADY ALICIA: She was present at the wedding of Lord St. Simon and Hatty Doran. *The Adventure of the Noble Bachelor*, I, 285.

WHOLE ART OF DETECTION, THE: Holmes intended to devote his declining years to the composition of a one-volume textbook on this topic. *The Adventure of the Abbey Grange*, II, 492.

WHYTE, WILLIAM: As Holmes sat down to await the expected arrival of the murderer of Enoch J. Drebber, he took up "a queer old book I picked up at a stall yesterday — *De Jure inter Gentes* — published in Latin at Liège in the Lowlands, in 1642."

"Who is the printer?" asked Watson.

"Philippe de Croy, whoever he may have been. On the fly-leaf, in very faded ink, is written 'Ex libris Guliolmi Whyte.' I wonder who William Whyte was. Some pragmatical seventeenth-century lawyer, I suppose. His writing has a legal twist about it." *A Study in Scarlet*, I, 180.

WIGGINS: At the time that Holmes was investigating the death of Enoch J. Drebber, Wiggins headed the Baker Street Irregulars. *A Study in Scarlet*, I, 185.

"One of their number, taller and older than the others, [Wiggins] stood forward with an air of lounging superiority which was very funny in such a disreputable little scarecrow." *The Sign of the Four*, I, 653.

WIGMORE STREET POST OFFICE: Observation told Holmes that Watson had been to the Wigmore Street Post Office earlier in the morning, while deduction let him know that his friend had been there to dispatch a telegram. *The Sign of the Four*, I, 613.

WILCOX, CHESTER: Of Marley Creek, Vermissa Valley. In an attempt on his life by the Scowrers, one of the Scowrers, Jim Carnaway, was killed. Wilcox was chief foreman of the Iron Dyke Company. Jack Mc-Murdo led another unsuccessful attempt on his life. *The Valley of Fear*, I, 542, 558.

WILD, JONATHAN: Holmes said, "He was a master criminal, and he lived last century — 1750 or thereabouts." *The Valley of Fear*, I, 479.

WILDER, JAMES: Secretary to the Duke of Holdernesse, "he was small, nervous, alert, with intelligent, light blue eyes and mobile features." *The Adventure of the Priory School*, II, 612, 626, 629.

WILLABY, ARTHUR: He stood guard with Jack McMurdo outside the editorial offices of the Vermissa *Herald*, while the other Scowrers beat up the editor. He and his brother were "men of action, tall, lithe young fellows with determined faces." *The Valley of Fear*, I, 545, 569.

WILLIAMS: A prizefighter, he had been lightweight champion of England. Once employed as a porter by Major John Sholto of Pondicherry Lodge, he was later employed by Sholto's son, Thaddeus, as a servant. He met Mary Morstan, Holmes, and Watson outside the Lyceum Theatre, at the third pillar from the left, to transport them on their journey to Thaddeus Sholto's house. *The Sign of the Four*, I, 622, 627.

WILLIAMS, CHARLIE: Murdered by the Scowrers. *The Valley of Fear*, I, 556.

WILLIAMS, JAMES BAKER: His large house, Forton Old Hall, lay near Aloysius Garcia's Wisteria Lodge, in Surrey. *The Adventure of Wisteria Lodge*, II, 246.

WILLIAMSON, MR.: Though his realty agent thought Williamson a respectable elderly gentleman, that assessment was quite mistaken: in truth, the white-bearded Williamson was an unfrocked clergyman. *The Adventure of the Solitary Cyclist*, II, 389.

WILLOWS, DR.: He felt that John Turner was a wreck, and that his nervous system was shattered after the violent death of his tenant, Charles McCarthy. *The Boscombe Valley Mystery*, II, 141.

WILSON: The sham chaplain aboard the barque *Gloria Scott* in 1855, he was in league with the convict Jack Prendergast. He was also instrumental in the convict uprising aboard ship, for he slew the captain with a pistol. He was presumed dead when the barque was destroyed by an explosion. *The "Gloria Scott"*, I, 118.

WILSON: Manager of the district messenger office in which worked the boy Cartwright, whom Holmes employed in his pursuit of the murderer of Sir Charles Baskerville. Holmes had helped Wilson in a little case which had saved the latter's good name, and perhaps his life. *The Hound of the Baskervilles*, II, 28.

WILSON: The year 1895 contained a number of cases of Holmes's memorable to Watson, one of which was Holmes's "arrest of Wilson, the notorious canary-trainer, which removed a plague-spot from the East End of London." *The Adventure of Black Peter*, II, 398.

WILSON: A Kentish constable, he met Holmes, Watson, and Stanley Hopkins at the garden gate of Yoxley Old Place, the country house in which Willoughby Smith had been murdered. *The Adventure of the Golden Pince-Nez*, II, 358.

WILSON: "A mere boy, in his teens," he volunteered for the murder of Andrew Rae. He was a member of the Scowrers. *The Valley of Fear*, I, 541.

WILSON, BARTHOLOMEW: District ruler of Lodge 29, Chicago, of the Ancient Order of Freemen. *The Valley of Fear*, I, 533.

WILSON, JABEZ: A pawnbroker, Wilson was fortunate to obtain an easy berth with the Red-Headed League, but came to Holmes when one day he found that it had been dissolved without notice. *The Red-Headed League*, I, 419.

WILSON, SERGEANT: Of the Sussex Constabulary, he received the first alarm of the tragic murder of John Douglas, of Birlstone Manor. *The Valley of Fear*, I, 485, 492.

WILSON, STEVE: Of Hobson's Patch. Jack McMurdo claimed that he was the Pinkerton operative on the trail of the Scowrers. *The Valley of Fear*, I, 565.

WINCHESTER: Five miles on the near side of the Copper Beeches. Holmes and Watson stayed in the cathedral town when they went down to Hampshire to investigate the strange situation of Miss Violet Hunter. *The Adventure of the Copper Beeches*, II, 117; see also *Silver Blaze*, II, 227; *The Problem of Thor Bridge*, II, 589.

WINDIBANK, JAMES: Mary Sutherland's stepfather. He traveled for Westhouse & Marbank, the great claret importers. Holmes said of him,

"There never was a man who deserved punishment more.... That fellow will rise from crime to crime until he does something very bad, and ends on a gallows." *A Case of Identity*, i, 413-14, 416.

WINDIGATE: The "ruddy-faced, white-aproned landlord" of the Alpha Inn who instituted a Christmas goose club. Holmes and Watson had two beers and obtained information from him. *The Adventure of the Blue Carbuncle*, i, 459.

WINDLE, J. W.: Division Master of the Ancient Order of Freemen, of Merton County, Lodge 249. He petitioned the Vermissa Valley Lodge to eliminate Andrew Rae, of Rae and Sturmash, coal owners. *The Valley of Fear*, i, 541.

WINDSOR: After his successful recovery of the stolen submarine plans, Holmes "spent a day at Windsor, whence he returned with a remarkably fine emerald tie-pin." *The Adventure of the Bruce-Partington Plans*, ii, 452.

WINTER, JAMES: The criminal who called himself John Garrideb was also known as "James Winter, *alias* Morecroft, *alias* Killer Evans." *The Adventure of the Three Garridebs*, ii, 651.

WINTER, MISS KITTY: A woman "ruined" by the notorious Baron Adelbert Gruner, she vowed to drag him beneath those depths to which he had driven her, and she aided Holmes in foiling Gruner's plans of marriage to the lovely Violet de Merville. *The Adventure of the Illustrious Client*, ii, 677.

WISTERIA LODGE: Near Esher, in Surrey, it had been rented by the mysterious Aloysius Garcia, who invited Scott Eccles to stay with him. But Garcia then disappeared, along with his house staff, before the next morning. He was later found horribly murdered. The house was about two miles on the south side of Esher. *The Adventure of Wisteria Lodge*, ii, 241.

WOKING: The unfortunate Percy Phelps's residence, Briarbrae, was "among the fir-woods and the heather of Woking." *The Naval Treaty*, ii, 169.

WOMBWELL: He was "one of the greatest showmen of his day," and the rival of Sanger and Ronder. *The Adventure of the Veiled Lodger*, ii, 455.

WOMEN: Watson observed "that Holmes had, when he liked, a peculiarly ingratiating way with women, and that he very readily established terms of confidence with them." He used his rapport to good advantage with Mrs. Marker, the housekeeper of Yoxley Old Place. *The Adventure of the Golden Pince-Nez*, II, 361.

Holmes said, "And yet the motives of women are so inscrutable.... How can you build on such quicksand? Their most trivial action may mean volumes, or their most extraordinary conduct may depend upon a hairpin or a curling-tongs." *The Adventure of the Second Stain*, I, 311.

Mrs. Warren, who finally persuaded Holmes to take the case of her mysterious lodger, "had the pertinacity, and also the cunning, of her sex." *The Adventure of the Red Circle*, II, 691.

Holmes tells us that "women have seldom been an attraction to me, for my brain has always governed my heart." But he was so struck by the beauty of Maud Bellamy that he concluded that she would "always remain in my memory as a most complete and remarkable woman." *The Adventure of the Lion's Mane*, II, 781, 782.

WOOD, DR.: "A brisk and capable general practitioner" from the village of Birlstone, in Sussex, he was the first called in to examine the dead body of John Douglas, of Birlstone Manor. *The Valley of Fear*, I, 485.

WOOD, HENRY: Once the smartest man in the 117th Foot, he had competed with Sergeant James Barclay for the hand of Nancy Devoy, daughter of a color-sergeant. He had fallen into an ambush by six rebels, during the Indian Mutiny. Captured, he was taken to Nepal, but he escaped, and wandered in Afghanistan and the Punjab, where he "lived mostly among the natives, and picked up a living by... conjuring tricks." *The Crooked Man*, II, 233, 235, 236.

WOOD, J. G.: A "famous observer" and author. One of Wood's books, *Out of Doors*, detailed, among other things, his aquatic confrontation with "the fearful stinger, *Cyanea Capillata*." *The Adventure of the Lion's Mane*, II, 788.

WOODHOUSE: A criminal, he was, according to Holmes, one of the fifty men who had "good reason" for taking Holmes's life. *The Adventure of the Bruce-Partington Plans*, II, 432.

WOODLEY, MISS EDITH: A resident of Carstairs, she had at one time been engaged to Ronald Adair. The engagement had been broken off by mutual consent some months prior to Adair's murder, however, "and there was no sign that it had left any very profound feeling behind it." *The Adventure of the Empty House*, II, 330.

WOODLEY, JACK: "Roaring Jack" had been "the greatest brute and bully in South Africa, a man whose name [was] a holy terror from Kimberley to Johannesburg." In league with Bob Carruthers, he had come back to England to defraud an innocent woman. Holmes saw that he received his just reward. *The Adventure of the Solitary Cyclist*, II, 385ff.

WOODMAN'S LEE: Home of Captain Peter Carey in Sussex, whose death was surrounded by very obscure circumstances. *The Adventure of Black Peter*, II, 398, 404.

WOOLWICH ARSENAL: Arthur Cadogan West, who was found dead on the London Underground tracks with stolen submarine plans in his pocket, was a clerk at the Woolwich Arsenal. *The Adventure of the Bruce-Partington Plans*, II, 434.

WORCESTERSHIRE: Jonathan Small was born in Worcestershire, near Pershore. *The Sign of the Four*, I, 673.

WORTHINGDON BANK GANG: Five conspirators, Biddle, Hayward, Moffat, Sutton, and Cartwright, robbed the Worthingdon bank in 1875. In their getaway, the bank's caretaker, Tobin, was killed. All five criminals were eventually caught. Sutton turned informer, and on his evidence, Cartwright was hanged, and the other three got fifteen years each. When the three were finally released, they vowed, and achieved, revenge on Sutton. *The Resident Patient*, I, 279.

WRIGHT, THERESA: Lady Brackenstall's maid and occasional nurse. She had served her mistress since the latter was a baby; so, it was hardly surprising that Theresa detested the unkind way Lady Brackenstall was treated by her husband, Sir Eustace. Theresa claimed that she had seen three men outside the Abbey Grange on the night Sir Eustace was murdered. *The Adventure of the Abbey Grange*, II, 493ff.

Y

YORK: Mr. and Mrs. Vandeleur ran St. Oliver's private school, in York. *The Hound of the Baskervilles*, II, 95.

YORK COLLEGE: Among the many billets that Jefferson Hope held in America during his life of wandering, he "was once janitor and sweeper-out of the laboratory at York College." There, he obtained the deadly South American arrow poison with which he hoped to extract vengeance. *A Study in Scarlet*, I, 227.

YOUGHAL: Of Scotland Yard's C.I.D., he arrested the villains who had stolen the Crown diamond. *The Adventure of the Mazarin Stone*, II, 738.

YOUNG, BRIGHAM: "A man who could not have been more than thirty years of age, but whose massive head and resolute expression marked him as a leader," Brigham Young welcomed John and Lucy Ferrier into the Mormon caravan on the condition that they accept the Mormon faith. "Brigham Young has said it, and he has spoken with the voice of Joseph Smith, which is the voice of God." Later, Young paid a visit to John Ferrier and told him of his [Ferrier's] primary failing in the true faith: that his daughter, Lucy, was rumored to be engaged to a Gentile. He gave Ferrier the ultimatum that his daughter choose her husband from one of the elect within thirty days. *A Study in Scarlet*, I, 202, 208.

YOXLEY OLD PLACE: This country house was down in Kent, seven miles from Chatham and three from the railway line. Some years prior to 1894, it had been taken by an elderly man who gave the name of Professor Coram. Professor Coram's secretary, Willoughby Smith, was killed in the study of Yoxley Old Place. *The Adventure of the Golden Pince-Nez*, II, 352, 353.

Z

ZAMBA, SIGNOR: An invalid, he was half of the great firm of Castalotte & Zamba, the chief fruit importers of New York. Because of his disability, Signor Zamba was no longer a viable force in the organization; indeed, "Castalotte [had] all power within the firm." *The Adventure of the Red Circle*, II, 702.